N

GUIDE TO

Brittany

Keith Spence

ROBERT NICHOLSON PUBLICATIONS

Also available:

Nicholson's Guide to the Loire Region
Nicholson's Guide to Normandy

A Nicholson Guide

First published 1985

© **Robert Nicholson Publications Limited 1985**

Maps © Robert Nicholson Publications Limited 1985
City plans © Robert Nicholson Publications Limited 1985

Line drawings by Richard Reid
Touring maps by Rodney Paull
City plans by Seagull Limited

The author would like to thank Brittany Ferries
The publishers would like to acknowledge the assistance
of the French Government Tourist Office

Robert Nicholson Publications Limited
17–21 Conway Street
London W1P 6JD

Great care has been taken throughout this book to be
accurate, but the publishers cannot accept responsibility
for any errors which appear

Phototypeset in England by Input Typesetting Limited
London SW19 8DR

Printed and bound in Great Britain by
Philip Print Limited, London

ISBN 0 905522 85 0

Contents

An introduction to Brittany

A country about the size of Denmark, which is a part of France and yet does not feel itself fully to belong to France; a country with its own language and traditions, going back for 1500 years and linking it with other Celtic lands from Ireland and Wales to Galicia in northern Spain; a country whose 'mountains' seldom exceed 1000ft (300m), yet which can be as rugged and wild as hill regions three times as high; a country whose 750 miles (1200km) of coastline contain tremendous cliffs and tiny sandy coves, great harbours where fleets can anchor, and strange moon landscapes of rock splintered into savage pinnacles or worn into animal, human or abstract shapes; a country whose sculptors and architects —working in granite, the toughest and most durable of all types of stone—produced churches and calvaries of the greatest originality and power: these are only a few of the qualities that distinguish Brittany not just from the rest of France, but from the rest of Europe.

Church, Pleubian

Brittany's rugged landscape has bred a rugged people. Like their cousins the Welsh, the Bretons do not necessarily take the visitor to their hearts straight away. To the outsider, they can seem dour and uncommunicative, busy about their own affairs and having little time for strangers; but anyone who enters sympathetically into their lives, even on such tourist terms as choosing Breton pancakes and cider for a meal, or attending one of the dozens of religious festivals (*pardons*) or open-air folk celebrations (*festou-noz*) that take place throughout much of the year, will be drawn into the Breton family circle and find a friendliness and hospitality that are rare elsewhere in France.

Most people spending a holiday in Brittany go to one of the many seaside resorts—either large sophisticated places like La Baule or Dinard, which can offer the visitor everything from roulette to windsurfing, or the smaller, less pretentious towns and villages, with little beyond a sandy beach and a simple restaurant serving crêpes and seafood. These visitors are experiencing only one half of Brittany—the half that Bretons for centuries have called '*Armor*', or the sea. There is, however, another inland half, known as '*Argoat*', or the forest, from the vast woodland that once covered the whole of inland Brittany and is still haunted by the ghosts of Merlin and the druids, King

Arthur and Sir Lancelot, and the army of Breton saints who lived as hermits in their forest caves. It is in the Argoat that the true Brittany lies. Though the forest has shrunk to a few small patches as agriculture and industry have encroached on it, the Argoat still keeps much of its timeless quality. Few of Brittany's inland towns have grown much beyond village size, and with the exception of Rennes they are without the featureless stretches of suburb found in the big coastal towns such as Brest, Lorient and St-Brieuc. Many of them have some remains of château or town wall to remind us of a warring past, and among them are castles that can compare with the finest in Europe.

Anyone coming to Brittany expecting to see lush landscapes, or to bask in the kind of sun that guarantees a tan, will come home disappointed. But those who go abroad to make their own discoveries of rivers and villages, moorlands and fishing ports, and a way of life that is more self-contained than most, will come home as members of that growing army for whom a holiday means simply 'Brittany'.

How to get there

Since Brittany Ferries opened up its cross-Channel car-ferry routes in the 1970s, they have been the natural choice for most people holidaying in Brittany. With their services between Plymouth and Roscoff, and Cork and Roscoff, Brittany Ferries have opened up the western part of the country that in the past was too often neglected by the tourist. The Portsmouth–St-Malo route has been well tried and tested down the years, and has the advantage of arriving at the magnificent walled town of St-Malo. An alternative is to cross to one of the other Channel ports (in order of proximity to Brittany: Cherbourg, Le Havre, Dieppe, Boulogne, Calais and Dunkirk) and then drive down to Brittany. This means a shorter and cheaper sea crossing; but it also means one or two days' additional driving at each end of the holiday, with the possible expense of overnight stops.

Though most people will travel to Brittany by sea, there are a number of regular flights by various carriers. Air France have services from Heathrow to La Baule and Nantes; BritAir fly from Gatwick to Morlaix, Quimper and Rennes; Brymon Airways fly from Plymouth to Brest and Morlaix; Touraine Air Transport have flights from Gatwick to Dinard.

Details of carriers are given below; current and seasonal prices can be obtained from any High Street travel agent or from the French Government Tourist Office (FGTO), 178 Piccadilly, London W1V 0AL, tel (01) 491–7622.

With frequent daily sailings it is not strictly necessary to book, but it is highly advisable to do so, especially at weekends, on public holidays, at Easter and during the summer months *from mid-Jun to mid-Sep.*

Cross-Channel ferry services
Brittany Ferries
Norman House, Millbay Docks, Plymouth PL1 3EF. Tel Plymouth (0752) 21321 or Portsmouth (0705) 27701. Services

from Plymouth to Roscoff and from Portsmouth to St-Malo. Overnight services are recommended, as the crossings take six to eight hours and the ferries are large and well equipped with cabins, restaurants, shops and entertainment areas.

Hoverspeed

International Hoverport, Ramsgate, Kent CT12 5HS. Tel Thanet (0843) 54881 or (01) 499-9481. Services from Dover to Boulogne and Calais. Hovercraft travel is the quickest and simplest way of getting to France for travellers on foot or in cars, but the journey can be uncomfortable in rough weather for those with delicate stomachs.

P & O Ferries

Arundel Towers, Portland Terr, Southampton SO9 4AE. Tel Southampton (0703) 34141. Services from Dover to Boulogne and from Southampton to Le Havre. Well equipped and comfortable boats, with good overnight facilities on the Southampton–Le Havre service.

Sally Line

81 Piccadilly, London W1V 9HF. Tel (01) 409-0536. Services from Ramsgate to Dunkirk. Although this route is a long way from Brittany, new and well equipped boats and competitive prices make it attractive.

Sealink

Sealink Car Ferry Centre, PO Box 303, 52 Grosvenor Gdns, London SW1W 0AG. Tel (01) 834-2345. Services from Dover to Calais and Dunkirk, from Folkestone to Boulogne and from Newhaven to Dieppe. Although offering the most services, Sealink ships are sometimes small and old-fashioned. British Rail's ships have still to come to terms with competition from private companies. The most old-fashioned, and therefore the most tedious, is the slow Newhaven–Dieppe service.

Townsend Thoresen

Car Ferry Centre, 1 Camden Cres, Dover CT16 1LD. Enquiries: tel (01) 734-4431 and (01) 437-7800. Services from Dover to Calais, from Portsmouth to Le Havre and Cherbourg, and from Southampton to Le Havre. Large and modern boats with good overnight facilities on the Le Havre and Cherbourg services are particularly convenient for travellers to Brittany.

All companies offer promotional fares, inclusive holidays, short breaks and day trips, so it is a good idea to read all the brochures carefully and shop around before booking. Bookings can be made directly with the companies or through a travel agent. Foot passengers should bear in mind that, except for Sealink, Hoverspeed and some special services, trains do not necessarily coincide with boats. Bicycles can be carried on all services, but booking in advance is generally necessary. Anyone wanting a cabin on any service is advised to book in advance.

Cross-Channel rail services

British Rail and SNCF (French Railways) operate a number of regular services between London and Paris which utilise Sealink ferries or Hoverspeed hovercraft. However, there are no through trains and so all these services involve a certain amount of walking between trains and the ferry or hovercraft. Luggage trolleys are usually available, but the journey can be problematic for elderly or disabled people, or for those with heavy luggage. Connecting trains to other parts of France leave from the various stations in Paris, which are all linked by *Métro* (Underground), bus or taxi. Journey times vary considerably, the fastest taking about 6½ hours, the slowest overnight service taking up to 11 hours. There are also considerable variations in cost, depending on the time of travel and the season, as well as various promotional or short break fares. Bookings can be made through a travel agent, a British Rail Travel Centre, or French Railways, 179 Piccadilly, London W1V 0BA, tel (01) 493-4451.

For those seeking a more luxurious way to travel from London to Paris there is 'The Parisienne', an overnight service operated jointly by British Rail, French Railways and P & O Ferries. The cost of the ticket includes a cabin on the boat between Southampton and Le Havre and reserved seats on the trains.

Bicycles can be taken on many services between London and Paris but they have to be registered in advance and often travel separately, to be collected again at their destination.

Travel by air

Air France
158 New Bond St, London W1Y 0AY. Tel (01) 499-9511. Service from London Heathrow to Deauville, Paris, La Baule, Nantes and from Manchester to Paris.

Air UK
Main office: Berkeley House, 51–3 High St, Redhill, Surrey; flight enquiries, tel Bishop's Stortford (0279) 506301. Services from London Stansted and Leeds /Bradford to Paris.

Britair
Address & tel as Air France. Services from London Gatwick to Caen, Le Havre, Morlaix, Quimper and Rennes.

British Airways
London Heathrow Airport, Hounslow, Mddx. Tel (01) 759-5511. Services from London Heathrow to Paris, from Birmingham to Paris, from Manchester to Paris and from Glasgow to Paris.

British Caledonian
London Gatwick Airport, Horley, Surrey. Tel (01) 668-9311, reservations (01) 668-4222. Services from Gatwick to Paris.

British Midland Airways
East Midland Airport, Castle Donington, Derbyshire. Tel Derby (0332) 810741. Services from East Midland to Paris.

Brymon Airways
City Airport, Crownhill, Plymouth, Devon. Tel Plymouth (0752) 707023. Services from Plymouth to Brest and Morlaix.

Lucas Air Transport
London Gatwick Airport, Horley, Surrey. Tel Horley (0293) 513631. Services from London Gatwick to Deauville.

Touraine Air Transport
Address & tel as Air France. Services from Gatwick to Dinard.

Travel by coach

There are many scheduled coach services linking British cities with Paris and other parts of France. For information and bookings contact a travel agent, or your local coach station.

Visas, passports & insurance

British citizens and those Commonwealth citizens entitled to British residence will be admitted to France on production of a full British passport or a British visitor's passport (valid for one year). No visas are required. Visitors from other countries should check with British Immigration officials before leaving for France, to see if any special documentation is required or any new arrangements are currently in force. French port officials are well used to visitors and are usually helpful; in fact, passport control and customs are often a formality when entering or leaving France.

Although insurance is not compulsory, all travellers to France are advised to take out an adequate personal policy to cover theft, loss of possessions or money and, particularly, medical expenses. A visit to a doctor can cost at least 70 francs, and to a specialist at least 100 francs, while hospitalisation, emergency treatment and transport can be very expensive. Insurance, by comparison, is very cheap. Ask your travel agent or your normal insurance broker. Under EEC regulations it is possible for British visitors in France to receive free medical attention, but only if they have obtained a current form E111 from their local Social Security office *before* leaving; this is not available to the unemployed or self-employed.

First aid, medical advice and the night service rota are available from pharmacies, marked by a green cross.

Internal transport

Once in France the independent traveller will have no trouble moving about on the internal transport services, which are excellent, although it will help if he or she speaks a little French. Driving in France is also easier than many people think.

Motoring in France

A full UK licence is required but an international driving licence is not necessary. Provisional licences are not valid. Motorists should hold Green Card insurance since the normal UK insurance only gives third party cover overseas.

Car travellers will be expected to comply with French motoring regulations. Seat-belts must be worn and any children under ten years of age must be carried in rear seats. A 'GB' plate must be displayed. Motorcyclists must wear crash helmets. Full or dipped headlights must be used at night or in poor visibility, and although yellow-tinted headlights are not compulsory, headlights must be adjusted to suit left-hand drive. Spare bulbs must be carried. All traffic travels on the right. Speed limits are as follows:

60km (37mph) max in towns, unless otherwise indicated.
90km (56mph) max on single track roads.
110km (69mph) max on dual carriageways.
130km (81mph) max on motorways (*autoroutes*).

In wet weather these upper limits are reduced to 110km (69mph) on motorways and 80km (50mph) on all other roads. Unless equipped with hazard flashlights, all cars must carry a red warning triangle and display this when necessary as, for example, when changing a wheel or after an accident.

Two further points are worth mentioning. It is a sad fact that most accidents concerning British motorists in France occur within 50mi/80km of the coast. This is usually attributed to British motorists on arrival being unused to driving on the right and to French road conditions, but people hurrying to get away from the port and tired travellers racing back to catch their ferry home also contribute to the statistics. Be sure to exercise extreme care in this high-risk zone, close to the coast. The breathalyser (*alcooltest*) is widely in use, and the French police can and do make on-the-spot fines. The *minimum* fine for speeding at the time of writing is 600 francs (approx £55).

A second fact, for which no statistics are available, is that British cars, marked with GB plates and loaded with luggage, are an easy target for thieves. Find secure parking whenever possible, or unload the car completely. Even a locked boot is vulnerable. If possible leave someone in the car when shopping, or park in a very public place with the car in plain view. Should your car be broken into and items taken, the fact must be reported to the police with a list of the missing contents. The police will provide the traveller with written proof of the theft and without such proof no UK insurance company will entertain a claim. The chances of recovering stolen property are slim.

Car hire

Many visitors prefer to hire a car in France, and thus overcome the problems posed by right-hand drive cars. France is well stocked with car hire companies and details can be obtained from Syndicats d'Initiative or Offices de Tourisme. Major international hire companies are also well represented, including Avis, Godfrey Davis/Europcar and Hertz. The advantages of these are that cars can be booked and paid for in England, that special package rates are often available and that they operate their own credit and charge cards. Many travel agents include a car in the cost of package holidays, and there are also many fly-drive and rail-drive schemes operated by airlines, travel companies and British and French Railways.

Driving in France

Driving a right-hand drive car in France does require a little caution, especially when pulling away in the morning, when it is easy to forget which side of the road one should be on, at roundabouts, and when overtaking. French drivers are good but fast, and not noticeably considerate. Foreign drivers should make clear signals and avoid indecision at road junctions.

Garages

French garages are quicker and cheaper than most UK garages, and usually very helpful. As a rule they will act at once to help the foreign traveller, and if the motorist has had the foresight to carry a few spare parts the French mechanics, who are usually highly efficient, will quickly get the car back on the road again. French garages will also help cyclists in case of need, and every French town has a cycle shop. Many French garages accept credit cards, particularly VISA.

Road networks

As a general rule, French roads are excellent and road signs are clear. Fast, safe travel is usually possible, on the extensive network of autoroutes. These are nearly all toll roads (*péages*) with regular payment stages. The bulk of the network is made up of 'N' roads (*Routes Nationales*) and 'D' roads, maintained by the départements; this arrangement is in a constant state of change, which can be confusing. Do not be surprised if a 'D' road on the map is an 'N' road on the ground, or vice-versa.

Taxis

Even the smallest village will have a taxi, which can usually be located at the hotel, bar or local garage. It is always advisable to agree the price for the distance before departure. In towns all taxis have meters. A tip of 10–15% is usual.

Travel by air

Air Inter is France's domestic airline, linking Paris with 30 towns and cities. For details of the routes and for bookings contact Air France, 158 New Bond St, London W1Y 0AY, tel (01) 499-9511. There are also a number of small independent airlines operating local services in France.

Travel by bus

There are very few long-distance bus or coach services in France, but there are good local services which usually operate within the départements from bus stations (*gares routières*) in the main towns, often found at or close to the main railway station. A bus or coach is a *car*, a car is an *auto* or a *voiture*, a ferry or shuttle bus is a *navette*. A water ferry is a *bac*.

Travel by train

Train services are fast, clean, regular, inexpensive by UK standards, and generally excellent. Tickets can be purchased ahead of the journey but must be stamped or *composté* at one of the yellow/orange machines which stand at the entrance to every platform, before boarding the train. Failure to 'composte' the ticket may result in a fine from the ticket inspectors of up to 20% of the basic fare.

As well as standard rail fares, visitors can take advantage of a number of special concessionary fares, such as the 'France-Vacances' ticket which gives unlimited 1st- or 2nd-class rail travel over the entire network for 7, 15 or 30 days. French Railways are also very efficient at transporting bicycles, and on certain trains, coded 40 on the timetables, cyclists can take their cycles as hand-baggage, loading and unloading them from the train personally. On longer journeys it is usually necessary to send cycles ahead, but full details can be obtained from any French Rail information office. The SNCF also operate a number of other services, including self-drive car hire and cycle hire.

Details of train and bus services can be obtained from local railway stations or tourist offices (*Syndicats d'Initiative*) in France, and from the offices of French Rail, 179 Piccadilly, London W1V 0BA, tel (01) 493-4451.

Tourist offices

Throughout France there are 5000 local Syndicats d'Initiative and Offices de Tourisme. They can give advice on local features of interest, accommodation, restaurants, entertainment, festivals and local transport. In practice, it is best to concentrate on those offices in major towns and cities, for they will not only have most of the information available in the smaller offices but they will also be open on a more frequent and regular basis. Some of the smaller offices are frankly a waste of time; their opening hours are often erratic and, if you are lucky enough to find them open, the information they supply can be very inadequate. Despite these warnings, it is noticeable how much better served the tourist is in France than in England.

Accommodation

Even today the vast majority of French country hotels are owned and run by a family. A high standard of service and a certain friendly, laissez-faire attitude can therefore be anticipated. In high summer it is better to book a day or two ahead, or arrive at the chosen hotel *not later than 18.00* to be sure of a room. The proprietor may enquire if the visitor intends to eat at the hotel as well as sleep there, before admitting that rooms are available. Most hotels have a good dining room, so agreeing to eat there, while not compulsory, is usually a good idea. Always inspect the rooms before accepting them and ask to see others if they are not acceptable. The price displayed on the door will be the price on the bill, but note that hotel breakfasts can be expensive. Remember also that in French cafés and bars it is cheaper to stand at the counter, as a percentage is added for table service. *En-pension* terms, or full-board, are only offered for a stay of three days or longer.

French hotels are graded from one to four stars, with an extra standard of four-star-de-luxe. A four-star-de-luxe will be an international hotel, a one-star hotel room will be very simple, with perhaps a shower but no private lavatory, and a choice of soap or towels, but not always both. Wise travellers will therefore always carry soap and towels, and remember that the pillows are in the wardrobe. It is useful if the hotel has covered parking, off the main street; car thieves are all too common nowadays and they tend to prey on foreign cars. The hotel price quoted is per room, not per person; it is based on two people per room, and an additional bed for a child will be provided for around 30% of the basic room rate. As a rule, French hotels are much cheaper and offer far better value for money than any of an equivalent standard in the UK.

If accommodation proves difficult to obtain, the local tourist office or Syndicat d'Initiative will be helpful. They can also advise on *gîtes*, which are country flats or cottages, and *chambres d'hôte*, which are guest rooms or 'bed-and-breakfast'. Chambres d'hôte, although still not widely available in France, are starting to be developed in the country districts and are the perfect way to meet local people and improve one's French.

The final option is camping, always a very popular way to see France. Like hotels, campsites are graded from one to four stars, and offer facilities which can range from a heated pool and a restaurant down to a simple shower and a cold water tap. There are many private and municipal campsites in France and even in high season it is usually possible to find a pitch. In the country districts away from the coast *camping-à-la-ferme*, or farm camping, is increasingly available. These farm sites are very simple but they offer green, pleasant, never crowded pitches and a touch of the real thing.

Climate

Brittany juts out far into the Atlantic, and so is more at the mercy of cloud, rain and wind than are the more favoured inland regions of France. As a general rule, you should never expect any two days in Brittany to be the same, and more often than not, never expect the afternoon to be the same as the morning. Travel in Brittany expecting the same kind of weather as you would in Wales, though a good deal warmer. This means that if you are camping, or expecting to walk for any distance from your hotel, it is worth taking a cagoule and wellingtons.

The best time to go to Brittany is in May and June, when the weather is beginning to warm up and the flowers in the gardens, both public and private, are at their best. During these months the sea is too cold for comfort, unless you are particularly hardy, and so the crowded months of July and August are more suitable for a seaside holiday. Average temperatures range from 3°C (37°F) in January to 18°C (64°F) in July; but there is no real average that covers the whole of the region, since Vannes in the Morbihan may well be several degrees warmer on a sunny day than St-Malo in Ille-et-Vilaine. The same difference applies to the sea temperature, which in August averages 18°C (64°F) on the north coast and 20°C (68°F) on the south.

Food & wine

Though Brittany is not the place to go for regional food of subtlety and sophistication, what Breton dishes can offer are the best of raw materials. First and foremost is the excellent quality of the seafood, which includes oysters from Cancale and the Morbihan, *langoustines* (giant prawns), lobsters and mussels from most fishing ports round the coast, and deepwater fish of all sorts, often served as a mixed dish of *fruits de mer*. The best meat produced here is the young lamb fed on the saltings round the Bay of Mont-St-Michel; while excellent artichokes and cauliflowers come from the Ceinture Dorée (Golden Belt) of rich agricultural land round Roscoff. Plenty of apples are grown, and the strawberries from round Plougastel are famous.

The best Breton food is the cheapest: the crêpes (pancakes), served with every variety of flavouring from jam to fish and made of ordinary wheat (*froment*) if they are sweet, or buckwheat (*sarrasin*) if they are savoury. Traditional peasant dishes are being revived in Breton homes, though you will not find them yet in many restaurants. They are mainly of the stew-and-dumpling variety, filling and energy-giving rather than gastronomically ingenious.

Breton food is best eaten with the local drink, which is flat cider (*cidre bouché*). Wine is produced in the Loire-Atlantique, round Nantes, and is of three sorts: Muscadet, a fairly dry white wine; Gros Plant, another white, slightly drier than Muscadet; and Gamay, a rosé produced in small quantities. The Bretons also produce a certain amount of mead (*hydromel*), known as Chouchen, and drunk as a sweet and rather heavy apéritif.

History & tradition

Customs & traditions

As a race, the Bretons cling tenaciously to all aspects of their past. In summer every town of any size, and almost every village, has its *pardon* or religious festival, in which the statue of the patron saint or the Virgin Mary is carried in solemn procession from the church, through the streets, and back again to the church, with the population following in their Sunday-best. This is the ideal time to see the traditional Breton costume being worn, the women in elaborate lace *coiffes*, or head-dresses, and richly embroidered skirts, the men in be-ribboned hats and traditional broad, baggy trousers. Some of the *pardons*, like those at Ste-Anne-d'Auray and Le Folgoët, have evolved into far more than merely local events, bringing thousands of pilgrims not only from Brittany but from all over France. Others, like the Fêtes de Cornouaille at Quimper or the Fête des Filets Bleus at Concarneau, are now purely secular, attracting groups of musicians and dancers from the whole of Brittany and serving as a focus for the nationalism that is never far below the surface of Breton celebrations.

In music and dance, too, the Bretons are unique. Their favourite dance is the gavotte, in which the whole population, from toddlers to grandparents, link hands and dance through the streets in a happy outburst of energy. Like the Scots, their typical musical instrument is the bagpipe (*biniou*), smaller and shriller than the Scottish variety. The *biniou* is normally played with a *bombarde* (shawm or oboe), to form the nasal sound of a *couple*, while bagpipes and oboes may be joined by drums to form a *bagad* or band, which evokes as much local support as the town football team.

Generally speaking, the further west you go in Brittany—in

other words, the further you are from the influence of
metropolitan France—the stronger grows the attachment to local
traditions. In Ille-et-Vilaine, except for a few places like St-
Malo, you could really be anywhere else in France; but once you
are in Finistère, with its unique architecture and atmosphere,
you know you could not be anywhere but in Brittany.

Famous people

As you might expect, the earliest Bretons to be remembered are
its army of saints, mostly from Wales and Ireland, who in the
5th and 6th centuries crossed the
Channel to bring Christianity to
pagan Brittany. Of these the most
famous are the 'Seven Founding
Saints'—Samson, Malo, Brieuc,
Tugdual, Paul-Aurelian, Corentin
and Patern. Of these Malo, Brieuc
and Paul-Aurelian have towns
named after them (St-Malo,
St-Brieuc and St-Pol-de-Léon),
while Corentin is the patron saint
of Quimper and Samson that of
Dol-de-Bretagne. Of later saints,
the most fondly remembered is
the 13thC St-Yves of Tréguier,
the patron saint of lawyers.

*St-Yves—16thC statue in
the cathedral at Tréguier*

From the great days of Breton
independence, between the 9th
and the 16th centuries, the first
and last rulers are the best
remembered. Nominoë, the first duke of Brittany, defeated
Charles the Bald of France in AD845 and established Brittany
as an independent duchy. The last ruler of the country, Duchess
Anne, is still recalled by street names all over Brittany. Married
to two kings of France, she managed to keep Brittany
precariously independent, but only 18 years after her death, in
1532, it finally came under the rule of France.

Brittany's fighting tradition was maintained down the years by
a succession of warriors. Best known is Bertrand du Guesclin,
born near Dinan, who throughout much of the 14th century
hammered both the English and the French. Made Marshal of
France, he died on a campaign in 1380. A later hero was the
extraordinary La Tour d'Auvergne, created France's 'First
Grenadier' by Napoleon, who was killed in action in 1800.

Brittany has produced great seafarers as well as soldiers, many
of them from the little town of St-Malo. Among them were the
corsaires—not pirates as we think of them today, but captains
granted by the crown the right to *'faire la course'*, that is, to
raid foreign shipping under well-defined rules. The greatest of
them, René Duguay-Trouin and Robert Surcouf, are
commemorated by statues on the ramparts of St-Malo, as is
Jacques Cartier, the 16thC discoverer of the St Lawrence River.

In literature, Brittany has produced only one name to be
counted among the really great—the arch-prophet of

romanticism, François-René de Chateaubriand. Born in St-Malo, he spent much of his childhood at the beautiful Château de Combourg. A century earlier, Mme de Sévigné, a court lady of Louis XIV's time, lived at the Château des Rochers and left a picture of her times in hundreds of descriptive letters to her friends. In this century, the poet Max Jacob, friend of Picasso and Cocteau and an artist in his own right, spent his early life in Quimper. He died in 1944 at the hands of the Nazis.

In the field of art, the name of Gauguin stands out. Born in Paris, he came to Pont-Aven in the 1880s and established the School of Pont-Aven, before going on to paint his best known works in the South Sea Islands. Brittany has produced a host of lesser artists, many of whose works are in the galleries up and down the country.

Statue of du Guesclin, Dinan

A short history of Brittany

Though it looks slightly different, the name of Brittany is the same as that of our country. The Bretons live in Petite Bretagne, which has lost its adjective, while we live in Grande Bretagne, which has kept it. The reason for this goes back to the 5th century, when the Celtic races from Wales and Ireland, driven ever further westward by the invading Angles and Saxons, took to their boats and sailed south to the westernmost peninsula of northern Europe, a country very similar in many respects to their own.

They were not the first people on the scene. Stone Age man had hunted through the thick forests and fished the rich coastal waters, and towards the end of the Stone Age, in the centuries round about 2000BC, tribes with a high degree of organisation had built tombs and stone circles over much of Brittany, and left at Carnac the rows of standing stones that still remain one of the ancient wonders of the world.

Some time in the 6th century BC the Gauls arrived, calling the country Ar-mor, the Country of the Sea—a name taken over by the Romans, who conquered the Gallic tribes in 56BC and set up the province of Gallia Armorica. With the decline of Rome in the 5th century and the chaos of barbarian invasions, the stage was set for the Celtic colonisation that led to modern Brittany. The Celts set up their own religious organisation, based on bishoprics which were loosely knit, rather than the territorial organisation favoured by the Roman Catholic church—another distinction, besides language and origins, that set the Bretons apart from the rest of France.

Conquered by Charlemagne at the end of the 8th century AD, Brittany threw off the Frankish supremacy within less than 50 years when Nominoë, the first duke of Brittany, defeated the Franks in AD845 and declared Brittany an independent duchy. Anarchy took over again at the beginning of the 10th century, when the Norsemen in their longships plundered and pillaged their way through Brittany almost unchecked. Then in AD939 Alain Barbe-Torte drove out the Norsemen, and the duchy was re-established on a far more secure basis—so secure that it lasted for almost 600 years, through the centuries of warfare with invading English and French armies, and the constant squabbles between the various claimants to the dukedom.

Brittany reached the height of its power, prestige and artistic glory under the last of the dukes, members of the House of Montfort. This was the period of superb Gothic churches and of the earliest of the noble stone calvaries that adorn most of the towns and villages of western Brittany. The last of the line, the much-loved Duchess Anne, after marrying two French kings in the hope of a son to carry on the ducal line, died in 1514, and her daughter married the future François I of France. Thus Brittany finally came by marriage under the French crown—an event officially recognised in 1532, when the Breton parliament handed over their autonomy to François I.

However, Brittany kept a measure of self-determination until 1790, when the Revolution abolished it by decree and set up five départements in its place. In many ways the period from 1532 to 1790 was a golden age for Brittany. It still had a semi-independent parliament, established at Rennes; and the building of fine churches and calvaries continued. During this period, Brittany was shaken by two major upheavals: during the 1590s, when the religious conflict known as the Wars of the League led to large-scale banditry in the west of the country; and again in 1675, when the so-called 'Stamped Paper' revolt, against a tax on documents, led to a full-scale peasant uprising. These were also the years of fine châteaux built in the Classical style, and the growth of Lorient and Brest into major international seaports.

After the Revolution of 1789, Brittany had a final spasm of revolt when the Chouans (anti-Revolutionary Royalists) made a short-lived

Château de la Bretesche, Missillac

attempt to get control of the country, but only succeeded in staging an unsuccessful invasion of the Quiberon Peninsula. Throughout the 19th century Brittany stagnated, under a central government that discouraged the Breton language and any other non-French manifestation. During World War I a quarter of a million Bretons were killed (Breton nationalists say they were deliberately put in the front line), and in World War II the Breton resistance fighters were some of the most dedicated and effective in the whole of France.

Resistance monument, Saffré

During the past 40 years the nationalists have kept alive the hope of an independent Brittany by fostering the language and other cultural aspects of Breton life. Agriculture has seen a great revival, especially in the north round Roscoff, where Brittany Ferries carries not only passengers but mountains of vegetables across the Channel. A blow was dealt to the unity of Brittany in the 1960s by the removal of Loire-Atlantique and the great city of Nantes from the five Breton départements, leaving only four behind. But the Bretons have seen bigger disasters and survived them, and Brittany remains today the same tough and independent country as it was in the days of Nominoë.

Language

The division between east and west Brittany is seen at its strongest in the distribution of the Breton language. The French call the eastern half of Brittany (the half nearest to themselves) Haute Bretagne or Upper Brittany; while the western half is Bas Bretagne or Lower Brittany. (This has nothing to do with the height above sea level, as the highest hills are all in Bas Bretagne.) Traditionally, Breton was spoken only in Bas Bretagne, west of an imaginary line running roughly from St-Brieuc in the north to Vannes in the south. Since the French Revolution this difference has become blurred, through the deliberate encouragement of the French language all over Brittany, and the more recent revival of Breton in universities in both Bas and Haute Bretagne. But the basic distinction still holds, and you are unlikely to hear the locals talking Breton except in Finistère, and parts of the Côtes-du-Nord and Morbihan.

The Breton language lives on mainly in place names, where it shows its kinship with Welsh. Here are a few common names, or components of names, met with as you go further west.

Aber	Estuary	*Kozh, koz*	Old
Aven, avon	River	*Lann*	Monastery
Beg	Cape, promontory	*Manac'h, monac'h*	Monk
Bihan	Small	*Menez*	Mountain
Bras, braz	Big	*Meur*	Large
Du	Black	*Mor*	Sea
Enes	Island	*Palud*	Marsh
Feunteun	Spring	*Penn, pem*	End, top
Glas, glaz	Blue (slate), green (vegetation)	*Plou*	Parish
Goat, goet	Wood	*Pont*	Bridge
Gwenn, guen	White	*Porz*	Harbour
Hen	Old	*Roc'h*	Rock
Ilis	Church	*Sant*	Saint
Kastell	Castle	*Ti, ty*	House
Ker	Town, village	*Toull*	Hole

Money

Under current legislation visitors may take any amount of English or French currency into France, but they may only export 5000 francs in bank notes or cash. Customs regulations and allowances are clearly displayed at all entry and departure points but it is worth reading the small print carefully as there are some anomalies. For example, despite popular belief to the contrary, it is possible to bring many species of plants and trees into England from France. Also the wine allowance into England varies depending on whether the purchase was made in France or at a duty free shop. Money can be changed before leaving England through the major banks, at the airport or main station, at some ferry terminals, on some ferries (but not on hovercraft), at French banks or at some major international railway stations. It is generally best to change money at banks. The Offices de Tourisme will advise where money can be changed. Some large hotels may change money, but at very unfavourable rates.

Banks

French banks open early, but close for a long lunch hour. Typical opening times are *08.15–12.00, 14.00–16.00*. Most banks are closed *on Sat & Sun* and many are also closed *on Mon*. They also close on the 11 public holidays in France, which are as follows:

Jan 1 (New Year's Day)	Whit Monday (Pentecôte)
Easter Monday	Jul 14 (Bastille Day)
May 1 (May Day)	Aug 13 (Assumption Day)
May 8 (Victory in Europe, VE Day)	Nov 1 (All Saints' Day)
	Nov 11 (Remembrance Day)
May 12 (Ascension Day)	Dec 25 (Christmas Day)

Currency

French currency is a decimal system based on the franc. Each
franc equals 100 centimes. There are 5, 10 and 20 centime coins
which are bronze coloured, and 50 centime and 1, 2 and 5 franc
coins in silver. These are all of a traditional design. There is
also a bronze 10 franc coin, a distinctive modern design. Notes
of 10, 20, 50, 100, 200 and 500 francs are all readily available.
Over the last few years the exchange rate has varied between 9
and 13 francs to the pound, but most banks display a board
showing the current rate of exchange.

Travellers' cheques
Travellers' cheques and cash can be changed at most banks, and
those banks displaying the EC (Eurocheque) sign will cash
British bank cheques up to a daily value of £100 (in two × £50
cheques) if the cheques are supported by a Eurocheque card.
This is *not* the normal UK cheque card but a special card issued
on demand by any British bank. Credit cards, while widely used,
are not always accepted in the smaller hotels and restaurants.
They can be used in many petrol stations but not in supermarkets. To save embarrassment, adequate cash should support
travellers' cheques and credit cards when possible.

Tipping & taxes

One of the pleasant things about travelling anywhere in France
is that the price on the menu is the price on the bill. As a rule,
most French restaurants offer a *carte* listing separate dishes at
various prices and at least one *menu* at a fixed price. The menu
can range, according to the dishes involved, from 40 to 200 francs
or more—and this price will not normally include wine or
coffee. Items not included are often referred to on menus as *en
sus* (extra). Tax and service at 15% is usually included on the
bill (*compris*) and no further tip is therefore expected, although
a small addition for good service will be much appreciated. If
the service is not included (*service non compris*) leave about
15%, depending on the quality of the service.

The same rule applies in hotels, where the price displayed in
the window, at the reception desk and behind the door of the
room will be the price on the bill in the morning. It is customary
to tip anyone providing a special service—such as carrying
luggage or parking the car; the amount depends on the effort
involved but between two and ten francs is adequate.

Other people who may expect a tip include cinema usherettes
(about one franc per seat); lavatory attendants will expect about
50 centimes; porters at airports and railway stations have a fixed
charge per item of baggage; extra services at a garage like having
the windscreen washed or the oil checked should be rewarded
with a small tip.

Taxi drivers can be tipped at the rate of about 10–15% of the
amount on the meter, and if they feel that you have undertipped
them be sure that they will inform you of the fact.

In all other cases where a tip seems reasonable, a maximum
of 15% of the bill is quite adequate. In general, tipping
expectations across the Channel are the same as in Britain.

Post offices & telephones

Post offices

Post offices are marked *Poste* or *PTT* (Poste, Téléphone,
Télégraphe) or indicated by a stylised blue bird on a white background, and can be found in all towns and villages. They provide
a full range of postal services, and the staff will help visitors to
make long-distance or international telephone calls. The central
post office in any town will also handle letters sent to await
collection (*Poste Restante*). When addressing letters to anywhere
in France, always include the five-digit postal code (eg 35000
Rennes). Should the post office be closed, stamps for letters and
postcards to most countries can be obtained from yellow coin-
operated machines in the street or from tobacconists (*tabacs*),
which are indicated by a red cone on the outside of the building.

Poste Restante

If you have arranged to have letters sent to a post office,
remember to take your passport with you as proof of identity
when you go to collect them. The post office will normally hold
mail for a fortnight; letters will then be returned to the sender,
whose name and address should be marked on the envelope.

Telephones

The French telephone service has improved greatly in recent
years and direct-dial telephone boxes, remarkably unvandalised,
can be found everywhere. Most are push-button and can be used
to make international calls. The telephones are coin-operated
and any money remaining at the end of the call will be indicated
on a display window.

    Calls can also be made from a post office. The caller goes to
a booth, and the call can be put through by the counter clerk
or by the caller. Remember that calls from a hotel, restaurant or
café incur a surcharge of up to 40%. Cheap-rate calls can be
made *from 20.00–08.00, Sun & hols*, when charges are halved,
and you can call England for three minutes for about five francs.

Dialling tones

French dialling tones are very different to those used in the UK.
Very rapid, shrill pips mean that the call is being connected;
slightly slower, less shrill pips or alternating long and short beeps
mean that the number is engaged; three rapid pips in ascending
pitch precede a special announcement. To hear a recording of
French telephone tones, in Britain dial 104 and ask the operator.

Telephone numbers

French telephone numbers are composed of six digits, shown in
the telephone directory as three pairs of digits. If you are making
a call within the same département (eg from Rennes to
Combourg) you need dial only these six figures.

    To call a number in another département, dial
16—inter-départemental code, then (for example)
99—area code (Ille-et-Vilaine), then the six-digit local number.
Thus to dial the Musée des Beaux-Arts in Rennes, Ille-et-Vilaine,
from a different département, one would dial 16 (99) 30 83 87.

To call the UK from France, dial
19—international code, wait for the tone, then
44—code for the UK, then (for example)
734—area code (Reading) omitting the initial zero, then the
seven-digit local number.
Thus to dial the French Government Tourist Office in London
from France, one would dial 19 44 (1) 491–7622.

To call France from the UK, a similar system obtains but with
different codes:
010—international code, then
33—code for France, then (for example)
99—area code (Ille-et-Vilaine), then the six-digit local number.
Thus to dial the Hôtel de la Plage in Dinard, Ille-et-Vilaine,
from Britain one would dial 010 33 (99) 46 14 87.

Emergency numbers
Directory enquiries—**12**   Fire—**18**   Operator—**13**   Police—**17**

Useful phrases

Where is the nearest post office?
Où est le bureau de poste le plus proche?

I would like X number of Y-franc stamps.
Je voudrais X timbres-poste à Y francs.

How much is it to send this letter/card to . . . ?
Combien coûte cette lettre/carte postale pour . . . ?

Is there a post office open on Sunday morning?
Y a-t-il un bureau de poste ouvert le dimanche matin?

I should like to telephone to England.
Je voudrais téléphoner à l'Angleterre.

Please give me the telephone directory for . . .
Voulez-vous me donner l'annuaire téléphonique à. . . .

My call has been cut off. Please reconnect me.
La communication a été coupée. Veuillez la rétablir.

Can I have some change, please?
Je voudrais de la monnaie, s'il vous plaît.

Using the guide

Modern Brittany is divided into four administrative regions, or
départements—Finistère, Côtes-du-Nord, Morbihan and Ille-et-
Vilaine—and the information in this book is organised and
presented on that basis. We have also included Loire-Atlantique
north of the Loire, since historically and culturally this is very
much a part of the region. Detailed facts are given on towns
and villages, hotels, restaurants, museums and buildings of
historic interest. Tours are suggested which cover all the best
parts of the province, and sights and events which the wise
traveller may wish to see are highlighted.

The guide has been based on selective information, for the five
départements covered are by no means homogeneous, and the
traveller should choose to visit those parts which, on the evidence

presented, offer the kind of trip which appeals to his or her individual taste. Brittany, with the exception of La Baule and certain smaller resorts in summer, is not a high fashion area like the Côte d'Azur. It offers simpler, if more cultured delights. Holidaymakers will find more nightlife and activity round Dinard and on the Pink Granite Coast than they will in the whole of central Brittany, which, on the other hand, has great possibilities for the countrylover, the walker and the cyclist.

Travellers using this guide should employ it especially to plan ahead, and so avoid disappointment, supplementing the information it contains with some background reading of a more general nature. Detailed help is also available from the French Government Tourist Office in London and from Offices de Tourisme and Syndicats d'Initiative in Brittany.

As a first and final piece of advice, wise travellers in any part of France will always: travel on minor roads; stay in small hotels; eat in local restaurants. With that advice, and this book, an enjoyable visit to Brittany is just a ferry ride away.

Structure, abbreviations & symbols

The guide is divided into five gazetteer sections, each covering one *département* or administrative province. Each section opens with a map of the département, showing its position in the region, towns and villages mentioned in the text and major roads. The text is conveniently separated into a wide range of topics. Entries are listed alphabetically and clearly map-referenced to the départemental map at the beginning of the section. The word **Charge** denotes an entry fee. City plans are included at the end of the gazetteer text and are indicated in the text by an *italic* heading. There is a comprehensive index at the end of the book.

The following symbols and abbreviations are used in the guide:

Pop	Population		Credit cards accepted:
MD	Market day	A	Access (also Master Card,
ft	Foot/feet		Eurocard)
mi	Mile(s)	Ax	American Express
m	Metre(s)	Dc	Diners Club
km	Kilometre(s)	V	Visa (including Barclaycard)

Price brackets are used as follows:

Accommodation: price of a double room for one night

F	100 francs and under
FF	100–300 francs
FFF	300 francs and over

Restaurants: price of a three-course meal for one including tax, service, cover and house wine

F	50 francs and under
FF	50–100 francs
FFF	100 francs and over

NB These prices were accurate when researched but, as prices fluctuate rapidly, should be used for comparison only.

Finistère

To the ancient Celts, the western end of Brittany was literally the end of the world—*Penn ar Bed* in Breton, *Finis Terrae* in Latin and thus Finistère. Shattered and fragmented by the might of the Atlantic, and cut into three separate peninsulas by the Rade de Brest and Douarnenez Bay, Brittany faces towards the sunset across the limitless waters.

The further west you go, the more Breton the land, the buildings and the people become. The countryside is harsher here, with the only two ranges of hills remotely resembling mountains—the Monts d'Arrée and the Montagnes Noires—in the whole country. The buildings have evolved forms uniquely suitable to the granite from which they were built, the churches with spiky pinnacles, crockets, towers and spires, the houses crouching low against the forces of wind, rain and sea. Taken as a whole, the people of Finistère are more conscious of their Breton heritage than their compatriots in the rest of Brittany. More of them speak Breton and wear their regional costumes, and it is in Finistère that most of the great religious festivals or *pardons* take place.

On the map, Finistère is a highly irregular rectangle, with the sea on three of the four sides, so not surprisingly its history has been largely shaped by the sea. The oldest towns—Quimper, Quimperlé, Morlaix, Landerneau—grew up on estuaries, at the first practicable place to build a bridge across the river, and until the 19th century nearly all their trade was water-borne. Apart from these major centres, almost every creek has its own small fishing harbour, once prosperous, then fallen into decay, and now often rescued in the nick of time by small-boat sailors who bring them a share, if only a small one, of the consumer wealth of the late 20th century.

Further inland too the wealth of Finistère came originally by water. Those unique examples of Breton architecture, the parish closes (*enclos paroissiaux*), are found mainly along the rivers, the finest of them inland from Landerneau along the Elorn. Farmers and merchants grew wealthy from flax planted on the uplands and shipped downstream, and the money they made was ploughed back into the land, and into the churches, calvaries and triumphal arches they built for the good of their souls and the delight of their eyes.

Inland Finistère as well as the coast is now beginning to recover from centuries of indifference. The harsh mountain heartland, like the Welsh hills, is seeing the growth of regional craft centres where ancient skills are revived, while inland resorts like Huelgoat are luring tourists away from the crowded coast to the beauty of rock, woodland and hillside. It is only fitting that all aspects of Breton culture should be celebrated each *Jul* in Finistère's superb capital city, Quimper, when Breton dance, music, costume, food and drink provide a week-long festival of regional pride that can be found nowhere else in France, and perhaps nowhere else in Europe.

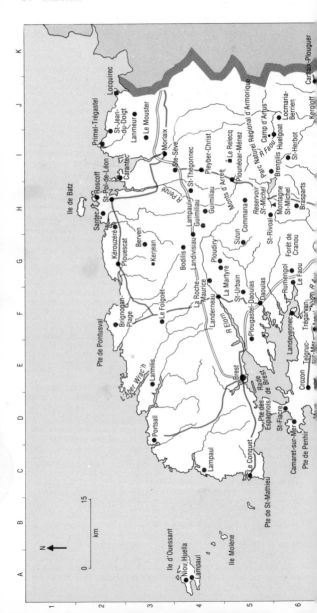

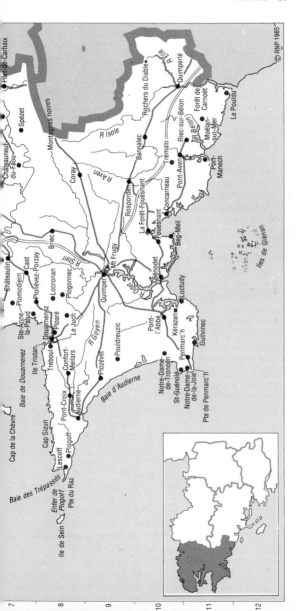

Towns & villages

Audierne   **D 8**
22mi/35km W of Quimper. Pop
3600. MD Wed & Sat. Once a
tunny-fishing centre, this small port
in an attractive setting by the
Goyen estuary is now mainly
concerned with catching lobsters
and crayfish. From the bridge over
the estuary there is a fine view of
the town, with its waterfront sweep
of houses.

Beg-Meil   **G 10**
12.5mi/20km SE of Quimper. Pop
280. This small, quiet resort,
reached down a dead-end road,
looks east across the bay to
Concarneau. The beach, sandy and
with rounded rocks, is reached
from a headland planted with pine-
trees. Beg-Meil still has a good
many large 19thC villas in their own
gardens, and cannot have changed
much since Marcel Proust came
here on holiday in 1895.

Bénodet   **G 10**
9.5mi/15km S of Quimper. Pop
2100. MD Mon. The most popular
resort on the south coast of
Finistère, Bénodet's population rises
to some 35,000 at the height of the
summer season. It has been a
favourite with British
holidaymakers since the 19th
century, and still remains so. Built
on the east side of the Odet
estuary, it has no bridge to the other
side (though there is a toll bridge
a short way upstream), and so it has
expanded inland and along the
coast. There are two main beaches,
the town beach and the Plage du
Letty, east of the headland.
Bénodet is the starting point for
river trips up the beautiful Odet
Valley to Quimper.

Brest   **E 5**
37.5mi/60km W of Morlaix. Pop
172,000. MD Mon & Fri. The
dockyards and industrial
installations of Brest sprawl along
the north shore of the Rade de
Brest, from the mouth of the Elorn
River to the narrows called the
Goulet de Brest, across from the
Pointe des Espagnols on the Crozon
Peninsula. Once one of the major
ports of western Europe, it has
shared with other European ports
in the general decline in western

shipping. Fortunately its superb
natural harbour has been improved
to take modern ships of the largest
size, and it has diversified into
industries of all sorts.
Brest was certainly a maritime
centre in pre-Roman times. The
Romans fortified it; throughout the
Middle Ages it was much fought
over; and it began to take on its
modern importance under Louis
XIV in the 17th century, when it
became the chief port of the
French navy. It reached the height
of its prosperity with the advent of
the railway and steam-powered
ships in the 19th century,
expanding from the banks of the
Penfeld River, on which old Brest
was built, east and west along the
Rade de Brest.
During World War II Brest was
largely obliterated, first by Allied
bombing, but mainly at the time of
the Liberation in 1944, when the
Germans put up a last-ditch
defence, and were only defeated
after a siege of six weeks followed
by savage house-to-house fighting.
So, like St-Nazaire in Loire-
Atlantique, which suffered in a
similar way, Brest is now virtually
a new town, with wide streets of
boxlike, concrete buildings. What
is left of old Brest can best be seen
from the vast Pont de Recouvrance
across the Penfeld—the largest
vertical-lift bridge in Europe, with
two huge pylons from which the
central lifting section is suspended.
Upstream is the Arsénal Maritime,
the naval dockyard, which stretches
along both sides of the river but
can only be visited by French
citizens. Looking downstream, the
castle—now the Admiralty Office
(Préfecture Maritime)—is on the
left, facing the 15thC Tour Tanguy
now a museum.
Brest is a centre of the revival of
Breton language and culture, based
on its university. At its western end
is a new centre for research into
oceanography, the Centre National
d'Etudes Océanographiques.
A variety of boat trips start from
the Port de Commerce—round the
harbour, to Ushant via Le Conquet
and Molène, and across the Goulet
de Brest to the Crozon Peninsula.

Brignogan-Plage   **F**
13mi/21km N of Landerneau. Pop
1100. A pretty little seaside resort,

round a sweeping sandy bay, where strange-shaped rocks are uncovered at low tide. In former times the men of Brignogan were renowned as wreckers, tying lights to their cows' horns to lure ships on to the rocks, like their opposite numbers in Cornwall.
Just north of the village, towards the Pointe de Pontusval, is a tall *menhir* (standing stone), Christianised by having a cross carved on its summit.

Camaret-sur-Mer   **D 6**
26mi/41.5km NW of Châteaulin. Pop 3300. MD daily in season. The only town of any consequence on the Crozon Peninsula, with a pretty harbour protected by a natural breakwater of shingle. In former times it was a leading lobster-fishing port, though the trade has now declined. Camaret played its part in the frequent wars between England and France. In 1694 an Anglo-Dutch invasion fleet landed on the shingle bank (the Sillon de Camaret) to attack the town and were repulsed, but not before they had knocked off the chapel belfry with a cannon ball. The chapel, built right out on the Sillon, dates originally from the 1500s and has been a sailors' shrine for centuries. Beyond it is the fortified tower known as the Tour Vauban, now a small museum. In 1801 the American inventor Robert Fulton carried out the earliest submarine experiments in Camaret harbour.

Carantec   **I 2**
9mi/14.5km NW of Morlaix. Pop 2500. MD Thur. Just across the estuary of the Penzé from Roscoff, this is a popular seaside resort for holidaymakers crossing the Channel from Plymouth. There are several good beaches round the promontory on which Carantec stands; their one slight disadvantage for swimmers is the distance to which the sea ebbs at low tide. On the other hand, this means that a number of small islands, notably the Ile Callot with its chapel, can be reached on foot as the tide falls.

Carhaix-Plouguer   **J 6**
31mi/49.5km SE of Morlaix. Pop 9900. MD Sat. An important crossroads town since pre-Roman times, Carhaix was the capital of a Gaulish tribe, the Osismii. In the Middle Ages it prospered from lead-mining, and in later centuries it was a centre of local agriculture. It has seen a recent revival with the coming of light industry.

Statue of La Tour d'Auvergne, Carhaix

Carhaix is famous among Bretons as the birthplace of La Tour d'Auvergne, born Théophile-Malo Corret in 1743. He was a pioneer of Breton language and literature, and won his place in French military glory during the Napoleonic wars, when Napoleon declared him 'the first grenadier of France'. He was killed in action in 1800. There is a statue of him in the main square of Carhaix, and a few relics are kept in the *mairie* (town hall). On the *last Sun in Jun* the town holds a festival in his honour.
With its roads radiating in every direction, Carhaix makes a good centre for exploring central Brittany.

Châteaulin   **G 7**
18mi/29km N of Quimper. Pop 6500. MD Thur. A peaceful little town, built on either side of the River Aulne, with tree-shaded riverside walks. The Aulne is a salmon river, and the fish appears on the town's coat of arms. In earlier times the salmon run was so vast that local workmen stipulated in their contracts that they would not eat salmon more than three times a week. After a serious

decline since World War II, the numbers of salmon have started to revive since 1980.

On the bluff above the town are the ruins of a castle, and a fine 16thC chapel containing a large number of statues of saints.

Châteauneuf-du-Faou   I 7

22mi/35km NE of Quimper. Pop 4000. MD Fri. Built high above the valley of the Aulne, on the edge of the Montagnes Noires, this is an unpretentious little town popular with fishermen. The tree-clad slopes below the town are said to be haunted by the ghosts of King Arthur's cavalry, who patrol the mountains whenever Brittany is threatened by war. The 19thC chapel of Notre-Dame-des-Portes, above the river, has a 15thC Gothic porch and is a centre of pilgrimage. A *pardon* (religious procession) is held here on the *3rd Sun in Aug*.

Concarneau   H 10

14mi/22.5km SE of Quimper. Pop 19,000. MD Mon & Fri. The Medieval walled city of Concarneau, first glimpsed from the main road along the coast, is an unforgettable sight. Built on a small island and linked to the mainland by a narrow causeway, it preserves the medieval illusion complete, in total contrast to the busy shipping all around, the modern harbour buildings, and the sprawl of Concarneau resort on the mainland.

Concarneau is now the chief tunny-fishing port of France, with its own canning factories, boatyards and a marine laboratory. Its Breton name is *Konk-Kernev*, the 'Creek of Cornouaille'—a creek that has made it a major port since at least the 13th century, when the island was first fortified. Visitors come to Concarneau to see the Medieval town (the Ville Close), to walk round the circuit of its ramparts, to buy curios and eat the local crêpes, and to visit the small museums within its walls. The fortifications were modified down the centuries, most recently by Louis XIV's great military engineer, Vauban, in the 17th century.

Every *Aug* Concarneau's maritime past and present are commemorated in the week-long Fête des Filets Bleus (Festival of the Blue Nets), originally a simple blessing of the fishermen's nets, but now a full-scale Breton folklore celebration.

Concarneau's sandy beaches are on the opposite side of the headland from the Ville Close, facing west towards the Beg-Meil Peninsula. From the harbour there are boat excursions across the bay to Beg-Meil, and out to sea to the Glénan Islands.

Le Conquet   C 5

15mi/24km W of Brest. Pop 1900. MD Tue. The most westerly town in the whole of Brittany, Le Conquet is a pretty little port built on the southern side of a picturesque estuary. Its small fishing boats are mainly used to catch lobster and crayfish. Though it is ancient in origin (the Breton name is *Konk-Léon*, the 'Creek of Léon', which was the old name for northern Brittany), not much of the historic town survives as it was largely burnt down by the English in 1558.

There are two good beaches nearby and there are boat services to the islands of Molène and Ushant.

Douarnenez   E 8

14mi/22.5km NW of Quimper. Pop 19,300. MD Mon & Fri. Douarnenez, the fifth most important fishing port in France, looks north across a wide bay towards the Crozon Peninsula. The 'New Harbour' faces out to sea, but small fishing boats and pleasure craft moor in the sheltered waters of Port-Rhu, the deep estuary that separates Douarnenez from the neighbouring holiday resort of Tréboul, immediately to the west. Though Douarnenez is now a workaday harbour town, its origins are buried deep in Breton legend. Its name is said to come from the Breton *Douar Nevez*, meaning 'New Land'—the land that appeared when the mysterious city of Ys was swallowed up by the sea. Ys, so the story goes, was ruled over by the good King Gradlon, who kept round his neck the keys to the sluice-gates that protected Ys from being flooded by the sea. Alas, Gradlon's daughter fell in love with the Devil in the guise of a young prince, who persuaded her to steal the keys from the king's neck while he lay asleep. The Devil opened the sluice gates, the sea flooded in, and the city of Ys was engulfed. Only Gradlon survived, outstripping the flood on his horse. On calm nights the ghostly church bells of Ys can still be heard, chiming far below the surface of Douarnenez Bay.

Another famous legend, the tragic love affair of Tristan and Isolde, is recalled by the tiny tree-covered Ile Tristan, just offshore. At the end of the 16th century the island was the stronghold of the brigand Le Fontenelle, who held Finistère in a state of terror for a decade before being captured and executed in 1602.

Douarnenez has its own small beach, but there are better beaches nearby at Ploaré to the east and Tréboul to the west.

Le Faou   **G 6**
7.5mi/12km N of Châteaulin. Pop 1500. A pretty harbour village on the tidal estuary of the Faou. It has a few 16thC houses with slate-hung façades, and a church overlooking the river.

Fouesnant   **G 10**
9.5mi/15km SE of Quimper. Pop 6700. MD Fri. An overgrown village rather than a town, Fouesnant is an agricultural centre said to produce the best cider in Brittany. It is set in an orchard landscape of apples, cherries and chestnut trees.

Fouesnant has given its name to one of the most distinctive of all the Breton lace head-dresses (coiffes)—the Giz Foen, or 'Style of Fouesnant', which has high 'wings' on either side of the head, and is worn with a wide lace collar. These are worn especially at the Fête des Pommiers (Apple-tree Festival) in Jul.

Guilvinec   **E 11**
6mi/9.5km SW of Pont-l'Abbé. Pop 6600. MD Tue. A busy fishing port, with trawlers that go out after tunny and sardine.

Huelgoat   **I 6**
9mi/14.5km S of Morlaix. Pop 2300. MD Thur. Huelgoat has a small town centre, with a lake on its west side, and superb scenery

to explore on its east (see 'Countryside' section). The parish church, in the wide main street, has a statue of St-Yves between a rich man and a poor man (see Tréguier, Côtes-du-Nord).

Landerneau   **F 4**
12.5mi/20km E of Brest. Pop 15,700. MD Tue & Sat. Built at the point where the estuary of the Elorn narrows to river width, Landerneau was for centuries an important commercial centre, and was at one time the capital of the region of Léon. It is an attractive riverside town, with an ancient bridge that links two bishoprics, Léon to the north and Cornouaille to the south. A traditional expression, "Ça fera du bruit dans Landerneau" ("That will make a noise in Landerneau"), is said to arise from the local practice of making an uproar outside the house of any widow who decided to get married again.

Landivisiau   **G 4**
14mi/22.5km W of Morlaix. Pop 7800. MD Wed. A busy market town, and the centre of an important cattle trade. Near the town centre is a fountain dedicated to St-Thivisiau, made largely of relief sculptures from 15thC tombs. Landivisiau is only a few km from the great parish closes of Lampaul-Guimiliau, Guimiliau and St-Thégonnec.

Locquirec   **J 2**
12mi/19km NE of Morlaix. Pop 1050. A small resort and fishing port, at the western end of the Corniche d'Armorique. It is built on a peninsula, mainly rocky but with some small, sandy beaches, and is a good centre for exploring the coastal region westwards into Finistère, and north east to the Côtes-du-Nord.

Locronan   **F 8**
10.5mi/17km NW of Quimper. Pop 700. Seemingly little altered for the past three centuries, Locronan is a gem of a stone-built town, deservedly one of the most popular places in Finistère for tourists to visit. Its 16th and 17thC merchants' houses have been largely turned into craft workshops and salerooms, where visitors can buy pottery, woven materials and sculptures,

and also watch them being made.
St-Ronan, after whom the town is
named, was a 5thC Irish monk who
is said to have died near St-Brieuc
(Côtes-du-Nord), from where his
body was miraculously transported
westwards on a cart drawn by two
wild buffalo. In the Middle Ages
the citizens grew wealthy from
weaving sailcloth—an industry that
lasted well into the 18th century.
Just east of the town is a hill called
the Montagne de Locronan. Every
six years, on the *3rd Sun in Jul*, the
chapel at its summit is the goal of
a great religious procession, the
Grande Troménie. Before reaching
the chapel, the procession wends its
way across the countryside for
about 7.5mi/12km, stopping at
numerous small shrines along the
way. (The next Grande Troménie is
due in 1989.) In the intervening
years there is a shorter procession,
the *Petite Troménie*, also held
in *Jul*.

Loctudy   F 10
4mi/6.5km SE of Pont-l'Abbé. Pop
3500. A small family seaside resort
and fishing port, with a fine
Romanesque church. Boats sail
from Loctudy to the offshore
Glénan Islands (1.5hr trip).

Morgat   D 6
22mi/35km W of Châteaulin. Pop
(with Crozon) 3500. A small resort
near the west end of the Crozon
Peninsula, linked to the town of
Crozon. Its east-facing beach is a
fine sweep of sand, sheltered by a
headland. Just to the south are
shore caves known as the Grandes
Grottes, which can be visited by
boat from Morgat.

Morlaix   I 3
15.5mi/25km SE of Roscoff. Pop
21,000. MD Sat. One of the oldest
towns in Brittany, Morlaix still has
enough half-timbered houses to
remind the visitor of its prosperity
in the 15th and 16th centuries. It
is dominated by a lofty viaduct,
built to carry the railway in the
1860s, which divides it into two
sections: inland, the streets of old
Morlaix, and on the north side the
River Dossen, lined with quayside
houses and popular with small-boat
sailors.
Called *Montroulez* in Breton, the
town's French name was used in a

punning way for its motto: "*S'ils te
mordent, mords-les*" ("If they bite
you, bite them"). This refers to a
raid by the English in 1522. The
invaders found Morlaix
undefended, as most of the
inhabitants were out of town for a
festival. After looting the houses,
the troops drank themselves
insensible in the cellars. When the
locals returned, they cut them down
without any trouble, so that the
town fountain ran red with English
blood. Fortunately, Morlaix is now
a good deal more hospitable to
visitors from across the Channel.
With the growing importance of
Brest in the 17th and 18th
centuries Morlaix declined, but it
has seen a recent revival with the
growth of light industry. A tobacco
factory on the quayside, founded
as long ago as 1736, is still in
operation.
The hamlet of St-Sève (2.5mi/4km
SW of Morlaix) has been claimed
as the birthplace of Napoleon, in
1769. The story probably stems
from the fact that his mother is
known to have spent the autumn
of 1768 at a nearby château
belonging to the governor of
Corsica.

Penmarc'h   E 1
9mi/14.5km W of Pont-l'Abbé. Pop
7000. Though the present
atmosphere of this small town is one
of sleepy decay, it was once one of
Brittany's main harbour towns.
Its large 16thC church, built in
Flamboyant Gothic style, harks
back to far wealthier times.
Penmarc'h suffered greatly in the
1590s, when the brigand
Fontenelle raged through south-
west Brittany with fire and sword
(*see Douarnenez*), and never
recovered its prosperity in the
centuries that followed.

Plouescat   G
9.5mi/15km W of St-Pol-de-Léon.
Pop 4100. MD Sat. A small
agricultural town, worth visiting for
its 16thC covered market, which
has a roof supported by massive
carved beams.

Plougastel-Daoulas   E
6mi/9.5km E of Brest. Pop 8200.
MD Thur. The chief strawberry-
growing centre in Brittany, and the
only town in the peaceful

Plougastel Peninsula, which juts
out into the Rade de Brest.
Strawberries were introduced here
from Virginia towards the end of
the 18th century. Outside the
church in the centre of the town is
one of the finest calvaries in
Brittany, built about 1600 after an
outbreak of plague. It has more
figures than any calvary except the
one at Guimiliau, which probably
inspired it.

Plozévet E 9
15.5mi/25km W of Quimper. Pop
3200. MD 1st Mon each month. A
village at the western limit of the
Bigouden country (see Pont-
l'Abbé). It has a fine 16thC church,
with 13thC interior arcading. Near
the town hall is a lifelike bronze
group of the typical Breton musical
duo of bombarde (shawm or oboe)
and biniou (bagpipe), by the Breton
sculptor René Quillivic
(1879–1969).

Statue of bombarde and biniou
players, Plozévet

Pont-Aven I 10
10.5mi/17km W of Quimperlé. Pop
3500. MD Tue. Pont-Aven is
famous for its connection with Paul
Gauguin and a group of lesser
artists, who came here to paint in
the 1880s. It is still a pretty little
town, with a neat square named
after Gauguin and a watermill
below the bridge; but, as it lies
along the main coast road, in
summer its narrow main street is
choked with traffic. Upstream
from the bridge there is a delightful
walk beside the Aven through the
Bois d'Amour ('Wood of Love'). At
the end of the path (20 minutes'
walk) is a trout farm where trout
are netted from the rearing-pools,
killed by a blow to the head, and
sold fresh to the public.

Pont-Croix D 8
10mi/16km W of Douarnenez. Pop
1900. MD Thur & Sun. Apart from
Audierne, Pont-Croix is the only
town of any size between
Douarnenez and the Pointe du Raz.
It has several narrow lanes of old
houses, and a fine church, 13thC
and with a tall spire, 220ft/67m
high, above a 15thC bell-tower.

Pont-l'Abbé F 10
12.5mi/20km SW of Quimper. Pop
7900. MD Thur. A quiet riverside
town, Pont-l'Abbé gets its name
from a bridge built here in the
Middle Ages by the abbots of
Loctudy. It is the capital of the Pays
Bigouden, a region with imprecise
boundaries, running from the west
bank of the Odet and taking in the
Penmarc'h Peninsula and the
coastal area to a point short of
Audierne. This has always been a
country apart, in all aspects of
living, including the women's
clothes—the Bigouden head-dress
(coiffe) is immensely tall and the
most recognisable of them all.
Bigouden-produced lace is also
famous. The 14thC château
contains a museum devoted to the
life of the region.
Everyday life in the Pays Bigouden
between the wars has been vividly
recreated in the most widely read
book to have come out of Brittany
in recent years, 'Le Cheval
d'Orgueil' ('The Horse of Pride'),
by Pierre-Jakez Hélias, born in
1914 in the village of Pouldreuzic,
8mi/13km NW of Pont-l'Abbé.

Le Pouldu J 11
7.5mi/12km S of Quimperlé. Pop
370. A tiny seaside resort at the
mouth of the Laïta River. Gauguin
spent some time here painting in
1889, preferring it to Pont-Aven.

Primel-Trégastel I 2
13mi/21km N of Morlaix. Pop 195.
A small seaside resort near the rocky
Pointe de Primel, from which there
are magnificent views west towards
Roscoff and east to Trégastel.

Quimper G 9
49mi/78.5km SE of Brest. Pop
61,000. MD Wed & Sat. The capital
both of Finistère and that imprecise
region of south-west Brittany
known as Cornouaille, Quimper is
a delightful town, large enough to

offer all the resources of an important provincial centre, yet not too large to be easily explored on foot. Its Breton name, *Kemper*, means 'river junction', and Quimper owed its early prosperity to its position at the junction of the Odet, which still runs fast through the centre of the city, and the Steir, smaller and now channelled through a pipe along the lowest part of its course.

The area has been inhabited since prehistoric times and the Romans had a colony at Locmaria, downstream from today's city. Quimper itself traces its origins back to a period a little later than the Romans: to the earliest days of Brittany, in the 4th and 5th centuries, and to the two semi-mythical figures of St-Corentin and King Gradlon, who were closely associated. (*For Gradlon, see Douarnenez.*) They are still associated in Quimper's splendid cathedral, a stone's throw from the river, which dominates the centre of the city; it is dedicated to St-Corentin, while on top of the parapet between the two towers Gradlon sits on his horse and looks out over the city he founded.

South of the cathedral, part of the Medieval city wall runs alongside the river. Quimper's Medieval streets, notably the rue Kéréon—consisting largely of well preserved half-timbered houses with jutting upper storeys—are across the main square (pl St-Corentin) to the west and north of the cathedral. In the old town, names like the pl au Beurre recall the days when each commodity had its own market and vendors. At the far end of the rue Kéréon the pl Terre-au-Duc is a reminder that this part of the city was ruled by the dukes of Brittany, whereas Quimper within the town walls was ruled by the bishop.

On the south side of the river is a tree-covered hill, Mont Frugy, with alleyways below it leading along the river to Locmaria. Below Frugy, the wide pl de la Résistance is the setting for the annual Fêtes de Cornouaille, a week-long festival held each *Jul*, culminating in a weekend of Breton music and dance. Here performers come together from all over Brittany to

vie with one another in the splendour of their regional costumes, the agility of their dancers, and the virtuosity of their musicians on drums, bagpipes, oboes, accordions and other outdoor instruments. The festival ends with a grand fireworks display and a *fest-noz* (night celebration) in which thousands of Quimpérois and visitors take part, all dancing the Breton gavotte under the plane trees and through the ancient streets of Quimper, with time off for litres of cider and quantities of crêpes to restore their energies.

Quimper has an excellent art gallery (the Musée des Beaux-Arts) and historical museum (Musée Breton) together with the potteries (*faïenceries*) at Locmaria, where the brightly coloured Quimper ware is made. Though it is not the most accessible of cities, it makes a good centre for exploring the south-west corner of Brittany, and for visiting coastal resorts like Bénodet and Concarneau. There are regular boat trips down the river to Bénodet, as often as six times a day in summer.

Quimperlé   J 1

27.5mi/44km E of Quimper. Pop 11,000. MD Fri. Like Quimper, Quimperlé's name derives from the Breton *Kemper*, meaning 'river junction'—in this case the River Ellé (Quimper-Ellé, shortened to Quimperlé), which joins the Isole in the heart of the town and flows down to the sea, renamed the Laïta. The charms of the town are summed up by an old saying: "If Quimper is the smile of Cornouaille, then Quimperlé is its kiss".

Quimperlé is in two parts: the Medieval Ville Basse, built where the rivers meet; and the more recent Ville Haute, on the hill in the direction of Pont-Aven and reached by flights of steps from the Ville Basse. In the lower town is Quimperlé's extraordinary Romanesque church, the Eglise Ste-Croix (Holy Cross), in the style of Jerusalem's Holy Sepulchre; and a few alleys of half-timbered houses, among them the fine Maison des Archers. The town's quaysides below the bridge are popular moorings for yachtsmen.

Riec-sur-Bélon   **I 11**
9mi/14.5km W of Quimperlé. Pop
4200. The centre of the Bélon
oyster trade. The oysters, known
simply as Bélons, grow in the
muddy shallows of the Bélon River
south of the town.

La Roche-Maurice   **G 4**
2.5mi/4km E of Landerneau. Pop
1200. The 19thC author Flaubert
described the ruins of the 13thC
castle of La Roche-Maurice as "a
vulture's nest on top of a
mountain". The little town also has
a fine parish close, with an ossuary
on which Death threatens dancing
humans with the words: "I kill
you all".

Roscoff   **H 2**
3mi/5km N of St-Pol-de-Léon. Pop
3700. MD Wed (summer only).
Since the 1970s, the port
installations of Roscoff have
become familiar to the thousands of
British tourists who each year
choose the Roscoff rather than the
St-Malo Channel crossing. Since
the road southwards from the port
misses out Roscoff altogether,
most travellers never get to see it;
which is a pity, as it is well worth
spending an hour or two exploring
its streets of granite houses.
Roscoff has a long seafaring history,
reaching its height in the days of
the corsairs from the 16th to the
18th centuries. Many of the old
houses date from those great days,
clustered round the main square
with its elaborate 16thC church.
The church tower, with its
carefully graded stages and corner
turrets, is one of the most fanciful
in Brittany. By the seafront are the
remains of the Medieval fortified

Unloading artichokes near Roscoff

town wall, with a stone inscription
stating that Mary Stuart (later
Mary, Queen of Scots) landed at
Roscoff in 1548, aged only five, to
be engaged to the Dauphin. Only
slightly less ancient is a giant fig-
tree, known as 'Le Grand Figuier'
in the garden of the Capuchin
convent, inland from the seafront.
It was planted in about 1620, and
its gnarled branches, supported by
columns, cover an area about
22yds/20m square.
Apart from its relics of the past,
Roscoff has an up-to-date Centre
of Marine Biology, which includes
an aquarium (*open May–Sep*). The
artichokes and cauliflowers that
form the bulk of the exports from
Roscoff's harbour grow right up to
the walls of the houses on the
outskirts of the town. From the
jetty, a regular boat service crosses
to the Ile de Batz, just offshore, in
about 15 minutes.

Rosporden   **H 9**
12.5mi/20km E of Quimper. Pop
7300. MD Thur. A small country

Roscoff

town, well off the tourist track,
standing where the Aven River
widens into a series of small lakes.
It is Brittany's main producer of
chouchenn or mead, the favourite
drink of the ancient Celts.

St-Pol-de-Léon   H 2

3mi/5km S of Roscoff. Pop 8100.
The main agricultural centre for
the rich belt of land known as the
'Ceinture Dorée' ('Golden Belt'),
St-Pol is a compact town, built
round two imposing churches: the
former cathedral and the chapel
with its lofty tower known as the
Kreisker. The town gets its name
from St Paul (*Pol* in Breton)
Aurelian, a 6thC Welsh monk who
became the first bishop of Léon
(north-west Brittany) and died on
the Ile de Batz, off Roscoff,
aged 104.
Just outside the town is the
headquarters of the SICA (the
controlling body that runs the local
artichoke and cauliflower trade).
Early each morning the farmers
drive up with their trailers of
produce, which they sell by Dutch
auction, beginning at a maximum
price and working down. The SICA
is linked with Brittany Ferries,
which started its operations as a
carrier of vegetables, not
passengers.

Interesting buildings

Churches and other ecclesiastical
buildings are normally *open
10.00–12.00, 14.00–17.00 (18.00 in
summer)*.

Note on parish closes

The parish close (*enclos paroissial*) is
western Brittany's contribution to
the art of church building. Nearly
all the finest closes are to be found
in Finistère. They reached their
culmination in the 16th and 17th
centuries, when the most elaborate
examples (eg Guimiliau and
Pleyben) were built. Though they
vary somewhat in the emphasis of
their four elements, they always
take the same basic form: a parish
church surrounded by a wall; a
triumphal arch forming an
impressive entry; an ossuary or
mortuary chapel, where the bones
of the dead were stored; and a

calvary surmounted by a sculpted
Crucifixion group.

Abbatiale de Daoulas   F

10mi/16km SE of Brest. The
ancient abbey church of Daoulas
dates from the 12th century, but
stands on the site of a far older
building. The cloisters, also 12thC
have been much restored, but
remain one of the finest examples
of the Romanesque style in Brittan

Abbaye de St-Gwénolé   F

Landevennec. 19mi/30.5km NW o
Châteaulin. The ruins of the
Benedictine abbey, founded in the
5th century by St Gwénolé, look
out across the estuary of the Aulne
at the end of an enchanting little
peninsula. Destroyed by the
Normans in the 10th century, the
abbey was rebuilt and survived
until the Revolution. In the 1950s
the Benedictines built a new abbey
on a site nearby. All that is left of
the old abbey are the ruins of the
Romanesque church. *Open 1
Jun–30 Sep 10.00–12.00,
15.00–18.00, closed Sun morn; 1
Oct–31 May Sun only 15.00–18.00.*

Argol, parish close   F

14mi/22.5km W of Châteaulin.
This village, at the base of the
Crozon Peninsula, has a fine parish
close. The church is 16thC, while
the triumphal arch dates from
1659. Over the arch is a figure on
horseback said to be Gradlon, king
of the mythical city of Ys, which
was drowned beneath the waves
(*see Douarnenez*).

Basilique du Folgoët   F

15mi/24km NE of Brest. Le
Folgoët owes its existence to the
great annual pilgrimage or *pardon*
that takes place each year in *Sep*.
The name Folgoët is Breton for
'Fool in the Wood', and derives
from a local simpleton who lived i
a wood here in the 14th century.
Called Salaün or Solomon, he
survived on bread dipped in the
water of a fountain, and spent his
time calling on the Virgin Mary,
either at Mass or from the branche
of a tree. After his death, a lily
took root in his mouth, with the
words AVE MARIA in gold on its
white petals. A chapel was built o
the site, miracles were reported,
and Le Folgoët's fame was assured
The basilica is 15thC, with more

recent additions; the story of Salaün is told in stained glass at the east end. The pardon is held on the *1st Sun after Sep 8*.

Brasparts, parish close **H 6**
27.5mi/44km N of Quimper. On the edge of the Armorique Regional Nature Park, Brasparts has a superb 16thC parish close, only 6mi/9.5km from the famous close at Pleyben. On the ossuary is an Ankou, the Bretons' skeletal personification of death. The calvary, with its three mourning figures supporting the dead Christ, is a highly expressive sculpture.

Cathédrale de St-Corentin **G 9**
In the centre of Quimper. The cathedral's graceful twin spires dominate the view of Quimper from every direction, but though they look genuinely Medieval they were in fact built as recently as the 1850s. The cathedral itself is one of the finest and most elaborate Gothic buildings in Brittany, dating mainly from the 13th century. An unusual feature is the pronounced angle between the axes of the 13thC nave and the 15thC choir, said to symbolise the drooping angle of Christ's head on the cross. Much of the stained glass in the choir is 15thC. The finest of the furnishings is the organ, built in the 1640s by the English organist and builder Robert Dallam. St-Corentin, the cathedral's dedicatee, was probably born about AD375 and spent his early life as a hermit in the woods near Ménez-Hom, beside a spring. Here he lived on a miraculous fish, which would swim up to him each morning, whereupon the saint would cut off a piece to eat and throw the fish back in the water. During the day the flesh of the fish regrew, and the next day the miracle was repeated. One day it was witnessed by King Gradlon, the legendary founder of Quimper, who was out hunting in the forest and was given some of the fish by Corentin. Naturally impressed, the king made him the first bishop of his new city. Gradlon's equestrian statue is between the twin towers of the cathedral. Until the Revolution this statue was the centre of a unique annual custom. A town official would raise a glass of wine to the statue's lips, then hurl it down to the square below. A prize was offered to anyone who could catch the glass before it broke, but no-one ever succeeded in doing so. The present statue is a copy of the 15thC original, destroyed in the Revolution.

**Cathédrale de
St-Pol-Aurélien** **H 2**
St-Pol-de-Léon. Though the twin towers of the cathedral, at 160ft (50m) high, would seem tall in most other towns, they are dwarfed by the enormous Kreisker tower close by (*see below*). A splendid Gothic building, dating mainly from the 13th–14th century, it remained a cathedral until the Revolution, when the ancient bishopric of Léon was abolished. Unusually for Brittany, the nave is built of limestone from Caen, in Normandy; the façade, transepts and chancel are of Breton granite. Inside there are some good 16thC choir stalls, and tombs of various bishops of Léon. There are also a number of caskets containing the skulls (*chefs*) of St-Pol's notabilities. On the north side of the choir is a reliquary with the head, finger and armbone of St-Pol himself.

**Centrale nucléaire des
Monts d'Arrée** **I 5**
Brennilis. 31.5mi/50.5km N of Quimper. Built in the 1960s in the heart of the Monts d'Arrée, the futuristic blocks of this atomic power station are in striking contrast to the bare, harsh landscape. Together with the reservoir beside them, they form an inescapable part of the panorama from the Montagne-St-Michel. To arrange a visit write, specifying the date you wish to go and the number of visitors, to: Monsieur le Chef de Centrale des Monts d'Arrée, EDF BP NI, La Feuillée, 29218 Huelgoat. Tel (16) 98 99 63 10.

Chapelle de St-Herbot **I 6**
St-Herbot. 4.5mi/7km SW of Huelgoat. On the southern edge of the Monts d'Arrée, the Gothic chapel of St-Herbot is in one of the most remote regions of Finistère. Herbot (like St-Cornély at Carnac) is the patron saint of horned

animals, and inside the chapel are
two stone tables for offerings made
in his honour. Each year on the *Fri
before Trinity Sun*, there is a *pardon*
at which local farmers leave tufts
of hair from their cattle on these
tables, to guarantee Herbot's
favour in the coming year.

Chapelle de St-Vennec   H 8
Briec. 9.5mi/15km NE of Quimper.
Dedicated to St-Vennec, this
16thC chapel contains some
interesting painted sculptures.
Among them is a group of Ste-
Gwenn and her triplet sons, Sts
Gwénolé, Jacut and Vennec.
According to legend, God was so
impressed with her merits as a
mother that he supplied her with a
third breast, so that she could feed
them all simultaneously.

**Chapelle de
Ste-Anne-la-Palud**   F 7
10mi/16km NE of Douarnenez.
Looking west across the wide
sweep of Douarnenez Bay, the
19thC chapel of 'St Anne of the
Marsh' has one of the most popular
pardons in Brittany, held each year
on the *last Sun in Aug*. (There is a
fine 19thC painting of this pardon
by Charles Cottet, in the Rennes art
gallery.) Inside the chapel is a
16thC granite statue of the saint.
The mother of the Virgin Mary,
she is greatly venerated in Brittany.

Chapelle de Trémalo   I 10
Trémalo. 1.5mi/2.5km N of Pont-
Aven. This little chapel is worth
hunting out, as it contains the
yellow figure of Christ on the cross
which was used by Gauguin as the
centrepiece of his great picture 'Le
Christ Jaune'. Gauguin puts the
figure in the typical orchard setting
he would have seen round Pont-
Aven.

La Chasse de St-Hubert   G 7
Cast. 4.5mi/7km SW of Châteaulin.
In front of the village church is a
unique sculptured group, dating
from the 16th century and green
with lichen, known as 'St Hubert's
Hunt' (La Chasse de St-Hubert).
The saint, accompanied by a groom
and two hounds, has dismounted
from his horse and is kneeling
before a stag, which has the
crucifix between its antlers.
Religious historians trace the cult

La Chasse de St-Hubert

of St-Hubert back to the ancient
Gauls, who worshipped a horned
god called Cernunnos.

Château de Kerjean   G 3
7mi/11km N of Landivisiau. Tel
(98) 69 97 03. In a remote part of
north-west Finistère, Kerjean is a
splendid 16thC Renaissance
château, reached down a noble
avenue of beech trees. The granite
outer walls rise from a dry moat;
much of the main building is little
more than a shell, as it suffered a
disastrous fire in 1710 and was
never rebuilt. Some of the rooms
have been restored and can be
visited. *Open 1 Apr–30 Sep
09.00–12.00, 14.00–18.00;
1 Oct–31 Mar 09.00–12.00,
14.00–17.00. Closed Tue.* **Charge**

Château de Kérouzéré   H 2
5mi/8km W of St-Pol-de-Léon. Tel
(98) 29 96 05. The castle was built
in 1425 by Jean de Kérouzéré, and
is a fine example of 15thC military
architecture, with pointed turrets at
three of its corners, and a 17thC
lodging at its fourth. *Open on request
only, 1 Jul–mid-Sep.* **Charge**

Circuit des Trois Enclos

Guimiliau   H 4
10mi/16km SW of Morlaix.
Guimiliau is the central close of the
trio that form the 'Circuit des Trois
Enclos' (the others are Lampaul-
Guimiliau and St-Thégonnec). It
exhibits all the elements of a parish
close more perfectly than any other
in Brittany. The church, reached
through a triumphal arch simple in
design, is amazingly rich on the
outside, and even more ornate
internally. Built in the early 17th
century, it has an elaborate porch
carved round the archway with
scenes from the Bible and lined
with brightly coloured statues of

saints. Inside the church there is a profusion of carved and painted reredoses, statues and other woodwork. But the masterpiece at Guimiliau is its 16thC calvary, covered with over 200 stone figures taken both from the Bible and from Breton legend. The story of Christ's Passion is told in a series of tableaux in which the figures are often grotesque caricatures, with the Last Supper portrayed as graphically as Katel-Golet being swallowed by the mouth of Hell. The close is completed by a sober ossuary, or mortuary chapel.

Lampaul-Guimiliau   **H 4**
11.5mi/18.5km SW of Morlaix.
One of the finest of all the closes.
The church has a curious truncated spire; originally 230ft/70m high, it was struck by lightning in the 19th century and never rebuilt. Inside it has numerous carvings of saints, including St-Miliau, decapitated by his brother and shown holding his severed head. The 16thC rood-beam, surmounted by a painted Crucifixion, is carved with a painted frieze showing the Passion and is a remarkable work of vernacular art. In one of the aisles is a lifelike 17thC stone Entombment. The calvary in the churchyard is austerely simple.

Calvary, St-Thégonnec

St-Thégonnec   **H 4**
7.5mi/12km SW of Morlaix. The easternmost of the three closes that make up the 'Circuit des Trois Enclos', St-Thégonnec is also the largest and the latest in date. The oldest element is the massive triumphal arch, built about 1590. The calvary is comparatively simple, with a single processional row of figures at the foot of the three crucifixes. The church, with its lofty Renaissance tower inspired by the one at Pleyben, has some rich furnishings, notably the pulpit which is alive with carved angels and allegorical figures, the intricate choir stalls and the sumptuous Baroque high altar. The ossuary, built in the 1670s, is classical in style, with a double row of columns separated by niches. Inside the ossuary is a highly naturalistic Entombment from about 1700, with lifesize figures of saints round the body of Christ, carved in oak and painted.

Le Diable du Juch   **F 8**
Le Juch. 4mi/6.5km E of Douarnenez. The 'Devil of Le Juch'—a statue of St Michael slaying the dragon—is the main feature of Le Juch's little church. The east window is also worth a look as it contains 17thC stained glass.

Eglise de Notre-Dame   **G 9**
Locmaria. On W side of Quimper. Locmaria, on the left bank of the Odet, is best known for its pottery (*see Faïence in Museums section*). It also has a superb Romanesque church, dedicated to Our Lady; the nave is 11thC, while the transepts and choir are 12thC. Beside it is a quiet little cloister, planted with flowers.

Eglise St-Germain   **H 7**
Pleyben. 20mi/32km N of Quimper. Pleyben is certainly the grandest of all the parish closes, if not perhaps the most immediately appealing. The church is large and sumptuous, while the calvary is one of the most elaborate in Brittany.
The church, dedicated to St-Germain, is immediately striking for its two towers, one 15thC Gothic, with a pierced stone belfry cage, and the other in 16thC Renaissance style, foursquare and topped by a large domed turret with four little turrets on the corners. Outside is a curious detached 18thC sacristy, all curved domes and rounded apses. Inside, the church is a riot

of carved woodwork, with statues of saints, wall plates (*sablières*), beams and reredoses all brightly painted. At the east end is some fine 17thC stained glass.

The calvary was probably begun about 1550 and completed a century later. Among its superb carvings are a realistic Last Supper, signed by 'Ozanne, Archetecte' along the stretcher; the women at the foot of the cross are carved with tears running down their cheeks, and a dignified Pontius Pilate in a turban and the mouth of Hell gaping for the souls of the damned are vividly depicted.

Between the calvary and the church is a plain cross called in Breton the *Croas an Holen* ('Salt Cross'), because merchants from Guérande, in Loire-Atlantique, used to sell their salt at its foot.

Eglise de St-Jean I 2

St-Jean-du-Doigt. 11mi/17.5km N of Morlaix. The village of St-Jean-du-Doigt owes its name, and its fame, to a miracle-working finger of John the Baptist which is kept in the church treasury in a reliquary. On *Jun 23* a grand *pardon* is held, in which the finger is carried in solemn procession. In former times the pardon was attended by the sick from all over Brittany, who believed that touching the finger would cure blindness, deafness and all kinds of diseases. The finger arrived in Brittany about 1440 and the church, in Flamboyant Gothic style, was founded as a shrine for the precious relic.

Outside the church is a pretty Renaissance fountain, carved with images of God the Father, Christ and John the Baptist.

Eglise de St-Mélar J 3

Lanmeur. 7.5mi/12km NE of Morlaix. Though modern externally, Lanmeur church has a pre-Romanesque crypt, probably 6thC, that is one of the most ancient constructions in Brittany. The crypt is associated with St-Mélar, said to have been buried here. The son of Miliau, murdered by his brother (*see Lampaul-Guimiliau above*), Mélar had his right hand and left foot cut off by his evil uncle. An angel miraculously cured him, giving him a silver hand and a bronze foot—early examples of spare-part surgery!

Eglise de St-Pierre I 4

Pleyber-Christ. 5mi/8km S of Morlaix. A fine parish church, partly Gothic and partly Renaissance. The furnishings include noteworthy carved beams, choir stalls and reredoses. A rare 16thC processional cross is kept in the treasury.

Eglise St-Ronan F 8

Locronan. In village square. This big church, dedicated to the Irish monk St Ronan, is flooded with light from enormous windows. Built in the 15th century, it is a rare example in Brittany of a church with a stone-vaulted ceiling. The Chapel of Le Pénity, attached to the side of the church and opening into it, contains the empty tomb of the saint, with a 15thC effigy on it. The chief events of Ronan's life are depicted in a series of ten medallions on the 18thC pulpit.

Eglise de St-Trémeur J 6

Kergloff. 2.5mi/4km W of Carhaix. The church has a large assemblage of 15th and 16thC statues of Breton saints, among them St-Trémeur carrying his head (*see Carnoët in Countryside section*); Languis, who cures backward ('languishing') children; and St-Diboan, who cures deafness and is shown holding his hand to his ear.

Eglise de St-Tudy F 10

Loctudy. 4mi/6.5km SE of Pont-l'Abbé. Behind the 18thC façade and bell-tower is the best preserved Romanesque interior of any church in Brittany. Built in the 12th century, it has unusual capitals, decorated both with abstract carving, and with animal and human figures.

Eglise de Ste-Anne H 5

Commana. 15.5mi/25km SW of Morlaix. The church, mainly 16th and 17thC, with its tall spire, is mainly worth visiting for the interior. Its chief treasure is the brilliantly painted Baroque reredos, showing Ste-Anne with Mary and Jesus.

Eglise Ste-Croix J 10

Quimperlé. In the Lower Town (Ville Basse). Modelled on the

Church of the Holy Sepulchre in Jerusalem, Quimperlé's Eglise Ste-Croix is a remarkable Romanesque building, in spite of wholesale restoration in the 1860s. Built in the 11thC, it was the church of a Benedictine abbey, of which a few traces survive. In contrast to the later, angular Gothic style, it is like a Greek Orthodox church in its round overall plan, central tower and rounded apses. Inside the main entrance is a striking stone Renaissance screen, depicting Christ in Majesty and the Four Evangelists.

Enclos paroissial de St-Sullian G 5

Sizun. 10.5mi/17km SE of Landerneau. Yet another splendid close, entered through a unique triple-arched triumphal arch. The church tower has a vast spire, 200ft/60m high and one of the tallest in Brittany. Inside, the brightly painted and gilded statues, altars and reredoses make it one of the most exuberant of Breton church interiors. The ossuary is gravely Classical, with a row of bearded statues filling the upper niches. The three crosses are placed above the triumphal arch, rather than on a separate calvary.

Manoir de Kérazan F 10

2mi/3km S of Pont-l'Abbé. Tel (98) 87 40 40. Once the home of the lords of Loctudy, Kérazan dates from the 16th century. One wing survives from this period, though most of the house is 18thC, with a 19thC upper storey. There is a fine collection of French paintings of all periods, including historic scenes of Breton life. *Open 1 Jun–mid-Sep 10.00–12.00, 14.00–18.00.* **Charge**

Morlaix, old buildings I 3

Most of old Morlaix lies inland from the giant 19thC railway viaduct, on the side away from the river. In spite of massive rebuilding in the 19th and 20th centuries, there are still plenty of half-timbered houses, built by wealthy Morlaix merchants in the 15th and 16th centuries. The Grand' rue has a number of these, as does the rue du Mur. In the pl des Halles one of the finest of them, the Maison de la Reine Anne, is *open to the public*

daily 10.00–12.30, 14.30–19.00. Closed Sun & hols.

The oldest church, St-Melaine, in Flamboyant Gothic style, is tucked away beside the viaduct. The church of St-Mathieu, largely 19thC, is on the other side of the Medieval town. It has one curiosity: a 15thC statue of the Virgin, with two doors in the front that open like a cupboard. For the Medieval monastery, *see under Jacobins in the Museums section.*

Notre-Dame-de-l'Assomption J 7

Cléden-Poher. 6mi/9.5km SW of Carhaix. A small but attractive close, of the late 16th century. The calvary shows angels collecting Christ's blood in a chalice—the theme of the Holy Grail. Inside the church are a number of statues, including one of the Virgin treading on a serpent with her right foot and on the crescent moon with her left.

Notre-Dame-de-Berven G 3

Berven. 11.5mi/18.5km SW of Roscoff. Berven's 16thC chapel, dedicated to Our Lady, is famous for its domed tower, balustraded and with small 'lanterns'. Built in 1576, it was the model for a number of later towers. The parish close is entered through a Renaissance triumphal arch.

Notre-Dame-de-Bodilis G 4

Bodilis. 15.5mi/25km W of Morlaix. The hamlet of Bodilis lies on a back road just outside Landivisiau. The church, built between 1570 and 1670, has a grand Renaissance south porch.

Notre-Dame-de-Bonne-Nouvelle F 8

Locronan. In lane near main square. The pretty 15thC chapel of Our Lady of Good News is well worth hunting out. It is down a steep alleyway near the square, and forms a most attractive group with the fountain beside it.

Notre-Dame-de-Confort E 8

Confort-Meilars. 7mi/11km W of Douarnenez. Inside the church is an unusual carillon-wheel, consisting of a wooden wheel with 12 small bells hung round the perimeter. When the wheel is turned, the bells ring in succession. In former times the wheel was believed to cure speech defects, and mothers would turn it above the heads of stammering or mute children.

Notre-Dame-du-Crann   I 7

Spézet. 10mi/16km SW of Carhaix. This chapel is a rarity in the Breton countryside, as it has remained virtually intact since it was built in 1532–5, with its original furnishings and stained glass. The windows are exceptionally fine, and show Italian and German influence. They illustrate scenes from the birth, childhood and Passion of Jesus, and from the life of St Eligius (St-Eloi), the patron saint of farriers.

Notre-Dame-des-Guérisons   G 6

Rumengol. Near Le Faou. 7.5mi/12km N of Châteaulin. Dedicated to Our Lady of Cures, this small country church is much visited by those seeking relief from all sorts of physical afflictions, and is the scene of an important *pardon* on *Trinity Sun*. It is mainly 16th and 17thC, and has a 15thC porch decorated with statues. The original foundation is said to go back to the legendary King Gradlon, in the 5th century.

Notre-Dame-de-la-Joie   E 11

Notre-Dame-de-la-Joie. 0.5mi/1km N of Penmarc'h. This dainty little chapel, with it beautiful dedication to Our Lady of Joy, stands above a sea-wall on the wild Penmarc'h coast. A *pardon* is held here on *15 Aug*.

Notre-Dame-de-Kreisker   H 2

St-Pol-de-Léon. The lofty Kreisker tower is a landmark of the landscape round St-Pol and Roscoff, soaring above the fields of cauliflowers and artichokes. Its slender spire, built in the 15th century, rises to a height of 250ft/78m, half as high again as the twin spires of the cathedral close by. From its top there are views over north Brittany as far as the Monts d'Arrée.

Notre-Dame-de-la-Martyre   G 4

La Martyre. 6mi/9.5km E of Landerneau. One of the oldest of all the closes, La Martyre dates largely from the mid-15th century. Its most fascinating feature is the south porch of the church, carved with angels, peasants and coats-of-arms, and crowned by a touching

Ornate 15thC porch, La Martyre

Nativity. Inside there are carved capitals, and an attractive painted frieze (*sablière*). The 17thC ossuary is carved with a Breton inscription warning the passer-by of "death, judgement and cold hell".

Notre-Dame-du-Relecq   I 5

Near Plounéour-Ménez. 12.5mi/20km S of Morlaix. This Cistercian abbey, built on the north edge of the Monts d'Arrée, was consecrated in 1132. It is said to stand on the site of a far older foundation, where in AD555 the tyrant Comorrus, the Bluebeard of Brittany, was defeated and killed—hence the name 'Relecq', meaning the remains or relics of those killed in the battle. The church is still largely Romanesque in style, though it was much altered in the 16th–18th centuries. Apart from the church, a few minor abbey buildings have survived, together with a 17thC fountain, and the ponds used by the monks to rear their fish. A festival of Celtic music is held at Le Relecq each *Jul*. Open daily 08.00–18.00.

Notre-Dame-de-Tronoën   E 10

Notre-Dame-de-Tronoën. 5.5mi/9km W of Pont-l'Abbé. Isolated and remote, the chapel and calvary of Notre-Dame-de-Tronoën are as far from the sophistication of the great parish closes as one could imagine. The calvary, thought to be the oldest in Brittany, dates from about 1465 and has never been restored. Among the carvings is a rarity: a bare-breasted Virgin suckling the infant Jesus.

'The Presentation in the Temple'—detail of frieze on calvary, Tronoën

Quimper, old streets   **G 9**

Any exploration of old Quimper begins with the rue Kéréon, still largely Medieval, which leads from the square in front of the cathedral. Quieter streets with less traffic are the rue des Gentilshommes and the rue du Sallé, much restored in recent years, which leads into the pl au Beurre, the old butter market. The rue Elie-Fréron was formerly called the rue Obscure, because the overhangs of the Medieval buildings on either side cut out most of the light. Nearer the river, the old market buildings (Les Halles) were replaced in the 1970s by an ultra-modern covered market with a sweeping wooden roof.

Museums & galleries

Beaux-Arts, Musée des   **G 9**

Pl St-Corentin, 29000 Quimper. Tel (98) 95 45 20. Based on the collection of a 19thC connoisseur, the Comte de Silguy, this is a fine art gallery, which was completely renovated in the 1970s. It has paintings by Italian, Flemish and French masters, including works by Fragonard and Corot and a number by artists inspired by Breton life and scenery. A section is devoted to the work of Max Jacob (1876–1944), poet and artist, and friend of Picasso and the Surrealists, who was born in Quimper. *Open 1 May–15 Sep 09.30–12.00, 13.30–19.00; 16 Sep–30 Apr 10.00–12.00, 14.00–18.00. Closed Tue & hols.* **Charge**

Bigouden, Musée   **F 10**

Le Château, 29120 Pont-l'Abbé. Tel (98) 87 24 44. Pont-l'Abbé is the capital of the Bigouden country, which takes in the Penmarc'h Peninsula, west of Quimper, together with its coastal hinterland. The Bigouden people have always remained distinct from the rest of Finistère in their general lifestyle, and this museum, housed in Pont-l'Abbé's Medieval castle, collects together their clothes —including a fine array of *coiffes*, the traditional Breton head-dress—furniture and artefacts to give an all-round picture of their life. *Open 1 Jun–mid-Sep 09.00–12.00, 14.00–19.00. Closed Sun.* **Charge**

Breton, Musée Départemental   **G 9**

Rue du Roi Gradlon, 29000 Quimper. Tel (98) 95 21 60. A comprehensive museum, in the former bishop's palace next to the cathedral, covering the history, art and culture of western Brittany (Basse Bretagne). The exhibits include menhirs (standing stones) and other stone objects from prehistoric times, Gallo-Roman archaeology, medieval stone and wood sculpture, and a superb collection of traditional Breton furniture. *Open daily 1 Jul–mid-Sep 10.00–12.00, 14.00–18.00; closed hols. Mid-Sep–30 Jun daily 10.00–12.00, 14.00–16.30; closed Tue.* **Charge**

Ecole de Pont-Aven, Exposition de l'   **I 10**

Hôtel de Ville, 29123 Pont-Aven. Tel (98) 06 00 35. An exhibition of works by artists of the Pont-Aven school, from the time of Gauguin onwards, is held in the town hall during the summer. *Open 1 Jun–30 Sep 10.00–13.00, 14.30–19.00.*

Ecole Rurale, Musée de l'   **F 6**

Trégarvan, 29150 Châteaulin. Tel (98) 68 81 71. Trégarvan is a small village on the south side of the Aulne estuary, 2.5mi/4km N of Ménez-Hom. The village school, built in 1906, has been restored as it was at the beginning of the 20th century, with contemporary desks, wall-charts etc, to give a picture of Breton school life. *Open 1 Jul–30 Sep daily 14.00–18.00. Closed Tue.* **Charge**

Ville Close, Concarneau

Faïence, Musée de la **G 9**
Locmaria, 29000 Quimper. Tel (98)
90 09 36. The world-famous
Quimper potteries have been
producing their colourful wares
since the end of the 17th century.
An exhibition displays almost three
centuries of the potter's skill, and
there are guided tours of the
works. *Open all year, Mon–Fri
09.00–11.30, 14.00–17.30.* **Charge**

Jacobins, Musée des **I 3**
Rue des Vignes, 29210 Morlaix. Tel
(98) 88 14 68. This fine museum is
housed in the 13thC church of a
convent of Jacobins (Dominicans),
from which it takes its name. The
collections cover all aspects of life
in north Finistère (Léon):
archaeology, religious and popular
art, agriculture, shipbuilding etc.
*Open all year, daily 09.00–12.00,
14.00–18.00. Closed Tue & hols.*
Charge

**Monts d'Arrée,
Ecomusée des** **H 5**
Maison Cornec, St-Rivoal, 29190
Brasparts. No tel. A museum
devoted to the inter-relationship
between man and his environment,
in this remote part of Finistère.
Housed in a traditional farmhouse
of 1702. *Open daily 1 May–30 Sep
11.00–19.00; closed Tue. 1 Oct–30
Apr 14.00–17.00.* **Charge**

**Oeuvres de Coquillages,
Exposition des** **H 10**
3 pl St-Guénolé, 29110 Concarneau.
Tel (98) 97 27 02. A small private
museum, with marine and other
tableaux formed entirely from
seashells. *Open daily 1 Jun–mid-
Sep.* **Charge**

Ouessant, Ecomusée d' **A 4**
Niou Huella, 29242 Ouessant.
Enquiries: tel Syndicat d'Initiative,
(98) 48 85 83. A museum in a small
village on the island of Ushant,
displaying fishing and agricultural
techniques, as well as the day-to-
day life of the islanders. *Open daily
1 May–30 Sep 11.00–19.00; closed
Tue. 1 Oct–30 Apr 14.00–17.00.*
Charge

Pêche, Musée de la **H 10**
Ville Close, 29110 Concarneau. Tel
(98) 97 10 20. A fascinating museum
in the Medieval walled town,
devoted to the story of the
Concarneau fishing fleet. A number
of traditional fishing boats are displayed, together with fishing tackle
of all sorts, navigational
instruments, and historic paintings
and photographs. *Open Aug
09.30–20.30; rest of summer
10.00–12.00, 14.00–18.30.* **Charge**

Tour Tanguy, Musée de la **E 5**
29200 Brest. Enquiries: tel Office
de Tourisme, (98) 44 76 94.
Dominating the former harbour
entrance of Brest, the Tour
Tanguy was built in the 15th
century by a powerful Breton
nobleman, Tanguy de Chastel. It is
now an excellent museum devoted
to the history of Brest, mainly
naval, but also dealing with life in
Brest's convict prison, dating from
the 18th century and the
predecessor of Devil's Island. *Open
Jun daily 14.00–19.00; Jul daily
09.00–12.00, 14.00–19.00; 1
Aug–31 May, Wed, Sat & Sun
14.00–19.00.* **Charge**

**Tour Vauban, Musée
Marin de la** **D 6**
29129 Camaret-sur-Mer. Enquiries:
tel Syndicat d'Initiative, (98) 27 93
60. This 17thC tower, built at the
end of the shingle bank to guard
Camaret harbour, is now a nautical
museum. Among its relics is the

nameplate of the 'Torrey Canyon', the huge oil tanker that broke up in the Channel in 1967, causing devastating pollution. *Open Easter–mid-Sep 10.00–12.00, 14.00–18.00.* **Charge**

Accommodation

Campsites

Prices at campsites vary according to the facilities available but seldom exceed ten francs per person at present. There will usually also be a charge for the car and for the site.

Audierne   D 8

Camping Kerivoas
29113 Audierne. Tel (98) 70 26 86. A two-star site, with food available. *Open mid-Jun–mid-Sep.*

Beg-Meil   G 10

La Roche Percée
Beg-Meil, 29170 Fouesnant. Tel (98) 94 94 15. A flat, grassy site, just north of the village and 550yds/500m from the beach. *Open 1 Jun–mid-Sep.*

Le Vorlen
Beg-Meil, 29170 Fouesnant. Tel (98) 94 97 36. A large site, west of the village and 325yds/300m from the beach, with common room and many other facilities. *Open mid-May–mid-Sep.*

Bénodet   G 10

Le Letty
Plage du Letty, 29118 Bénodet. Tel (98) 91 04 69. A large site, with many facilities, beside the Letty beach. *Open late Jun–early Sep.*

Pointe St-Gilles
29118 Bénodet. Tel (98) 91 05 37. A flat, grassy site, ten minutes' walk from Bénodet's main beach, on the south side of the resort. *Open 1 Apr–30 Sep.*

Brennilis   I 5

Municipal de Nestavel Bras
29218 Huelgoat. Tel (98) 99 61 07. In the heart of the Armorique Regional Nature Park, by the St-Michel reservoir. A small site. *Open mid-Jun–mid-Sep.*

Brignogan-Plage   F 2

Kéravézan
29238 Brignogan-Plage. 1.5mi/

2.5km NW of village. Tel (98) 83 41 65. A flat site, consisting of mixed sand and grass. *Open mid-Jun–mid-Sep.*

Camaret-sur-Mer   D 6

Lambézen
29129 Camaret. 2mi/3km NE of town. Tel (98) 27 91 41. A gently sloping, grassy site, in the direction of the Pointe des Espagnols. *Open Easter–mid-Sep.*

Carantec   I 2

La Chaise du Curé
Rue de la Marne, 29226 Carantec. Tel (98) 67 91 76. A very small, gently sloping site, with limited facilities, 275yds/250m from the beach. *Open Apr–Sep.*

Les Mouettes
29226 Carantec. Tel (98) 67 02 46. By the sea, just south of the town towards St-Pol-de-Léon. *Open 1 Jun–mid-Sep.*

Châteauneuf-du-Faou   I 7

Penn ar Pont
29119 Châteauneuf-du-Faou. 0.5mi/1km SE of town. Tel (98) 81 81 25. A very attractive inland site, laid out in terraces and looking across the River Aulne. *Open 1 Apr–30 Sep.*

Concarneau   H 10

Lochrist
29110 Concarneau. 2.5mi/4km N of town on D783. Tel (98) 97 25 95. A flat, grassy site on the Quimper road. *Open mid-Jun–mid-Sep.*

Les Prés Verts
29110 Concarneau. 2mi/3km NW of town. Tel (98) 97 09 74. A grassy site, with common room and other facilities, within 275yds/250m of the beach. *Open mid-Jun–mid-Sep.*

Le Conquet   C 5

Municipal Le Théven
29217 Le Conquet. 3mi/5km NE of town. Tel (98) 89 06 90. A large site, across the estuary from the town, and 435 yds/400m from a good beach. *Open Easter & mid-Jun–mid-Sep.*

Crozon-Morgat   E 6

Les Pieds dans l'Eau
St-Fiacre, 29160 Crozon. 4mi/6.5km N of Crozon. Tel (98) 27 62 13. A grassy site by the hamlet of

St-Fiacre, and right by the sea as the name, 'Feet in the Water', suggests. *Open mid-Jun–mid-Sep.*

Les Pins
29160 Crozon. 1.5mi/2.5km W of Crozon. Tel (98) 27 21 95. A site among pine trees, towards the Pointe de Dinan. *Open 1 Jun–mid-Sep.*

Douarnenez   E 8

Camping Municipal
Tréboul, 29100 Douarnenez. Tel (98) 92 21 60. A quiet site, 550yds/500m from the beach, across the estuary west of Douarnenez. Difficult caravan access. *Open mid-Jun–mid-Sep.*

Trézulien
29100 Douarnenez. Tel (98) 92 40 52. Terraced site, inland from Tréboul and about 1.5mi/2.5km from the sea. *Open Easter–30 Sep.*

La Forêt-Fouesnant   H 10

Manoir de Pen Ar Steir
29133 La Forêt-Fouesnant. Tel (98) 56 97 75. A quiet site, with games room, tennis court and other facilities, just north of the village towards Quimper. *Open all year.*

Fouesnant   G 10

La Grande Allée
29170 Fouesnant. 0.5mi/1km S of town centre. Tel (98) 56 01 68. An attractive site, within a few mi/km of a wide choice of beaches. *Open Easter & 1 Jun–mid-Sep.*

Huelgoat   I 6

Le Fao
29218 Huelgoat. Tel (98) 99 71 55. At the end of Huelgoat's lake, near boating, swimming and other sporting facilities. May be crowded in summer. *Open mid-Jun–mid-Sep.*

Landerneau   F 4

Municipal
29220 Landerneau. Tel (98) 85 00 92. Near the river and town centre. *Open mid-May–mid-Oct.*

Locquirec   J 2

Du Rugunay
29241 Locquirec. 1.5mi/2.5km S of village. Tel (98) 67 41 06. A quiet site, with limited facilities, on the Plestin road. *Open Easter–early Sep.*

Locronan   F 8

La Motte
29136 Plogonnec. 1.5mi/2.5km E of town. Tel (98) 91 70 09. An attractive site with fine views, below the Montagne de Locronan. *Open mid-Jun–mid-Sep.*

Loctudy   F 10

Kergall
29125 Loctudy. 0.5mi/1km S of village. Tel (98) 87 45 93. A small site, 55yds/50m from the sea. Sailing nearby. *Open Easter–mid-Sep.*

Morgat   *See Crozon*

Penmarc'h   E 11

La Joie
29132 St-Guénolé. Tel (98) 58 63 24. A peaceful family site, flat and grassy, 55yds/50m from the beach and just outside the village of St-Guénolé. *Open late Jun–early Sep.*

Plogoff   C 8

Pointe du Raz Camping
29151 Plogoff. Tel (98) 70 62 94. A small site, outside the hamlet of Lescoff, near Brittany's Land's End. *Open mid-May–mid-Sep.*

Plomodiern   F 7

Ménez-Hom
29127 Plomodiern. 2.5mi/4km NW of Plomodiern. Tel (98) 81 55 23. A country site, in the Armorique Regional Nature Park near the foot of Ménez-Hom. *Open mid-Jun–mid-Sep.*

Plonévez-Porzay   F 8

International de Kervel
Kervel, 29127 Plomodiern. 3mi/5km SW of Plonévez. Tel (98) 92 51 54. A large site, with a wide range of facilities including a games room. In the hamlet of Kervel, near the Bay of Douarnenez. *Open 1 May–early Sep.*

Pont-Aven   I 10

Roz Pin
29123 Pont-Aven. 2.5mi/4km W of town on Concarneau road. Tel (98) 06 03 13. Large site, with separate emplacements and many facilities including a snack bar, and with plenty of trees. *Open 1 May–30 Sep.*

Pont-Croix   D 8

Municipal de Langroas
29122 Pont-Croix. Tel (98) 70 40
66. At the sports ground, on the
north-east side of the town. A fairly
basic site. *Open mid-Jun–mid-Sep.*

Pont-l'Abbé   F 10

L'Ecureuil
29120 Pont-l'Abbé. 2mi/3km NE of
town off Bénodet road. Tel (98) 87
03 39. A quiet site in wooded surroundings. *Open 1 Jun–mid-Sep.*

Quimper   G 9

L'Orangerie de Lanniron
29000 Quimper. 2mi/3km S of town
centre off Bénodet road. Tel (98) 90
62 02. A 'Castels et Camping' site
of the highest quality, set in
parkland in the grounds of
Lanniron Château, with swimming
pool, tennis court and common
room. *Open 1 May–mid-Sep.*

Riec-sur-Bélon   I 11

Château de Bélon
29124 Riec-sur-Bélon. 2mi/3km
from village. Tel (98) 06 90 58. A
fairly large site, on the right bank
of the Bélon and 325yds/300m
from the river. *Open all year.*

Roscoff   H 2

Perharidy
29211 Roscoff. Tel (98) 69 70 86.
A useful stop-over site for
travellers on the Roscoff ferry.
Sandy site, a little west of the town
along the Santec road. *Open mid-
Apr–30 Sep.*

St-Pol-de-Léon   H 2

Municipal Trologot
29250 St-Pol-de-Léon. 1.5mi/
2.5km from town centre. Tel (98) 69
06 26. A flat, grassy site, near the
sea. *Open 1 Jun–30 Sep.*

Sizun   G 5

Municipal Du Gollen
29237 Sizun. Tel (98) 68 30 13. A
small, grassy site, just south of the
village beside the Elorn River. *Open
1 Jun–mid-Sep.*

Telgruc-sur-Mer   E 6

Le Panoramic
Telgruc-sur-Mer, 29127
Plomodiern. Tel (98) 27 78 41. A
sloping, terraced site, just south of
the village on the road to Trez-

Bellec beach. Facilities include a
games room. *Open late May–
mid-Sep.*

Hotels

Audierne   D 8

Hôtel Le Cornouaille
Le Port, 29113 Audierne. Tel (98)
70 09 13. A small hotel overlooking
the harbour (bed and breakfast
only). One of the Logis de France
federation. *Closed 1 Oct–30 Jun.* F

Hôtel du Goyen
Pl Jean-Simon, 29113 Audierne.
Tel (98) 70 08 88. An attractive
modern hotel, overlooking the
harbour and hung with flowers
during summer. A 'Relais
Gastronomique' hotel. *Closed
1 Nov–31 Mar.* FF

Beg-Meil   G 10

Hôtel de Bretagne
Beg-Meil, 29170 Fouesnant. Tel
(98) 94 98 04. Hotel with a large
shady garden, 165yds/150m from
the beach. *Closed 1 Oct–Easter.*
Ax.V. FF

Hotel-Restaurant Au Bon Accueil
Beg-Meil, 29170 Fouesnant. Tel
(98) 94 98 14. In a quiet position
165yds/150m from the beach. The
restaurant specialises in seafood.
Closed mid-Sep–31 May. FF

Bénodet   G 10

Hôtel Belle-Vue
Av de la Plage, 29118 Bénodet. Tel
(98) 91 04 23. Hotel without
restaurant, near the main beach.
Closed 1 Sep–30 Jun. F

Hôtel Gwel-Kaer
Av de la Plage, 29118 Bénodet. Tel
(98) 91 04 38. *Gwel-Kaer* is Breton
for 'beautiful view', and this hotel
has a fine outlook on the sea, with
a panoramic restaurant. *Open all
year.* V. FF

Hôtel-Restaurant Le Cornouaille
Av de la Plage, 29118 Bénodet. Tel
(98) 91 03 78. A comfortable hotel
near the beach. *Closed 1 Oct–
Easter.* FF

Brest   E 5

Hôtel Bretagne
24 rue de l'Harteloire, 29200 Brest.
Tel (98) 80 41 18. Small hotel
without a restaurant, a littly way
from the town centre. *Closed
Xmas & New Year.* A.V. FF

Hôtel Continental
Sq La Tour d'Auvergne, 29200
Brest. Tel (98) 80 50 40. A large
hotel near the town centre. *Closed
Feb.* A.Ax.Dc.V. **FF**

Brignogan-Plage   **F 2**

Hostellerie Castel Régis
Plage du Garo, 29238 Brignogan-
Plage. Tel (98) 83 40 22. A hotel and
restaurant on a magnificent site,
above the harbour and rocky
shore, with swimming pool. *Closed
1 Oct–31 Mar.* A.Ax. **FF**

Hôtel Ar Reder Mor
29238 Brignogan-Plage. Tel (98) 83
40 09. A modern hotel, in the main
street and near the beaches. One of
the 'Logis de France'. *Closed mid-
Dec–30 Apr.* **F**

Camaret-sur-Mer   **D 6**

Hôtel de France
19 quai Toudouze, 29129 Camaret.
Tel (98) 27 93 06. A modern hotel,
overlooking the harbour, one of the
'Hôtes Bretons' association. The
restaurant specialises in seafood.
Closed mid-Nov–mid-Mar.
A.V. **FF**

Concarneau   **H 10**

Grand Hôtel
Av P-Guéguin, 29110 Concarneau.
Tel (98) 97 00 28. A big friendly
hotel, overlooking the harbour and
old walled town (Ville Close).
Closed 1 Oct–Easter. **FF**

Hôtel Modern
5 rue du Lin, 29110 Concarneau.
Tel (98) 97 03 36. In a quiet back
street, ten minutes' walk from the
Ville Close. *Open all year.* **FF**

Le Conquet   **C 5**

Hôtel Pointe Ste-Barbe
29217 Le Conquet. Tel (98) 89 00
26. A quiet hotel with a view of the
sea, situated on the tip of the Pointe
Ste-Barbe. *Closed Jan.* Dc. **FF**

Douarnenez   **E 8**

Hôtel Le Bretagne
23 rue Duguay-Trouin, 29100
Douarnenez. Tel (98) 92 30 44. A
small hotel near the town centre and
the Port-Rhu estuary. One of the
'Logis de France'. A. **FF**

La Forêt-Fouesnant   **H 10**

Hôtel de la Baie
Pl de la Baie, 29133 La Forêt-
Fouesnant. Tel (98) 56 97 35. Small

hotel with a view over a pretty
estuary. *Closed 1 Oct–31 Mar.* **F**

Huelgoat   **I 6**

Hôtel de Bretagne
13 pl A-Briand, 29218 Huelgoat.
Tel (98) 99 71 13. A traditional
stone Breton building overlooking
the main square. *Closed mid-
Sep–Easter.* **F**

Hôtel du Lac
12 rue de Brest, 29218 Huelgoat.
Tel (98) 99 71 14. Quiet hotel near
the lake and the woodland walks.
Closed 1 Nov–31 Dec. **F**

Landerneau   **F 4**

Hôtel Raould
Quai de Léon, 29220 Landerneau.
Tel (98) 85 00 79. A bed-and-
breakfast hotel by the Elorn River.
Closed winter. **F**

Landivisiau   **G 4**

Hôtel L'Etendard
Rue Général-de-Gaulle, 29230
Landivisiau. Tel (98) 68 06 60. A
modern hotel in the centre of the
town. *Closed mid-Dec–mid-Jan.*
A.Dc.V. **FF**

Locronan   **F 8**

Hôtel Au Fer à Cheval
Pl de l'Eglise, Locronan, 29136
Plogonnec. Tel (98) 91 70 67. A
modern hotel just outside the town.
One of the 'Inter-Hotel' group.
Its restaurant specialises in
seafood. *Open all year.* A.Ax.
Dc.V. **FF**

Manoir de Moëllien
Plonévez-Porzay, 29127
Plomodiern. Tel (98) 92 50 40. A
small 17thC stone-built manor
house, 2mi/3km NW of Locronan
on a minor road. The restaurant
serves imaginative dishes of all
sorts. *Restaurant closed 1 Oct–
30 Apr.* V. **FF**

Morlaix   **I 3**

Hôtel d'Europe
1 rue d'Aiguillon, 29210 Morlaix.
Tel (98) 88 22 58. A comfortable
hotel in the town centre. It contains
some 17thC panelling. *Closed mid-
Dec–mid-Jan.* A.Ax.Dc.V. **FF**

Hôtel Les Arcades
11 pl Cornic, 29210 Morlaix. Tel
(98) 88 20 03. A small,
unpretentious hotel near the
viaduct. *Closed 1st 2 wks Sep.* **F**

Pont-l'Abbé   **F 10**

Hôtel A La Tour d'Auvergne
22 pl Gambetta, 29120 Pont-
l'Abbé. Tel (98) 87 00 47. Modest
hotel in the town centre. *Closed
1 Oct–31 Jul.* **F**

Hôtel des Voyageurs
Quai St-Laurent, 29120 Pont-
l'Abbé. Tel (98) 87 00 37. A
'Logis de France' hotel, near the
château with a view over the
estuary. The restaurant specialises
in *fruits de mer. Closed Mon, Feb
& Nov.* A. **F**

Quimper   **G 9**

Hôtel Griffon
Rte de Bénodet, 29000 Quimper.
Tel (98) 90 33 33. A hotel in the
luxury class, 2mi/3km S of the city
on the Bénodet road. *Closed 15
Feb–20 Mar, Sat eve & Sun out of
season.* Ax.Dc.V. **FFF**

Hôtel La Tour d'Auvergne
13 rue des Réguaires, 29000
Quimper. Tel (98) 87 00 47. An old-
style hotel not far from the
cathedral. *Closed mid-Dec–early Jan.*
A.V. **FF**

Quimperlé   **J 10**

Hôtel L'Hermitage
29130 Quimperlé. 1.5mi/2.5km S of
town on D49. Tel (98) 96 04 66. A
quiet, comfortable hotel in its own
grounds. *Closed 1 Nov–31 Mar.*
A. **FF**

Hôtel Moderne
22 pl St-Michel, 29130 Quimperlé.
Tel (98) 96 01 32. A no-frills hotel
in the upper town, overlooking a
large square. *Closed mid-Dec–mid-
Jan.* A. **F**

Roscoff   **H 2**

Hôtel des Arcades
15 rue Amiral Réveillère, 29211
Roscoff. Tel (98) 69 70 45. This
hotel gets its name from the 16thC
granite arches in the entrance hall.
Its terrace overlooks the harbour.
Closed 1 Oct–Easter. **FF**

Hôtel des Bains
Pl de l'Eglise, 29211 Roscoff. Tel
(98) 61 20 65. A large, unfussy hotel,
near the church and with a sea
view. *Closed mid-Oct–mid-Mar.*
A.V. **F**

Hôtel Le Brittany
Bvd Ste-Barbe, 29211 Roscoff. Tel
(98) 69 70 78. A comfortable hotel,
near the ferry port and with a
harbour view. Its core is a 17thC
Breton manor house. A Brittany
Ferries 'Go As You Please' hotel.
Closed Feb. A.Ax.Dc. **FF**

Restaurants

Unless otherwise stated, all the
hotels listed in the previous section
have restaurants; they are not
included here to avoid repetition,
but many of them are worth
sampling nonetheless.

Bénodet   **G 10**

La Ferme du Letty
Plage du Letty, 29118 Bénodet. Tel
(98) 91 01 27. A small restaurant,
by the beautiful Letty beach (Plage
du Letty). *Closed Oct, Wed &
Thur.* A. **FF**

La Pizza
10 av de l'Odet, 29118 Bénodet. Tel
(98) 57 19 39. A lively pizzeria and
restaurant near the harbour. *Open
daily.* **F**

Brest   **E 5**

Le Poulbot
26 rue Aiguillon, 29200 Brest. Tel
(98) 44 19 08. Named after the
French for 'street-urchin', this is a
comfortable restaurant with a
selection of regional specialities.
Closed 21 Aug–12 Sep & Sun.
Ax.Dc.V. **FF**

Camaret-sur-Mer   **D 6**

Pizzeria del Mare
16 quai Toudouze, 29129 Camaret.
No tel. An attractive pizzeria, with
Italian ices and other specialities,
beside the harbour. *Open daily in
season. Closed 1 Oct–30 Apr.*
A.V. **F**

Carhaix   **J 6**

Auberge du Poher
Port-de-Carhaix, 29270 Carhaix.
3mi/5km S of town on D769. Tel
(98) 93 42 79. In the hamlet of Port-
de-Carhaix. *Closed Feb & Mon.*
A.V. **FF**

Châteaulin   **G 7**

Auberge des Ducs de Lin
29150 Châteaulin. Tel (98) 86 04
20. A small restaurant with garden,
just south of the town on the
Quimper road. *Closed Mar, late
Sep & Mon.* A. **FF**

Concarneau   H 10

La Bagatelle
12 rue Théophile Louarn, 29110
Concarneau. Tel (98) 97 49 98. An
unpretentious restaurant in the old
town (Ville Close). *Open daily.*
V. **F**

Le Galion
15 rue St-Guénolé, 29110
Concarneau. Tel (98) 97 30 16. In
an ancient granite house in the
'Ville Close'. Specialises in fresh-
caught fish. *Closed mid-Jan–mid-
Mar & Mon.* V. **FFF**

Noz ha Deiz
Ville Close, 29110 Concarneau. No
tel. The name of this crêperie in
the Old Town means 'Night and
Day' in Breton. It has a tearoom
attached. *Closed mid-Sep–
mid-Mar.* **F**

Douarnenez   E 8

Chez Fanch
Le Vieux Port, 29100 Douarnenez.
Tel (98) 92 31 77. Restaurant by the
harbour, specialising in *fruits de
mer. Closed mid-Sep–mid-Oct &
Thur in winter.* A. **F**

L'Océan
62 rue Anatole-France, 29100
Douarnenez. Tel (98) 92 60 98. A
small restaurant on a steep street
leading down to the harbour. *Open
daily.* A.V. **F**

Huelgoat   I 6

Auberge de la Truite
Locmaria-Berrien, 29218 Huelgoat.
Tel (98) 99 73 05. The small village
of Locmaria-Berrien is 4mi/6.5km
E of Huelgoat. This restaurant
specialises in lobster, trout and
other fish dishes. *Closed mid-
Nov–mid-Dec & Mon 1 Sep–30 Jun.*
A. **FF**

Landerneau   F 4

Auberge du Reveil Matin
Rue du Chanoine Kerbrat, 29220
Landerneau. Tel (98) 85 14 83.
Attractive creeper-covered
restaurant near the river. *Closed
Sun.* **F**

Morlaix   I 3

Auberge des Gourmets
90 rue Gambetta, 29210 Morlaix.
Tel (98) 88 06 06. Near the
Medieval town centre and only
33yds/30m from the station. *Closed
Mon.* V. **F**

La Fringale
8 venelle au Beurre, 29210 Morlaix.
Tel (98) 88 31 91. A quick-food
restaurant in the heart of the old
town serving hamburgers etc.
Closed Thur & Sun. **F**

Restaurant Pékin
4 venelle au Son, 29210 Morlaix.
Tel (98) 62 18 03. Restaurant
serving Chinese and Vietnamese
food. *Open daily.* **F**

Pont-Aven   I 10

Le Moulin de Rosmadec
29123 Pont-Aven. Tel (98) 06 00
22. A pretty restaurant by the
bridge in the centre of the town, in
an old watermill with Breton
furniture. *Closed mid-Oct–mid-
Nov & Wed.* A. **FF**

Quimper   G 9

Le Capucin Gourmand
29 rue des Réguaires, 29000
Quimper. Tel (98) 95 43 12.
Restaurant near the cathedral,
specialising in fish. *Closed late Aug,
Sun eve & Mon.* A.Dc.V. **FF**

La Krampouzerie
Rue du Sallé, 29000 Quimper. Tel
(98) 95 13 08. Lively crêperie in
the heart of the old city. *Closed
Tue.* **F**

La Rotonde
36 av de la France Libre, 29000
Quimper. Tel (98) 95 09 26. Small
restaurant north-east of the town
centre. *Closed 1st 2 wks May, 1st 2
wks Sep, Sat eve & Sun.* A.V. **F**

Quimperlé   J 10

La Vache Enragée
5 rue Jacques-Cartier, 29130
Quimperlé. Tel (98) 39 10 44. Small,
friendly restaurant on a cobbled
back street in the old town. *Closed
Mon.* **FF**

Roscoff   H 2

Auberge du Quai
Vieux-Port, 29211 Roscoff. Tel (98)
69 72 65. Restaurant and snack bar
overlooking the old harbour. *Closed
15 Oct–26 Mar & Tue.* V. **F**

Le Blockhauss
Ste-Barbe, 29211 Roscoff. Tel (98)
69 71 23. Restaurant and bar in a
concrete blockhouse, constructed
by the Germans in World War II
as part of their Atlantic Wall.
Cabaret in the evenings. *Open daily
in season.* **F**

Countryside

Les Abers   D 3–E 2
12.5mi/20km N of Brest. *Aber* is
Breton for estuary (it is Welsh as
well, as in Aberdovey). The name
Les Abers is applied to a stretch of
deeply indented and rocky coast in
north-west Finistère. The two
main estuaries are Aber Wrac'h and
Aber Benoît.

Baie des Trépassés   C 8
2mi/3km N of the Pointe du Raz.
The little 'Bay of the Dead' faces
due west across the Raz de Sein to
the island of Sein. Traditionally, it
was from this bay that the bodies of
the Druids were taken on board to
be buried on Sein. 'The dead' may
also refer to the hundreds of sailors
who down the years have drowned
in the Raz.

Cap de la Chèvre   D 7
6.5mi/10.5km S of Crozon. The
'Cape of the Goat', rising almost
330ft/100m from the sea, is the
southernmost point of the Crozon
Peninsula. From it there are
panoramic views southwards across
the bay to Douarnenez and the
Pointe du Raz, and westwards
across the Atlantic.

Cap Sizun   D 8
12.5mi/20km W of Douarnenez.
The seabird reserve of Cap Sizun
lies only 6mi/9.5km from the Pointe
du Raz, on the south side of
Douarnenez Bay. The cape's
mighty cliffs, over 230ft/70m high,
offer nesting-ledges and perches for
countless birds including
cormorants, gulls, puffins,
choughs, fulmars and razorbills.
The best time to see the reserve is
in the breeding season, roughly
*Apr–Jun. Open 10.00–12.00,
14.00–18.00.* **Charge**

Cornouaille   B 8–E 11
Much of Brittany was colonised in
the 5th and 6th centuries by
immigrants from Cornwall, who
gave the name of their homeland
to their new country across the sea.
Though Cornouaille originally
extended into north Finistère, the
name nowadays is confined to the
coastal region west of Quimper,
which still bears a remarkable
resemblance to Cornwall, with its
small fields and low-built cottages.
Each year at the end of *Jul* the old

*Breton dancers in their traditional
costume*

traditions of Celtic music and
dance are recalled in the week-long
Fêtes de Cornouailles, held at
Quimper.

Enfer de Plogoff   C 8
6mi/9.5km W of Audierne. The
'Hell of Plogoff' is a boiling cauldron
of sea, where the waves seethe
against the rocky coast. In the
1970s Plogoff entered the political
arena, when there was a much
disputed proposal to build a nuclear
power station there—a project that
has still failed to materialise.

Forêt de Carnoët   J 11
2mi/3km S of Quimperlé. The state
forest of Carnoët, mainly planted
with beech and oak, covers 1845
acres/750 hectares on either side of
the D49. According to legend, the
forest was once the lair of
Comorrus, the Breton Bluebeard,
who married successive wives and
put them to death. Among them
was Ste-Triphine, who gave birth
to St-Trémeur, decapitated in his
turn by Comorrus. This so enraged
the saint that he picked up his head
and walked to Comorrus's castle,
where he threw a handful of earth
against the wall, bringing the
building down on the monster.
(Trémeur is always carved or
painted in Breton churches carrying
his head.)

Fôret de Cranou   G 6
4mi/6.5km E of Le Faou. A
woodland area at the west end of
the Monts d'Arrée, surviving from
the vast forest that once covered
inland Brittany. In the Armorique
Regional Nature Park.

Huelgoat, rocks & rivers   I 6
19mi/30.5km S of Morlaix. In the
heartland of Finistère, the little
town of Huelgoat gives access to the
most picturesque small area in the

whole of Brittany. East of the town lies a jumble of boulders, fast-flowing streams and woodland, marked out with walks lasting anything from half-an-hour to three hours. The names give a good idea of the scenery: Chaos, Trembling Rock, Devil's Cave, Alley of the Clear Stream, Bridge of the Silver River. A little to the north is the impressive Camp d'Artus (Camp of King Arthur), which has only a legendary connection with the king. It is in fact a Gallo-Roman fortified site, probably from the 1st century.

Ile de Batz   H 2

2mi/3km N of Roscoff. Pop 800. This small island (pronounced 'Ba') is only 15 minutes by boat from Roscoff, yet it seems amazingly remote. The north shore is rugged, while the south shore has a small village and harbour, and several quiet little coves. The lighthouse can be visited *in summer*. One of Brittany's most famous saints, St-Pol, is said to have tamed a dragon on Batz and to have made it jump into the sea at the Trou du Serpent.

Ile de Molène   B 5

7.5mi/12km W of mainland. Pop 400. A small island, half-way between the mainland and Ushant. The few islanders are mainly fishermen. They also cultivate their tiny fields, which are so small that their cows are said to graze one field, stand in a second and deposit their manure in a third. The boat trip from Le Conquet takes about half-an-hour.

Ile d'Ouessant *See Ushant*

Ile de Sein   B 8

5mi/8km W of Pointe du Raz. Pop 600. Only 5ft/1.5m above sea-level, this narrow, rocky island surrounded by reefs remained isolated for centuries. It was the Druids' Isle of the Dead, and it remained pagan until well into the 17th century—1000 years after the conversion of the rest of Brittany. The island is without trees, and the only crops are barley and potatoes; the islanders live by fishing, or go to the mainland to work.
Sein's greatest historical moment came in June 1940, when every man of fighting age, 130 altogether, left the island for England, to join De Gaulle's Free French forces.

Iles de Glénan   G 12

12.5mi/20km S of Concarneau. A cluster of nine small islands, reached by boat in about one and a half hours from Concarneau, Bénodet or Loctudy. In earlier years the islands were pirate lairs; nowadays they are sanctuaries for cormorants, gulls and other seabirds.

Ménez-Hom   F 7

9mi/14.5km W of Châteaulin. *Ménez* is Breton for 'mountain' and is the same as the Welsh 'mynydd'. This rounded hill, 1080ft/330m high, guards the eastern end of the Crozon Peninsula. From its summit there are spectacular views along the peninsula, and inland to the Monts d'Arrée. By the road near its foot is the pretty little chapel dedicated to Ste-Marie-du-Ménez-Hom.

Montagne-St-Michel   H 5

11mi/17.5km N of Pleyben. At 1247ft/380m high, this is almost the highest point in Brittany, exceeded only by two other crags of the Monts d'Arrée, and then only by a few metres. At its summit is a chapel dedicated to St Michael, the patron saint of all high places. On a clear day there are magnificent views over the whole of north Finistère.

Monts d'Arrée   H 4–I 5

19mi/30.5km inland from Morlaix. Though hardly mountains in the Alpine sense of the word—the highest point is only just over 1247ft/380m high—the Arrée hills are nevertheless the survivors of a vast range far older than the Alps, worn down by millions of years of erosion. The chief landmark is the Montagne-St-Michel, giving spectacular views all over Finistère. The lake at the centre of the Monts d'Arrée is now used for cooling the Brennilis atomic power station.

Parc Natural Régional
Armorique   G 5–K 6

Throughout northern Finistère. Established in 1968, the Regional Nature Park is unusual in being in a number of distinct sections, covering some 160,000 acres/65,000 hectares in the remoter parts of Finistère. The largest section takes in the Monts d'Arrée, and preserves, round Huelgoat and in the Cranou Forest, vestiges of the vast forest that once covered the whole of inland Brittany. The other sections are: the picturesque estuary of the Aulne, including the mountain of Ménez-Hom; the western end of the Crozon Peninsula; and the islands of Molène and Ushant (Ouessant), off the west coast of Finistère.

Pointe des Espagnols   **D 5**
6mi/9.5km N of Camaret-sur-Mer. The northernmost of the three headlands of the Crozon Peninsula, it gets its name from Spanish troops who camped here in 1594 before being defeated by the French.

Pointe de Penhir   **D 6**
2mi/3km SW of Camaret-sur-Mer. The central 'prong' at the western end of the Crozon Peninsula. From its top, 230ft/70m high, there are wide views over to sea, and downviews to the jagged rocks known as the Tas de Pois ('Heap of Peas') at its foot.

Pointe de Penmarc'h   **E 11**
9mi/14.5km W of Pont-l'Abbé. A weed-covered stretch of rocks rather than a dramatic headland, the point lies beyond Penmarc'h village, at Brittany's south-western corner. Its name means 'Horse's Head' in Breton, possibly derived from one of the offshore rocks, which bears some resemblance to a horse. The Eckmühl lighthouse can be visited *in summer*.

Pointe du Raz   **C 8**
9.5mi/15km W of Audierne. Finistère means 'Land's End', and the Pointe du Raz is thus the Land's End of France. Like its Cornish counterpart, it is desecrated by a rash of shacks and curio shops; but if you stand with your back to these, you have the feeling of sea stretching to infinity

beyond the splintered terraces of rock. *Raz* is Breton for 'narrows' and refers to the dangerous channel, 5mi/8km wide and a prey to treacherous currents, between the jagged rocks of the mainland and the reefs that encircle the Ile de Sein. Prominent on the point is a statue of Our Lady of Shipwrecks (Notre-Dame-des-Naufrages).

Pointe de St-Mathieu   **C 5**
16mi/25.5km W of Brest. This grand headland guards the northern side of the approaches to Brest. From it on a clear day you can see west as far as Ushant and south as far as Sein. The clifftop buildings include a lighthouse and a ruined abbey, and there is a fine monument to sailors who died in World War I.

Presqu'île de Crozon   **E 5–7**
Between the Rade de Brest and Douarnenez Bay. The Crozon Peninsula is a small world within the larger world of Finistère. Shaped like a flattened trident, with three lofty headlands (the Pointe des Espagnols, Pointe de Penhir and Cap de la Chèvre), it is protected to the north by the Brest Peninsula and to the south by Cornouaille. Its only town of any size is the pretty port of Camaret, and it has a few seaside resorts, of which Morgat is the most important.

River Bélon   **I 11**
SW of Quimperlé. This little river on the south coast is famous for its oysters, known on menus simply as *Bélons*. The chief centre of oyster culture is at Riec-sur-Bélon.

Rochers du Diable   **K 10**
7.5mi/12km NE of Quimperlé. The 'Devil's Rocks' are a jumble of massive boulders above the fast-flowing waters of the Ellé River. St-Gwénolé is said to have had a

Camaret-sur-Mer

hermitage here, where he put the Devil to flight—hence the name.

Ushant (Ouessant)   **A 4**
12.5mi/20km from mainland. Pop 1450. Familiar from the shipping forecasts, Ushant is an ideal weather station, since it is far out in the Atlantic and subject to every wind that blows. The island is 4.5mi/7km long and 2.5mi/4km wide, and its combination of rocky coast, strong winds, dangerous currents and frequent fog have made it a ships' graveyard down the centuries. There is one small town, Lampaul, on the west side, and a number of smaller hamlets. On the north coast, the Cré'ach lighthouse throws its beam for 30mi/48km, and its foghorn can be heard for 11mi/17.5km.

In former times, it was the custom on Ushant for women rather than men to propose marriage, since the women greatly outnumbered the men, most of whom spent much of their lives away at sea.

Boats sail regularly from Brest to Ushant, stopping at Le Conquet and Molène. The journey takes about two hours.

Val d'Odet   **F 10**
S of Quimper. One of the prettiest rivers in Brittany, the Odet flows through Quimper and out to sea at Bénodet (Breton for 'Mouth of the Odet'). On its way it flows through peaceful, largely wooded scenery. The journey down the Odet by boat is a popular excursion from Quimper.

Entertainment

Casino

Casino de Bénodet   **G 10**
Av de la Plage, 29118 Bénodet. Tel (98) 91 04 16. Beside the beach, with pizzeria, cinema and swimming pool. *Open during season. Gaming rooms 21.00–03.00; disco 23.00–04.00.*

Discothèques

Bahia Club   **I 3**
Le Mouster, 29250 St-Pol-de-Léon. 2mi/3km S of town. Tel (98) 69 57 04. Grill and restaurant with disco. *Open daily to 24.00.* **Charge**

Le Flash   **I 3**
41 rue de Paris, 29210 Morlaix. Tel (98) 88 30 56. Night club and disco. *Open 22.00–03.00. Closed Mon.* **Charge**

Yannick Club   **G 10**
Rte de Fouesnant, 29118 Bénodet. Tel (98) 91 03 99. *Open all year.* **Charge**

Leisure activities

Craft centres

La Ferme St-Michel   **H 6**
29190 Brasparts. 4.5mi/7km N of Brasparts, on the Morlaix road (D785). Tel (98) 81 41 13. More than 200 artists and craftsmen exhibit and sell their products in this farm complex in the Monts d'Arrée. *Open daily 10.00–12.00, 14.00–18.30. Closed Tue out of season.*

La Maison des Artisans   **F 8**
Pl de l'Eglise, Locronan, 29136 Plogonnec. Tel (98) 91 70 11. Craftsmanship including Locronan's typical weaving exhibited in one of the town's finest old mansions. *Open daily all year.*

La Vieille Maison   **I 3**
27–8 pl des Otages, 29210 Morlaix. Tel (98) 88 02 46. Exhibits of Breton craftsmanship in Medieval houses. *Open summer only 08.00–20.00.*

Golf

Golf de Quimper et de Cornouaille   **H 10**
Manoir de Mesmeur, 29133 La Forêt-Fouesnant. Tel (98) 56 02 02. A nine-hole course with clubhouse. *Open daily in summer.* **Charge**

Parc des Loisirs de Lann-Rohou   **F 5**
St-Urbain, 29220 Landerneau. 3mi/5km S of Landerneau. Tel (98) 85 16 17. An 18-hole course in this country park. *Open all year.* **Charge**

Sailing

Centre International Léo Legrange   **D 6**
29129 Camaret-sur-Mer. Tel (98) 27 90 49. Sailing instruction given. **Charge**

Club Nautique   F 2
29238 Brignogan-Plage. Enquiries: tel Syndicat d'Initiative (98) 83 40 06. Sailing club with a school, teaching sailing skills on a variety of boats to learners from the age of seven. *Open 1 Jul–10 Sep.* **Charge**

Société Nautique de la Baie de Concarneau   H 10
29110 Concarneau. Tel (98) 97 34 84. Sailing taught. **Charge**

There are also sailing schools at Carantec, Locquirec and Roscoff.

Excursions

Boat trips

Brest   E 5
Port de Commerce, 1ᵉʳ Bassin, 29200 Brest. Tel (98) 80 24 68. Services to Ushant (Ouessant).

Vedettes Armoricaines, address as above. Tel (98) 44 44 04. Trips round Rade de Brest.

Iles de Glénan
Vedettes Aigrettes, 29118 Bénodet. Tel (98) 91 00 58. Excursions from Quimper, Bénodet and Loctudy.

River Odet   G 10
Vedettes Aigrettes, 29118 Bénodet. Tel (98) 91 00 58. From Quimper. *Jul & Aug 08.30–18.30, every 2 hours; May, Jun & Sep, 10.30 & 16.30.* Departures also from Bénodet and Loctudy.

Roscoff   H 2
Vedettes Blanches, Estacade vers l'Ile de Batz, 29211 Roscoff. Enquiries: tel Syndicat d'Initiative (98) 69 70 70. To Ile de Batz. *In summer, every hour from 08.00–20.00 (last boat back 19.00). In winter, every 90 mins.*

Festivals

The main *pardons* of Finistère are as follows:

Whit Mon Carantec.	I	2
Fri before Trinity St-Herbot.	I	6
Trinity Sun Rumengol.	G	6
23 Jun St-Jean-du-Doigt.	I	2
2nd Sun in Jul Locronan.	F	8
3rd Sun in Jul Douarnenez.	E	8
3rd Mon in Jul Roscoff.	H	2
4th wk in Jul Quimper (Fêtes de Cornouaille).	G	9
26 Jul Fouesnant.	G	10
1st Sun in Aug Brest.	E	5
1st Sun in Aug Pont-Aven.	I	10
15 Aug Plougastel-Daoulas.	E	5
3rd Sun in Aug Concarneau (Fête des Filets Bleus).	H	10
Last Sun in Aug Audierne.	D	8
Last Sun in Aug Ste-Anne-la-Palud.	F	7
1st Sun in Sep Camaret-sur-Mer.	D	6
8 Sep (or Sun before) Le Folgoët.	F	3
3rd Sun in Sep Notre-Dame-de-Tronoën.	E	10

Horse-drawn caravans

Roulottes de Bretagne   J 6
Gare de Locmaria-Berrien, 29218 Huelgoat. Tel (98) 93 73 28. Normally hired by the week or fortnight, the *roulottes* explore the byways of central Finistère, on specially marked routes, keeping to the level as far as possible.

Long-distance footpath

The Grande Randonnée (GR) no 380 takes a devious course from Morlaix to Lampaul-Guimiliau, taking in the three most famous parish closes (Guimiliau, St-Thégonnec and Lampaul-Guimiliau), and the remains of the Medieval Le Relecq abbey.

Tours by car (one day approx)

Round Morlaix

Parish closes & churches
From Morlaix, take the Brest road and turn off for St-Thégonnec, the first in the 'Circuit des Trois Enclos'. On to Guimiliau and Lampaul-Guimiliau, the other two of the trio. Then to Landivisiau, and south west cross-country to

La Martyre (fine south porch and church), near Ploudiry. To Sizun (towering spire, elaborate interior), Commana and back to Morlaix.

Round Quimper

Bigouden country

To Pont-l'Abbé (Bigouden Museum), Loctudy past Kérazan Château, then either main road (D53) or longer, slower coast road to Pointe de Penmarc'h (Notre-Dame-de-la-Joie chapel, St-Gwénolé and Tronoën calvary). Main road to Plozévet and Audierne, then out to Pointe du Raz (Brittany's Land's End). Return along north coast road (D7), looking at Cap Sizun bird reserve. If time, back via Douarnenez and Locronan.

Monts d'Arrée

North from Quimper to Briec and Pleyben (superb parish close). Into Regional Nature Park at Brasparts, view from Montagne-St-Michel. To Huelgoat with its magnificent woodland and rock walks, then south to Châteauneuf-du-Faou (walks by Aulne River). Across Montagnes Noires to Coray and back to Quimper.

South coast

Down left bank of Odet to Bénodet, then to Beg-Meil (dead end). North to Fouesnant, and round bay to Concarneau (Medieval walled town). To Pont-Aven (memories of Gauguin, riverside walk in Bois d'Amour). Riec-sur-Bélon (oyster centre), then either direct to Quimperlé along D783, or via Moëlan-sur-Mer and the Carnoët Forest. From Quimperlé (upper and lower towns and Romanesque cathedral), back along N165, or if time inland road through Bannalec and Rosporden.

Côtes-du-Nord

As its name suggests, the Côtes-du-Nord (literally, 'coasts of the north') consists largely of coastline, of a variety unparalleled in Brittany. Following it from west to east, you come first to the Pink Granite Coast (Côte de Granit Rose) round Trégastel and Perros-Guirec, where the rocks, eroded by millennia of wind and tide, have taken on monstrous animal or humanoid shapes. Next the estuaries of the River Jaudy and the River Trieux cut deeply into the rugged coastline, followed by the sweep of the Bay of St-Brieuc, lined with small resorts perfect for a quiet holiday. East of St-Brieuc the bay shades into the Emerald Coast (Côte d'Eméraude), with wonderful beaches, rock pools and little islets cut off by the tide. Yet, apart from Perros-Guirec, there are no substantial holiday towns to rival Dinard next door in Ille-et-Vilaine, or La Baule away to the south in Loire-Atlantique. It is very much a family-oriented coast.

Inland, too, this is a département of the greatest variety. In its south-west corner, the Black Mountains (Montagnes Noires) lead on to Finistère and the highland fastnesses of Brittany. There are beauty spots like the Lac de Guerlédan, a favourite place for water sports; the strange Gorges du Daoulas; and the wilderness of giant boulders known as the Gorges de Toul-Goulic. Large areas are almost without main roads, and so have preserved their rural remoteness to an extent found nowhere else in the country. The old inland towns, like Guingamp and Lamballe, have managed to keep their sense of the past alive in spite of modern developments, while in Dinan the Côtes-du-Nord possesses the most picturesque and unspoiled Medieval town in the whole of Brittany. Castles abound, from the frowning ruins of Tonquédec to the well preserved walls of Fort la Latte.

Ancient and modern meet in unexpected ways. Just outside Lannion, still at heart a Medieval town, the futuristic radome of Pleumeur-Bodou beams in on satellites hurtling round the earth hundreds of miles overhead. A few miles of coastline on the Bay of St-Brieuc link historic worlds almost 1500 years apart. It was here that Christian missionaries landed from Cornwall and Wales in the 5th century, while the 20th saw a very different traffic in the opposite direction: Allied pilots smuggled out of Brittany to safety by the French Resistance, under the nose of the German invader.

The Côtes-du-Nord is where the two halves of Brittany meet: the French-speaking half to the east, and the Breton-speakers to the west. In the old days a line could be drawn a little way west of St-Brieuc, beyond which Breton was the everyday spoken tongue. Though nowadays the line is almost non-existent, since so few people still speak Breton, the Côtes-du-Nord still seems Breton in the ancient way. This feeling is epitomised by the granite town of Tréguier, with its cathedral spire pierced like a colander to lessen the force of the wind, its half-timbered houses, and its memories of St-Yves, the patron saint of lawyers, who is revered throughout Brittany.

G H I J K L

N

0 15
km

Baie de St-Brieuc

Cap Fréhel

Cap d'Erquy

Sables-d'Or-
les-Pins

Fort la Latte

Erquy

Fréhel

St-Cast-le-Guildo

Pléneuf-Val-André

Bienassis

Pen Guen

Dahouët

Matignon

Lancieux

Légué

Le Guildo

Ploubalay

St-Jacut-
de-la-Mer

Brieuc

Yffiniac

La Poterie

Pléven

Plancoët

Plouër-sur-
Rance

Corseul

Houssaye

Lamballe

Hunaudaye

Dinan

Temple de Mars

Léhon

oncontour

Trédaniel

Jugon-les-Lacs

otre-Dame-
du-Haut

Touche-
Trébry

Grand Etang
de Jugon

Plénée-Jugon

Boquen

Broons

Guitté

Caulnes

R Rance

orêt de Loudéac

Merdrignac

R Arguenon

© RNP 1985

Towns & villages

Belle-Isle-en-Terre　　C 5
16mi/25.5km SE of Lannion. Pop
3400. At the heart of one of the
prettiest tourist regions of the
Côtes-du-Nord, this quiet small
town stands at the meeting-place
of two rivers, the Léguer and the
Guic. Its name dates back to the
Middle Ages, when monks from the
island of Belle-Ile (then called Belle
Isle en Mer) settled here. Formerly
an industrial centre for mining and
paper manufacture, it is now a
centre for excursions to the nearby
villages and countryside.

Binic　　F 4
9mi/14.5km NW of St-Brieuc. Pop
700. Binic is the southernmost of
the sailing harbours along the
western side of the Bay of St-
Brieuc. Its cafés and restaurants
look out across a waterfront
crammed with small craft,
successors to the fishing boats that
once left Binic to fish for cod off
Iceland.

Bréhec　　F 3
7.5mi/12km SE of Paimpol. Pop
200. A quiet little seaside village
reached down minor roads, Bréhec
is said to be where the first
immigrants from Great Britain
landed in 'Little Britain' (Brittany)
at the end of the 5th century. This
influx begin in about AD480, and
lasted for a century and a half.

Broons　　J 7
15mi/24km SW of Dinan. Pop
2000. This small country town has
a single claim to fame: it was here
that Bertrand du Guesclin,
France's greatest general of the
Hundred Years' War, was born in
1320 (see Famous People, in
introduction). A column beside the
N12 marks the site of the now-
vanished manor house where he
was born. The name Broons derives
from the Breton bronn (literally
'breast', also meaning 'hill').

Callac-de-Bretagne　　B 6
17.5mi/28km SW of Guingamp.
Pop 2200. In the heart of the
Breton countryside, this small town
is one of several Callacs in
Brittany. Above it are the ruins of
the church of Botmel, with a 17thC
bell-tower. Callac is a centre for the
breeding of Breton spaniels, for

horsebreeding (there is a statue of
a stallion beside the horse-stud),
and for trout-fishing.

Corseul　　K 6
6mi/9.5km W of Dinan. Pop 1200.
At the time of Caesar's conquest of
Gaul, in 57BC, Corseul was the
capital of a leading tribe, the
Curiosolites, from whom the
present name derives. The Romans
made it an important Gallo-Roman
centre, with a forum, public baths
and temples, but of this little
survives (see Temple de Mars).
Today Corseul is an
undistinguished crossroads village.

Farmhouse near Corseul

Dinan　　K 6
31mi/49.5km NW of Rennes. Pop
17,000. MD Thur. Dinan is the
most-visited town in the whole of
Brittany, and it well deserves its
fame, as in spite of the tourist
hordes it manages to preserve a
feeling of medieval timelessness.
With its ancient streets (the best of
them pedestrianised), ramparts,
towers and churches, it has been
luring visitors from Britain since
the 1830s, when it was possible to
live in a hotel in Dinan for £3 a
month. Suitably enough, the finest
viewpoint in Dinan, behind the
Church of St-Sauveur and looking
across the steep valley of the Rance,
is the tree-shaded Jardin Anglais
(English Garden), which makes a
marvellous place for a picnic on a
hot summer's day.
Until the tidal barrage was
constructed across the mouth of
the Rance, Dinan guarded the
river's first major crossing-point,
and was of great strategic
importance. The Romans had a fort
here, and William the Conqueror
besieged it; but it reached the
height of its glory during the wars
with England during the Middle
Ages, when the massive town walls

and castle were built. The hero of these years was Bertrand du Guesclin, who is commemorated by an equestrian statue in the main square of the town. Here in 1359 he fought and defeated an English knight, Sir Thomas Canterbury, in single combat. Du Guesclin's heart, in a silver casket, is in the Church of St-Sauveur.

The usual approach to Dinan is by the high-level road across the magnificent viaduct, but no one should visit Dinan without walking down the zigzag path from the Jardin Anglais to see the old bridge across the river and the picturesque houses lining the riverbanks. The town's ramparts have been classed as an historic monument since 1886, and they still remain remarkably complete, justifying Dinan's title of the 'Carcassonne of the North'.

Dinan is an excellent excursion centre: to the coast, to the towns and countryside inland, and by water down the Rance to Dinard and St-Malo in Ille-et-Vilaine.

Erquy   I 4
15mi/24km NE of Lamballe. Pop 3400. A pretty little harbour town, with a fleet of small fishing boats that make a living from shellfish, especially scallops (*coquilles St-Jacques*). Nearby is a spectacular headland, the Cap d'Erquy, and there are no fewer than ten fine beaches within easy reach.

Etables-sur-Mer   F 4
11mi/17.5km NW of St-Brieuc. Pop 2100. A small resort, with the village a short way inland from the beach, which lies at the foot of a steep hill. In summer it is best to leave the car in the village and walk down. The church is mainly 18thC, and there is a 15thC calvary beside the road.

Guingamp   D 5
20mi/32km W of St-Brieuc. Pop 10,800. MD Fri & Sat. The old town of Guingamp, with its austere granite houses, clusters tightly round its superb Medieval church. The name derives from the Breton *Gwen Camp*, meaning 'White Camp', and probably goes back to the Dark Ages, when its citizens fortified their town against Norsemen raiding the heart of Brittany from the sea. Today it is

Town centre, Guingamp

an important commercial centre, from which roads radiate to all parts of north Brittany. Guingamp is the easternmost town to be Breton in every sense of the term, as it stands on the dividing line between the Breton and the French language. In the *3rd wk in Aug* each year a Festival of Breton Dance is held here; while the annual *pardon*, on the *eve of 1st Sun in Jul*, is one of the most popular in Brittany. It is celebrated with a candlelit procession and bonfires, and in former times was the scene of wild debauchery.

Jugon-les-Lacs   I 6
12.5mi/20km W of Dinan. Pop 650. Jugon's Medieval château has disappeared, but the lakes from which it gets its name are still very much in evidence. Just upstream from the village the Arguenon has been dammed to form a reservoir (the Grand Etang de Jugon), which looms uncomfortably close but is excellent for swimming and sailing.

Lamballe   H 6
24mi/38.5km E of Dinan. Pop 5500. MD Thur. A quiet old town, whose centre is bounded by two important churches, the Eglise St-Jean on the west and Notre-Dame-de-Grande-Puissance (Our Lady of Great Power) on the east. The town is said to have been founded in the 6th century by St-Pol, one of Brittany's most famous saints, from which it gets its name (Lan-Pol becoming Lamballe). The Syndicat d'Initiative occupies the ground floor of the finest old house in the town, the 16thC Maison du Bourreau ('House of the Hangman'), in the pl du Martray. On the floor above is a small museum devoted to the work of the Lamballe-born artist Mathurin Méheut.

Near the town centre is the Haras National (National Stud), one of the most important horsebreeding centres in northern France. Many of the stallions kept here are the powerful Breton draught horses (the *Trait Breton*). *Open mid-Jul–mid-Feb, Mon–Fri 12.30–16.30.*

Lancieux   K 4

12.5mi/20km NW of Dinan. Pop 1085. A small seaside resort of the Côte d'Eméraude, with a fine sandy beach. The Anglo-Canadian poet Robert W Service (1874–1958), author of popular verses such as 'The Shooting of Dangerous Dan McGrew', died at Lancieux and is buried here.

Lannion   B 3

20mi/32km NW of Guingamp. Pop 22,000. MD Thur. Now an important centre for research into electronics and telecommunication, Lannion was founded in the 11th century on the banks of the River Léguer. The wide river gives a spacious feeling to the town centre. On the left bank, by the main bridge, are the large buildings of an 18thC Augustinian convent; while on the right bank the narrow streets of old Lannion lead up to the church at the top of the town (St-Jean-de-Baly). A little way to the north, the 12thC church of Brélévénez is reached up a flight of 144 steps.

Steps to Brélévénez Church, Lannion

Lannion is centrally placed for the beach resorts of the Côte de Granit Rose, and has good moorings for visiting small boats. Among its sporting facilities is a flying club, which runs trips round the Pink Granite Coast.

Lézardrieux   E

3mi/5km W of Paimpol. Pop 2900. A small town on the left bank of the River Trieux, chiefly remarkable for a fine suspension bridge, which gives spectacular views up and down the estuary.

Loc-Envel   B

2.5mi/4km S of Belle-Isle-en-Terre. Pop 450. Set in a pretty valley, this village stands at the edge of a forest which has a curious double name: the Koat-an-Noz ('Forest of the Night') and Koat-an-Hay ('Forest of the Day'). This twinning is paralleled by St-Envel, after whom the village is named, since there were said to be twin saints of that name. Historians have traced their origin back to the Druidic religion, which had a special reverence for twins. The 16thC church, in Flamboyant Gothic style, contains a richly ornamented rood-screen.

Loudéac   F

25mi/40km S of St-Brieuc. Pop 11,600. A small agricultural town, which stands virtually at the central point of Brittany. In the 17th century it was famous for the weaving of flax, which was grown in the surrounding countryside, and whose blue flowers were described as looking like 'lakes reflecting the blue of the sky'. It is now a centre for making *charcuterie* and animal feeds.

On its north-east side is the Forest of Loudéac, part of the great forest that once covered the whole of inland Brittany. Wolves were still shot here in the 19th century.

Moncontour   G

14mi/22.5km S of St-Brieuc. Pop 2400. A compact little town, still largely Medieval, built round a neat central square. It stands on a spur of ground where two river valleys meet, and during the wars of the Middle Ages was an important strategic town. It was besieged three times, in 1393, 1487 and finally in 1590. A good deal of the Medieval ramparts survive, together with several of the town gates.

Mur-de-Bretagne   E

12.5mi/20km W of Loudéac. Pop 2250. This small town is completely unwarlike and hardly justifies its name of the 'Wall of Brittany'. It has a 19thC Gothic Revival church

Yffiniac G
4.5mi/7km SE of St-Brieuc. Pop
3500. The motorway from St-Brieuc
to Lamballe now bypasses Yffiniac
but it is well worth visiting in
summer, when almost every house
in the straggling main street has
sacks of onions, strings of garlic and
vegetables of all sorts for sale at low
prices. It is the home town of one
of Brittany's heroes, the world
champion cyclist Bernard Hinault,
whose bust and shirt are displayed
in the entrance hall of the *mairie*
(town hall).

Interesting buildings

Churches and other ecclesiastical
buildings are normally open
*10.00–12.00, 14.00–17.00 (18.00
summer).*

Abbaye de Léhon K
1mi/1.5km S of Dinan. An abbey
was founded here in the 9th century
by a group of monks, who secretly
removed the relics of St-Magloire
from the island of Sark, to justify
their new foundation. The present
monastic church dates from the
13th century and has some of the
oldest stained glass in Brittany. The
17thC cloister and 14thC refectory
can also be visited. Legend says
that underground passages lead
from the abbey ruins to the castle
on the hill above.

**Abbaye de Notre-Dame-de-
Beauport** E
2.5mi/4km SE of Paimpol. The
picturesque ruins of this ancient
abbey, founded in 1202 for monks
of the Premonstratensian order,
stand surrounded by trees near the
Bay of Paimpol. Most of the
surviving ruins date from the 13th
century, including part of the
transept and the choir, and the
enormous refectory, opening on to
the Channel. Abandoned in 1790,
the abbey was used as a gunpowder
factory during the French
Revolution. *Open Jun Sat & Sun
only; 1 Jul–20 Sep, daily
09.00–12.30, 14.00–19.00. Charge.*

**Abbaye de Notre-Dame-du-
Bon-Repos** D
Near St-Gelven. 19mi/30.5km W of
Loudéac. In 1184 an abbey was
founded here by Alain de Rohan,

and a 17thC chapel, on a stretch
of grass surrounded by oak trees;
the chapel was a favourite subject
of the 19thC artist Jean-Baptiste
Corot. Nowadays it is mainly a
jumping-off point for the Lac de
Guerlédan, the Daoulas Gorges,
and other beauty spots of the region.

Paimpol E 2
15.5mi/25km N of Guingamp. Pop
8500. MD Tue. Paimpol owes its
existence to the 19thC cod-fishing
industry. Today it is mainly a
port for small pleasure craft,
though there are still a few offshore
fishing boats; but in the heyday of
the Icelandic cod fisheries Paimpol
maintained a fleet of over 80
schooners which made the annual
journey to the cod-banks. In 1886
it won a place in French literary
fame with the publication of Pierre
Loti's novel 'Pêcheur d'Islande'
('The Iceland Fisherman'), a study
of Breton fishing life; many of the
places mentioned have seen little
change since Loti's day.
Apart from its attractions as a
small-boat centre, Paimpol is
ideally placed for excursions—
north to the Ile de Bréhat; west to
Tréguier, Perros-Guirec and the
neighbouring seaside resorts; and
south to the beaches of the Bay of
St-Brieuc. Paimpol also continues
its seafaring tradition with a
training school for officers of the
merchant navy (Ecole Nationale de
la Marine Marchande), the oldest
such school in France.

Perros-Guirec C 2
.5mi/12km N of Lannion. Pop
7900. MD Fri. Second only to
Dinard among the seaside resorts of
north Brittany, Perros-Guirec has
ne superb beach (the Plage de
Trestraou) and three smaller
beaches, a casino, a fishing harbour
with a marina, and a modern
conference centre. The town centre
is on a ridge above the harbour and
beaches. Its old Breton name,
Penros or Pennroz, means 'top of
the hill'; while Guirec was a Welsh
monk who, according to legend,
sailed across to Brittany in a granite
drinking-trough.
West of Trestraou beach, a
delightful coastal path (the Sentier
des Douaniers, or Path of the
Customs Officers) leads to the
neighbouring resort of

Church, Perros-Guirec

Ploumanac'h, past groups of the
grotesquely shaped pink granite
rocks from which this stretch of
coast gets its name (Côte de Granit
Rose). A few kilometres offshore
are the Seven Islands (Les Sept
Iles), a magnificent seabird
sanctuary which can be visited by
boat from Perros. Just west of the
town, the village of La Clarté has
one of the most famous chapels of
the region.

Plancoët J 5
10mi/16km NW of Dinan. Pop
2500. A large village (or small town)
on the River Arguenon, famous
mainly for its connection with the
writer Chateaubriand, who
describes his childhood here in his
autobiography. Bottled water from
Plancoët is now sold all over
Brittany.

Pléneuf-Val-André H 4
9mi/14.5km N of Lamballe. Pop
4000. A popular small resort on the
Emerald Coast, with a fine sandy
beach along the front, and other
good beaches close at hand. Just to
the south is the little port and
yachting harbour of Dahouët,
which in former times maintained
a fleet of Icelandic cod-fishing
boats.

Pleumeur-Bodou B 2
4.5mi/7km NW of Lannion. Pop
3450. Like a giant white golfball, the
radome of the Pleumeur-Bodou
Space Telecommunications Centre
looms above the heathland inland
from the Pink Granite Coast. The
Centre was opened in 1962, and has
been used since then for satellite
tracking and picking up signals. It
forms part of the Intelsat network,
in which more than 100 nations take

part. *Open Jul & Aug daily
09.00–12.00, 13.45–18.00; Jun
daily 09.00–11.00, 14.00–16.45;
Easter–31 May & 1 Sep–15 Oct,
same times but closed Tue.* **Charge**

Plouër-sur-Rance **L 5**
6mi/9.5km NE of Dinan. Pop 600.
A riverside village, once famous for
producing both deep-sea fishermen,
and fine craftsmen in wood.
During the 19th century a pianist
called Kowalski lived nearby; half-
French and half-Polish, he was
Chopin's last pupil, and divided
his musical talents between church
accompaniments and playing the
piano at orgies organised by the
sous-préfet of Dinan.

Plouha **F 3**
19mi/30.5km NW of St-Brieuc.
Pop 2900. A small crossroads town,
from which lanes lead down to
secluded rocky coves, and inland
to the little-frequented region
between the Bay of St-Brieuc and
Guingamp.

Ploumanac'h **B 2**
9.5mi/15km N of Lannion. Pop: *see
Perros-Guirec*. This little resort,
packed in summer, is the centre for
exploring the amazing rock
formations of the Pink Granite
Coast, which have fanciful names
such as Napoleon's Hat and the
Death's Head (*see also Côte de
Granit Rose*). Ploumanac'h is in two
sections, divided by a headland: on
the south side the small harbour,
and on the north the Beach of St-
Guirec (after whom Perros-Guirec
is named). The saint has a small
oratory on the beach, sheltering a
granite statue. The original
wooden effigy, now kept in the
chapel above the beach, suffered in
the past from having pins stuck in
its nose by girls wanting husbands.

Quintin **F 6**
11mi/17.5km SW of St-Brieuc. Pop
3600. Once a prosperous weaving
town, Quintin still has its share of
17th and 18thC granite houses
built during wealthier times. The
17thC castle overlooks the River
Gouët, which flows below the town.
Traces of the 15thC ramparts
survive; and the church contains a
venerated relic, said to be part of
the girdle of the Virgin Mary,
brought back from Palestine by a
Crusader in the 13th century.

Rostrenen **C**
29mi/46.5km W of Loudéac. Pop
2800. A small town buried in the
heartlands of Brittany, Rostrenen
makes a good jumping-off point fo
exploring the central stretch of the
Brest–Nantes Canal. On *15 Aug*
each year the inhabitants celebrate
the festival of Our Lady of the
Bramble (Notre-Dame-du-
Roncier), which gets its name from
a miracle-working statue of the
Virgin, found buried in a thorn
thicket by a local peasant. There is
a similar statue and legend at
Josselin in the Morbihan.

Sables-d'Or-les-Pins **I**
4.5mi/7km E of Erquy. Pop 600.
A family seaside resort, consisting
almost entirely of hotels and
holiday cottages. The village is
strung out behind a magnificent
sandy beach, one of the largest in
the whole of Brittany.

St-Brieuc **G**
62.5mi/100km NW of Rennes. Pop
57,000. MD Sat. The départementa
capital of the Côtes-du-Nord, St-
Brieuc is an expanding and busy
city which well repays exploration,
though it is not as picturesque as
many of Brittany's more historic
towns. Yet it is as ancient as any
of them, and dates its foundation
back to about AD580, when
Brioc—a Welsh monk and one of
the 'Seven Founding Saints' of
Brittany—sailed across the Channel
and set up a monastic community
later named after him. St-Brieuc
stands on a magnificent site, on a
plateau between the valleys of the
Gouëdic and the Gouët, and owes
much of its drama, and its traffic
problems, to this hilly situation.
During the 10th century the people
of St-Brieuc fought the invading
Normans, and their battles
continued throughout the Middle
Ages. The frowning Medieval
cathedral in the town centre, which
looks as much like a fortress as a
church, was largely built in the
early 13th century by Guillaume
Pinchon, a 'battling bishop' who
fought the duke of Brittany and was
later canonised. Much of the centre
is now pedestrianised, which makes
it easy to enjoy what is left of old
St-Brieuc. There are a number of
fine public gardens, notably the
Grandes Promenades, with their

holes to lessen the force of the
wind, dominates the town.
Dedicated to St-Tugdual, one o
Brittany's 'Seven Founding Sain
it is a magnificent building dati
from the 13th–15th centuries.
Below it, streets of old houses d
to the wide waters of the Jaudy
used as an anchorage by boats o
all shapes and sizes. Tréguier w
the seat of a bishopric from the
century until the Revolution
abolished it in 1791.
Above all, the town is famous as
birthplace of one of France's be
loved saints, St-Yves. Born jus
outside Tréguier in 1253, Yves
both priest and lawyer. He spe
nearly all his active life in his h
town, and was renowned for
helping poor clients who could
afford legal fees. He is usually
portrayed between a poor man
a rich man, as in a carving in
Tréguier Cathedral. The story
that the rich man had sued the
man, on the grounds that the
lived on the smells of good foo
wafting out of the rich man's
kitchen. So Yves took a coin a
made it ring in the rich man's
giving as his judgment that the
sound would pay for the smell
Yves died in 1303, and his ton
Tréguier Cathedral soon becar
goal of pilgrimage. He was
canonised in the 14th century
became the patron saint of law
Every year on *19 May* membe
the legal profession from all o
France meet at Tréguier and
march in procession from the
cathedral to St-Yves' birthplac
Minihy-Tréguier.
Tréguier's other famous citize
at the opposite end of the relig
spectrum. Ernest Renan
(1823–1892), the philosopher
anti-clerical freethinker, is
commemorated by a statue in
square outside the cathedral.
mid-19th century his 'Life of
Jesus' scandalised Roman Cat
opinion by maintaining that C
was an ordinary human being
though an 'incomparable man
Renan's birthplace is now a
museum.
Tréguier makes an excellent
from which to explore the no
coast, and the many delightfu
intriguing towns and villages
this most Breton of areas.

on a beautiful site beside the River Blavet. The monks were Cistercians, from the Abbey of Savigny, in Normandy. Apart from the Medieval entrance gateway and the church, the ruins date from the 17th and 18th centuries. *Open Jun & 16–30 Sep Sat & Sun only; 1 Jul–15 Sep, daily 09.00–12.30, 14.00–19.00.* **Charge**

Abbaye de Notre-Dame-de-Boquen   I 7

Plénée–Jugon. 22mi/35km W of Dinan. An abbey was founded here in 1137 and soon became extremely wealthy, but in the 15th century it declined, fell into ruin and was used as a source of building stone. In 1964 reconstruction was taken in hand, and it is now a convent of nuns of the Order of Bethlehem. Of the 12thC Romanesque abbey, some fine capitals survive. The church alone can be visited, during *normal visiting hours.*

Bourbriac, church   D 5

6mi/9.5km S of Guingamp. The church with its lofty bell-tower stands in the centre of Bourbriac, which gets its name from the Irish St Briac, whose relics were famous for curing epilepsy and other mental ailments. The Romanesque crypt dates back to the 11th century, as does the high crossing arch. Much of the rest of the church is in Flamboyant Gothic style. A tomb in the church is said to have been the saint's burial place, but his bones have long since disappeared.

Cathédrale St-Etienne   G 5

St-Brieuc. Dedicated to St Stephen, the cathedral was built at the end of the 12th century on the site of the monastery founded by the Welsh St Brioc in the 6th century. It stands on marshy ground, on piles driven into the soil, and its twin towers, with battlements and pierced with arrow slits, give it the appearance of a fortress. It was destroyed by fire in 1353 and subsequently rebuilt by the duke of Brittany. The nave was rebuilt in the 18th century; during the Revolution it was used as stabling for horses. In the south aisle is the tomb of Bishop Guillaume Pinchon St-Guillaume), who died in 1234 after completing the cathedral. The

south transept has a magnificent 15thC rose window; the Stations of the Cross are modern work, by a professor from the Ecole Nationale des Beaux Arts.

Cathédrale de St-Tugdual   D 2

Tréguier. 19mi/30.5km N of Guingamp. St-Tugdual's Cathedral is one of the finest churches in the whole of Brittany, and dominates the town of Tréguier. It is of unusual design, with three towers over the transept; the southern tower is surmounted by a tall stone spire, pierced with holes against the force of the wind sweeping in from the sea to the north. The main entrance is from the pl du Martray, below this tower. Most of the cathedral dates from the 13th–15th century, though the northern tower is Romanesque of the 10th or 11th century. Inside the church there is a remarkable 13thC wooden statue of Christ, a sculptured wood group of St-Yves between a poor man and a rich man (*see Tréguier*), and 46 superb Renaissance choir stalls. The original tomb of St-Yves was destroyed during the French Revolution; the present tomb dates from the 19th century. The cathedral's most precious relic, the head (*chef*) of St-Yves, is kept in the sacristy. On the north side of the cathedral are the cloisters, built in the 15th century and the finest in Brittany.

Chapelle de Kerfons   B 3

Near Ploubezre. 4.5mi/7km SE of Lannion. This chapel, built in the 15th and 16th centuries, has a remarkable interior with a fine Renaissance rood-screen (late 15thC) and windows containing 16thC stained glass. In front of it is an ancient calvary set among chestnut trees.

Chapelle de Notre-Dame   C 4

Locmaria. 0.5mi/1km N of Belle-Isle-en-Terre. A 16thC chapel with a fine rood-screen, built on top of a small hill. In the cemetery is the funeral chapel of Sir Robert Mond, the 19thC nickel tycoon, and Lady Mond (1869–1949), who was born at Belle-Isle. The daughter of a local miller, as a young woman she made her way to Paris, where she met and married Sir

Robert. In later life she was a great benefactress of her home town.

Chapelle de St-Gonéry   D 2
4.5mi/7km N of Tréguier. A fascinating little chapel, with an odd twisting spire, almost in corkscrew shape. Inside, the wooden roof of the nave is painted from end to end with scenes from the Bible, dating from the 16th century. Visitors are shown a stone sarcophagus, in which the saint is said to have rowed himself across from Britain in the 6th century.

Chapelle de St-Miliau   B 3
Ploumilliau. 10mi/16km SW of Lannion. Ploumilliau's 17thC chapel is famous for its stone carving of the Ankou—the Breton figure of Death, shown as a dancing skeleton carrying a scythe. In former times the Ankou was invoked to bring about the death of an enemy.

Château de Bienassis   H 4
3mi/5km S of Erquy. Built in the 15th century, Bienassis is a dainty little château, with a moat, and an outer wall fortified with pointed turrets. The living quarters were rebuilt in Classical style in the 17th century, and formal gardens were laid out at the same period. During World War II Bienassis was occupied by the Germans, who shot a number of the local inhabitants in the garden in reprisal for Resistance activities. *Open 6 Jun–17 Sep 10.30–12.30, 14.00–16.30. Closed Sun.* **Charge**

Château du Guildo   J 5
15.5mi/25km NW of Dinan. The ruined castle of Le Guildo is half-hidden by trees on the east bank of the Arguenon River, just north of the bridge across the estuary. In the 15th century it was the home of Gilles de Bretagne (1424–1450), son of the duke of Brittany, who was brought up at the English court and later led a riotous life with his cronies at Le Guildo. Accused of plotting against his elder brother, who had inherited the dukedom, Gilles was strangled under mysterious circumstances at the age of 26.

Château de la Houssaye   G 6
7.5mi/12km SE of St-Brieuc. An 18thC château, 131ft/40m in length and built in classically

symmetrical design. The chapel was built in the 19th century, from older materials; and there is a fine granite dovecote. The château stands in a large park. *Open 20 Jul–31 Aug 10.00–12.00, 15.00–19.00.*

Château de la Hunaudaye   I 6
Near Pléven. 9.5mi/15km E of Lamballe. Once the most powerful fortress of the Breton duchy of Penthièvre, La Hunaudaye remains impressive even in ruins. The first château was built in the 13th century, but towards the end of the 15th it was rebuilt on a far grander scale, with granite towers and curtain wall. The largest of the towers formed the keep. Duchess Anne of Brittany and François I of France are said to have visited La Hunaudaye. It was largely destroyed during the French Revolution, and was used as a stone quarry throughout the 19th century. *Open 1 Jul–31 Aug 10.00–13.00, 15.00–19.00; Easter–30 Jun & Sep, Sun & hols only 15.00–19.00.*

Château de Quintin   F 6
11mi/17.5km SW of St-Brieuc. Begun about 1645, the château was never completed, since while it was being built the bishop of St-Brieuc told the king that it might become a Huguenot (French Protestant) stronghold, and work on it was stopped. The lower stages of the projected castle remain, together with ancillary buildings which were made into a château in the 18th century. *Open daily (exterior only).*

Château de la Roche-Jagu   D 3
4mi/6.5km SW of Paimpol. The castle stands at the top of a tree-covered slope, on the steep left bank of the Trieux River. Built in the 15th century, its fortified towers form part of the main building, which stands on the site of two earlier strongholds. It was restored in the 1970s and is now used as a cultural centre, where art exhibitions, concerts and other activities are held during the summer. *Open mid-Jun–mid-Sep, daily 10.00–12.00, 14.00–19.00.* **Charge**

Château de Rosanbo   B 3
Near Lanvellec. 9.5mi/15km SW of Lannion. Rosanbo stands above a

stream called the Bo (Breton *Roc'h an Bo*, meaning Rock above the Bo). Basically a fortified Renaissance manor house, it dates mainly from the 14th and 15th centuries, and was much altered in the 17th. Rosanbo has belonged to the Coskaër family since 1050. Inside there is a fine Louis XIV staircase, some notable tapestries, and a library of ancient books. The garden terraces give magnificent views over the surrounding countryside. *Open Sat & Sun only, 1 May–30 Jun 14.00–18.00; 1 Jul–31 Aug 10.00–12.00, 14.00–18.00.* **Charge**

Château de Tonquédec   C 3
6.5mi/10.5km SE of Lannion. The majestic ruins of Tonquédec loom among the trees above the valley of the Léguer. Completed at the beginning of the 15th century, it has powerful curtain walls guarded by turrets, and a central keep with walls 13ft/4m thick. It was dismantled on Richelieu's orders in 1622.

Château de la Touche-Trébry   H 7
3mi/5km E of Moncontour. Built at the end of the 16th century by Christophe de la Roche, governor of Moncontour, La Touche-Trébry is a typical Renaissance château, with a central courtyard and turrets with bulbous roofs. One of its 17thC owners was an eccentric who had a clock by his bed with a different sweetmeat in each of the twelve numbers. If he wanted to know the time during the night, all he had to do was to follow the hour hand along to the nearest number, which he would recognise by the taste of the sweetmeat. *Open Jul & Aug 14.30–16.30. Closed Sun.* **Charge**

Dinan, old houses   K 6
31mi/49.5km NW of Rennes. There is hardly a house in the centre of Dinan that is not old. The Office de Tourisme in the pl du Théâtre is a good starting point, as it is in a 16thC townhouse, the Hôtel Kératry. Nearby is the pedestrianised rue de l'Horloge, named after the lofty clock tower, 197ft/60m high, from whose top there are wide views over the town and the valley of the Rance (*open*

in summer 10.00–12.00, 14.00–18.00; **charge**). Some of the finest of Dinan's half-timbered houses are in the rue du Jerzual, which leads through a Medieval gateway to the rue du Petit Fort, and so down to the quayside and the old bridge across the river. At the opposite side of the old town from the Porte du Jerzual is another ancient gateway, the Porte St-Louis, which leads to the castle and a walk under the ramparts (the prom des Petits Fossés). The castle, known as the Château de la Duchesse Anne, was not built as such, but consists of a fortified main tower or *donjon* and a smaller tower (the Tour de Coëtquen), with a stretch of curtain wall between. It now houses a museum.
Dinan's main church is the Basilica of the Holy Saviour (Basilique St-Sauveur), on the eastern side of the old town. Built in the 12th century, it is a mixture of the Romanesque and Gothic styles, and was largely reconstructed in the 15th and 16th centuries. The three-storey bell-tower is 17thC, restored in 1981. The Romanesque west doorway is very fine. Inside, the treasures include a 12thC font, 15thC stained glass of the Evangelists, a 16thC alabaster statue of the Virgin and the 'heart-shrine' of Bertrand du Guesclin (died 1380), the great Marshal of France. The other important church is the Eglise St-Malo, begun at the end of the 15th century and built in Flamboyant Gothic style. It was not completed until 1865.

Eglise de Brélévénez   B 3
Lannion. 20mi/32km NW of Guingamp. On the north side of the town, this superb Romanesque church is reached up a flight of 144 granite steps, past houses built stepwise up the slope. Built by the Templars in the 12th century, it has a lofty 15thC bell-tower, and contains some fine paintings and altar-pieces, including a 17thC Entombment of Christ.

Eglise de Notre-Dame   C 7
Kergrist-Moëlou. 5.5mi/9km N of Rostrenen. Dedicated to Our Lady, the church dates from the early 16th century (restored in the 19th) and is built in Flamboyant Gothic style. The south façade is decorated with

sculptures, including one of a
drunkard holding a jug. Outside is
a large and elaborate calvary.

Fort la Latte   **J 4**
Near Cap Fréhel. 26mi/41.5km
NW of Dinan. Built on a rocky
peninsula, with the sea pounding
far below, this magnificent castle
has perhaps the most dramatic
situation of any building in
Brittany. It became familiar to
cinema-goers in the late 1950s, and
more recently to television viewers,
as the setting for the final battle
scenes in the Kirk Douglas–Tony
Curtis epic 'The Vikings'.

Fort la Latte

However, it was built at a period
far later than that of the Vikings,
in the 13th and 14th centuries, and
was adapted for artillery use in the
17th. Prince Rainier of Monaco is
descended from one of the lords of
Fort la Latte, which was called in
former times the Château de la
Roche-Goyon. *Open 1 Jun–30 Sep
10.00–12.30, 14.30–18.30; May,
Sat & Sun only; Sun out of season
14.30–17.30.*

Guingamp, old houses   **D 5**
20mi/32km W of St-Brieuc. At the
heart of the old town of Guingamp
is the pl du Centre, with most of
the streets of historic houses
opening off it. The best of the
buildings are 16thC half-
timbering, or granite from the 17th
and 18th centuries; some of them
have superb Renaissance doorways.
However, the main feature is not a
building at all but a splendid
fountain, known as 'La Plomée'.
Dating from the Renaissance and
restored in the 18th century, it is
crowned by a statue of the Virgin,
and adorned with dolphins,
nymphs and monsters.
The lower walls of the 15thC
château survive, but most of it was
demolished under Cardinal
Richelieu in the 17th century. The
imposing 17thC town hall (Hôtel de
Ville) was founded as a convent.
The glory of Guingamp's buildings,

and one of the finest churches in
the whole of Brittany, is the Basilica
of Notre-Dame-du-Bon-Secours
(Our Lady of Succour). An
extraordinary mixture of 14thC
Gothic and 16thC Renaissance, it
was largely rebuilt after 1535,
when the south-west tower
collapsed. The reconstruction was
entrusted to a young architect, Jean
le Moal, who was an enthusiast for
the new Renaissance style. Not only
did he rebuild the tower (the
north-west tower survives from the
earlier church), but he recast the
southern side of the nave, giving it
fanciful Renaissance decorative
motifs. The main spire was
destroyed by an American shell in
1944 and rebuilt after the war. A
rare feature of the church is the
porch on the north side (the Porche
Notre-Dame), which has a 'Black
Madonna', possibly 13thC, high on
the wall. The stone floor is inlaid
with a labyrinth, which leads to the
inscription 'Ave Maria' at the
centre. Madonnas made of black
stone were highly venerated, and
the worship of black stone cult
objects goes back to pre-Christian
times.

Gurunhuel, calvary   **C 5**
7.5mi/12km SW of Guingamp.
Near the 16thC church is a superb
calvary of the same date. On the
central shaft, two angels collect the
blood of Christ in a chalice; while
on two outer crosses the souls of
the crucified thieves are shown
leaving their mouths. The soul of
the good thief is gathered up by an
angel, and that of the unrepentant
thief by a demon.

Kermaria-an-Iskuit   **F 3**
2.5mi/4km NW of Plouha. This
chapel, whose name means 'the
house of Mary who heals', dates
from the 13th century with much
subsequent rebuilding. It was
originally a courthouse as well as a
chapel, and above the porch is the
courtroom and the balcony from
which sentence was read. In the
nave is a superb 15thC fresco of
the 'Dance of Death', with dancing
skeletons leading a parade of figures, from emperor to ploughman.

Lannion, old houses   **B 3**
The best of these are in the pl du
Général Leclerc, reached from the

river up the pedestrianised rue des Augustins. Built in the 15th and 16th centuries, several of the houses are hung with slates on the exterior. In the same square is a statue to Charles le Goffic (1863–1932), Lannion's most famous writer.

Notre-Dame-de-Bulat C 6
Bulat-Pestivien. 14mi/22.5km SW of Guingamp. In former times an important goal of pilgrimage, the church of Notre-Dame-de-Bulat has a pierced spire 217ft/66m high, the highest in the Côtes-du-Nord. It was added in 1865 to an ornate 16thC Renaissance tower. The porch contains statues of the Apostles, the sacristy is decorated with a 16thC frieze of the 'Dance of Death', and the lectern is carved with the figure of a young man in the costume of the Morbihan. Bulat has no fewer than three sacred fountains. A *pardon* takes place there annually on *8 Sep*.

Notre-Dame-de-la-Clarté B 2
La Clarté. 1.5mi/2.5km W of Perros-Guirec. The 15thC chapel of Notre-Dame-de-la-Clarté is one of the architectural jewels of the Trégor (the region near the town of Tréguier). It is said to have been built by a Breton nobleman in fulfilment of a vow. Caught in a fogbank off the rocky coast, he vowed to build a chapel to the Virgin if he came safely ashore. At that moment the fog lifted, giving a clear view (*clarté*) of the coast, and he was saved. Another explanation for the name is that the Virgin has the power to restore clarity of sight to the blind, or near-blind. Each year on *Aug 15* a *pardon* (pilgrims' procession) is held at La Clarté.

Notre-Dame-du-Guiaudet D 7
Lanrivain. 17.5mi/28km S of Guingamp. Just north of the small village of Lanrivain, set in some of the remotest countryside in Brittany, is the 17thC Chapel of Notre-Dame-du-Guiaudet. It has been a pilgrimage centre since 1692, when a local peasant had a vision and discovered an ancient statue of the Virgin buried in the ground; it is now displayed in the sanctuary. The electrified carillon has 16 bells, and plays two traditional Breton hymns to the Virgin.

Notre-Dame-du-Haut

Notre-Dame-du-Haut H 7
Trédaniel. 0.5mi/1km E of Moncontour. This pretty little chapel stands on a grassy knoll in the country outside Moncontour. Though it is dedicated to Our Lady, it is in fact a centre for Brittany's 'Seven Healing Saints' (Sept Saints Guérisseurs) and is visited by pilgrims each year on *Aug 15*. Inside, there are statues to all seven: St-Yvertin, who cures headaches; St-Houarniaule or Hervé (fears and depression); St-Hubert (wounds); St-Méen (insanity); St-Lubin (eye disorders and rheumatism); St-Mamert (digestive complaints); and Ste-Eugénie (childbirth).

Notre-Dame-du-Ruellou D 7
St-Nicolas-du-Pélem. 22.5mi/36km S of Guingamp. The 18thC chapel of Notre-Dame-du-Ruellou contains a wooden carillon wheel, dated 1777, with 12 little bells. Such wheels, rung by those hoping for heavenly favours, are thought to derive from pagan wheels dedicated to the sun-god Belen, from which the name Pélem may derive.

Notre-Dame-de-Runan D 3
Runan. 10.5mi/17km N of Guingamp. Runan's magnificent church, which dates from the 14th–15th century, was begun about 1300 by the Knights Templar and completed in the following century by the Hospitallers. It is set in a parish close, with a calvary and pulpit, and a Renaissance ossuary dated 1552. Outside it is decorated with stone-carved figures and coats-of-arms; inside it has carved beams and columns, and an east window with some fine 15thC Flemish glass. A torchlit religious procession is held at Runan on the *last Sat in Jul*.

Notre-Dame-du-Tertre E 5
Châtelaudren. 11.5mi/18.5km W of St-Brieuc. Dedicated to Our Lady

of the Hill, this 15thC church is famous for its unique series of paintings on wood panels (late 15thC). The choir ceiling has 96 paintings showing scenes from the Bible, while a further 32 in a side chapel illustrate the lives of St-Fiacre and St Margaret.

'Temple' de Lanleff　　　**E 3**
Lanleff. 7.5mi/12km S of Paimpol. The ruins of Lanleff's so-called 'Temple' were for centuries thought to be of Roman origin, but are in fact the remains of a 12thC Romanesque church. Dating from the time of the Crusades, its circular shape was copied from the Church of the Holy Sepulchre in Jerusalem.

Temple de Mars

Temple de Mars　　　**K 6**
Near Corseul. 5.5mi/9km W of Dinan. One of the few authentic Gallo-Roman remains in Brittany, the temple stands in a field beside the D794. Probably built at the end of the 1st century AD, it consists of part of a polygonal tower or apse, made of a double 'skin' of brick with rubble infilling between.

Museums & galleries

Aquarium de la Côte de Granit Rose　　　**B 2**
22730 Trégastel. Tel (96) 23 88 67. A fascinating aquarium, in spaces hollowed out beneath gigantic rocks. The collection includes fish native to the coasts of Brittany, together with many exotic species. *Open May, Sat, Sun & hols; Jun, Sep & early Oct, daily 14.00–18.30; Jul & Aug, daily 09.00–21.00.* **Charge**

Archéologique, Musée　　　**K 6**
La Mairie, Corseul, 22130 Plancoët. Tel (96) 27 90 17. Exhibits from prehistory to Gallo-Roman times, with special reference to the Curiosolites tribe, whose capital was at Corseul. *Open in summer, Mon, Tue & Fri 09.00–12.00, 14.00–17.00.* **Charge**

Château, Musée du　　　**K 6**
Château de la Duchesse Anne, 22100 Dinan. Tel (96) 39 45 20. In 1906 the 14thC château became the property of the town of Dinan, and a museum was begun here. Displayed throughout the rooms of the castle are costumes and furniture from the Dinan region, local history exhibits, and a fine collection of stone tomb effigies from the 12th and 13th centuries. *Open Wed–Mon 1 Mar–30 Apr 10.00–12.00, 14.00–17.00; 1 May–30 Sep 09.00–12.00, 14.00–17.00. Closed Tue.* **Charge**

Histoire, d'Arts et Ethnographie des Côtes du Nord, Musée d'　　　**G 5**
Rue Mireille Chrisostome, 22000 St-Brieuc. Tel (96) 61 29 33. A new museum devoted to all the historical and social aspects of the Côtes-du-Nord was opened in 1984. It includes audio-visual presentations, displays of documents, and both permanent and temporary exhibitions. *Open 10.00–12.00, 14.00–18.00. Closed Mon.* **Charge**

Mathurin Méheut, Musée　　　**H 6**
Syndicat d'Initiative, pl du Martray, 22400 Lamballe. Tel (96) 31 05 38. Born in Lamballe in 1882, Méheut studied painting in Rennes and Paris, before returning to Brittany, where he spent most of his creative life. He died in 1958, in Paris. The upper floor of the Syndicat building is devoted to his paintings and drawings, and also has exhibits of Breton art and culture. *Open 1 Jun–mid-Sep 10.00–12.00, 14.30–18.30, closed Tue & Sun; rest of year Tue & Fri only 14.00–17.00.* **Charge**

Renan, Maison de　　　**D 2**
22220 Tréguier. In town centre. Tel (96) 92 30 19. The 19thC freethinker and writer Ernest Renan was born in this 16thC half-timbered house in 1823. He spent his boyhood here, and kept the house as a holiday home throughout his life. It is now a museum devoted to his life and writings, including a reconstruction of his workroom. *Open 1 Apr–30*

Sep 10.00–12.00, 14.00–19.00.
Closed Tue. **Charge**

Accommodation

Campsites

Prices at campsites vary according
to the facilities available but seldom
exceed ten francs per person at
present. There will usually also be
a charge for the car and for the site.

Belle-Isle-en-Terre   C 5

Le Cleuziou
22540 Louargat. Tel (96) 43 07 76.
Set in the grounds of a 16thC
stone-built Breton manor house,
this is a four-star site with
swimming pool, tennis court and
many other facilities. *Open all year.
Closed Xmas hol.*

Caurel   E 8

Nautic International
22530 Mur-de-Bretagne.Tel (96) 28
57 94. Beside the Lac de Guerlédan
in the heart of Brittany, this is an
ideal centre for boating and other
water sports. *Open 1 Apr–31 Oct.*

Dinan   K 6

Municipal Beauséjour
22100 Dinan. 3mi/5km NE of
Dinan. Tel (96) 39 53 27. Near St-
Samson-sur-Rance, on a flat, grassy
site. *Open mid-Jun–mid-Sep.*

Municipal de la Hallerais
Taden, 22100 Dinan. 2mi/3km NE
of town. Tel (96) 39 15 93. A grassy,
terraced site, near the village of
Taden. There is direct access to
the banks of the Rance. *Open
1 Mar–early Nov.*

Erquy   I 4

Bellevue
22430 Erquy. Tel (96) 72 33 04.
2mi/3km S of the town, and about
1mi/1.5km from the sea, on a level
site and quieter than the seaside
campsites. *Open mid-Jun–mid-Sep.*

Le Vieux Moulin
22430 Erquy. Tel (96) 72 34 23.
Just east of the town, within easy
reach of several beaches. *Open
1 Apr–30 Sep.*

Etables-sur-Mer   F 4

L'Abri-Côtier
22680 Etables-sur-Mer. Tel (96) 70
61 57. Just north of the town, within

easy reach of the sea. *Open
1 Apr–30 Sep.*

Guingamp   D 5

Milin-Kerhré
Pabu, 22200 Guingamp. 2.5mi/4km
N of town on D787. Tel (96) 43 77
94. A terraced site beside the
Trieux River, by the village of
Pabu. *Open mid-Jun–mid-Sep.*

Jugon-les-Lacs   I 6

Municipal Le Bocage
22270 Jugon-les-Lacs. Tel (96) 31
60 16. A lakeside site, offering
facilities for water sports. *Open
1 Jun–30 Sep.*

Lamballe   H 6

St-Sauveur
22400 Lamballe. Tel (96) 31 00 61.
A small site not far from the town
centre. *Open mid-Jun–mid-Sep.*

Lancieux   K 4

Le Villeu
22770 Lancieux. Tel (96) 86 21 67.
Off the Ploubalay road, a short way
south of the town. Its facilities
include a common-room. *Open
1 May–30 Sep.*

Lannion   B 3

Beg-Léguer
22300 Lannion. Tel (96) 37 25 20.
A terraced site 550yds/500m from
the sea, off the Trébeurden road
just NW of the town. Has games
and television rooms. *Open
1 Jun–30 Sep.*

Mur-de-Bretagne   E 8

Le Rond-Point
22530 Mur-de-Bretagne. 1.5mi/
2.5km W of village. Tel (96) 26 01
90. A terraced, gently sloping site,
only 110yds/100m from the Lac de
Guerlédan, with its excellent
facilities for water sports. *Open
mid-Jun–mid-Sep.*

Paimpol   E 2

Cruckin-Kerity
22500 Paimpol. Tel (96) 20 78 47.
A large seaside campsite, with
boating and sporting facilities nearby. *Open mid-Jun–mid-Sep.*

Perros-Guirec   C 2

Le Ranolien
22700 Perros-Guirec. 4mi/6.5km N
of Perros. Tel (96) 23 21 13. A four-
star site, set among the strange
rocks of the Pink Granite Coast,

0.5mi/1km S of Ploumanac'h and 220yds/200m from the sea. Ideal for walkers and birdwatchers. *Open all year.*

Trestraou-Camping
Av du Casino, 22700 Perros-Guirec. Tel (96) 23 08 11. Near the town centre, within easy reach of the beach, shops and casino. *Open all year.*

Pléneuf-Val-André	H 4

Le Minihy
22370 Pléneuf–Val-André. Tel (96) 72 22 95. A site near the sea, at the south end of the town. *Open mid-Jun–mid-Sep.*

Plestin-les-Grèves	A 3

La Haye
22310 Plestin-les-Grèves. 1.5mi/2.5km NE of town. Tel (96) 35 62 53. In the direction of St-Efflam; a terraced, grassy site 325yds/300m from the sea. *Open 1 Apr–mid-Sep.*

Pleumeur-Bodou	B 2

Le Port
Landrellec, 22670 Pleumeur-Bodou. 4mi/6.5km N of town. Tel (96) 23 87 79. An attractively situated campsite, beside the sea. *Open Easter–30 Sep.*

Municipal
Landrellec, 22670 Pleumeur-Bodou. Tel (96) 23 87 92. A small, sloping site at Landrellec. *Open mid-Jun–mid-Sep.*

Plouha	F 3

Municipal de Kerjean
22580 Plouha. 2mi/3km NE of town. Tel (96) 20 24 75. A quiet site on the minor road to the Pointe de Plouha. *Open 1 Jul–mid-Sep.*

Quintin	F 6

Les Quinconces
22800 Quintin. Tel (96) 74 92 54. Small site near the centre of town and the lake. *Open 1 Apr–30 Sep.*

St-Brieuc	G 5

Municipal du Pont Chapet
Rue Pierre de Coubertin, 22000 St-Brieuc. Tel (96) 61 29 33. A fairly large site on the south edge of the town. *Open all year.*

St-Cast-le-Guildo	J 4

Ferme de Pen Guen
22380 St-Cast. 2mi/3km S of town. Tel (96) 41 92 18. A large site by

Pen Guen beach. *Open Easter–30 Sep.*

St-Jacut-de-la-Mer	J 5

La Manchette
22750 St-Jacut. Tel (96) 27 30 33. A large site, at the south end of the village near the beach of La Manchette. *Open mid-Jun–mid-Sep.*

Trébeurden	B 2

Armor-Loisirs
22560 Trébeurden. Tel (96) 23 52 31. A quiet, terraced site just south of the village and only a short distance from the sea. Suitable for caravans. *Open mid-Jun–mid-Sep.*

Kerdual
22560 Trébeurden. Tel (96) 23 54 86. Small site south of village, with direct access to Porz Mabo beach. *Open Whit Sun–30 Sep.*

Trégastel	B 2

Le Golven
22730 Trégastel. 1mi/1.5km N of village. Tel (96) 23 87 77. A flat, grassy site with a common-room, TV room and food shop. *Open late May–early Sep.*

Tréguier	D 2

Municipal
22220 Tréguier. Tel (96) 92 30 10. A smallish site, convenient for the town centre. *Open mid-Jun–mid-Sep*

Hotels

Dinan	K 6

Hostellerie du Vieux St-Sauveur
19 pl St-Sauveur, 22100 Dinan. Tel (96) 39 04 63. A small hotel above a bar, in an ancient, half-timbered building near the great basilica. *Open all year.* V. **F**

Hôtel d'Avaugour
1 pl du Champ Clos, 22100 Dinan. Tel (96) 39 07 49. An attractive hotel on the main square, with a garden under the ramparts. Afternoon tea is provided. *Closed Jan.* A.Dc. **FFF**

Hôtel-Restaurant Le Marguérite
29 pl Duguesclin, 22100 Dinan. Tel (96) 39 47 65. Modern hotel overlooking the main square. *Closed 1 Dec–31 Jan.* Ax.Dc.V. **FF**

Erquy	I 4

Hôtel Reflet de la Mer
Bvd de la Mer, 22430 Erquy. Tel (96) 72 30 55. Small family hotel by the beach. *Closed 1 Oct–31 May.* **F**

Hôtel de la Plage
21 bvd de la Mer. 22430 Erquy. Tel
(96) 72 30 09. Hotel by the beach,
no restaurant. *Closed 1 Oct–31
Mar.* **FF**

Hôtel-Restaurant Beauregard
Bvd de la Mer, 22430 Erquy. Tel
(96) 72 30 03. An unpretentious
family hotel on the seafront. The
restaurant specialises in *fruits de
mer. Closed Oct.* V. **F**

Hôtel-Restaurant Les Salines
1 rue de la Saline, 22430 Erquy. Tel
(96) 72 31 73. A quiet, small hotel
just off the seafront. *Open all year.*
A.Dc.V. **F**

Guingamp   **D   5**

Le Relais du Roy
42 pl du Centre, 22200 Guingamp.
Tel (96) 43 76 62. The only hotel in
the old town centre, near the
pedestrian precinct. It has a fine
Renaissance stone doorway. *Closed
last 2 wks in Sep & end Dec.*
Ax.Dc. **FFF**

Manoir de Kerhuel
Pabu, 22200 Guingamp. Tel (96) 43
94 19. A 15thC stone manor house,
2mi/3km N of Guingamp, in the
peaceful Trieux valley. It has four
large bedrooms. **F**

Lamballe   **H   6**

Hôtel d'Angleterre
26 bvd Jobert, 22400 Lamballe. Tel
(96) 31 00 16. A traditional-style
hotel, near the station. In both the
'France Accueil' and 'Destination
Bretagne' hotel groups. *Closed
1 Nov–30 Apr.* Dc. **FF**

Manoir des Portes
La Poterie, 22400 Lamballe. Tel
(96) 31 13 62. In the village of La
Poterie, 2mi/3km E of the town
centre, this is one of the 'Relais du
Silence' hotels chosen for their
peace and quiet. The restaurant
specialises in seafood. *Closed
1 Nov–end Feb.* **FF**

Lézardrieux   **E   2**

Relais Brenner
Pont de Lézardrieux, 22500
Paimpol. Tel (96) 20 11 05. A
member of the prestigious 'Relais
et Châteaux' association, this
comfortable hotel stands in peaceful
gardens overlooking the Trieux
estuary. *Closed mid-Nov–mid-Feb.*
Ax.Dc.V. **FFF**

Paimpol   **E   2**

Hôtel Berthelot
1 rue du Port, 22500 Paimpol. Tel
(96) 20 88 66. A small hotel near
the waterfront (bed and breakfast
only). *Open all year.* V. **F**

Hôtel-Restaurant L'Origano
Rue du Quai, 22500 Paimpol. Tel
(96) 22 05 49. A waterfront hotel,
which has a bed-and-breakfast
contract with Brittany Ferries.
Closed Feb. A.V. **F**

Perros-Guirec   **C   2**

**Grand Hôtel de Trestraou
et de la Plage**
Bvd J-le-Bihan, 22700 Perros-
Guirec. Tel (96) 23 24 05. This is
the grandest hotel in the town, and
overlooks the finest beach
(Trestraou Plage). Attached is the
Institut de la Cure Marine, for
those taking a seawater cure. The
hotel has a good restaurant, the
'Homard Bleu'. *Open all year.*
Ax.Dc.V. **FFF**

Hôtel Le Gulf-Stream
26 rue des Sept-Iles, 22700 Perros-
Guirec. Tel (96) 23 21 86. On the
steep hill leading from the upper
town down to Trestraou Beach,
this is a small hotel with a
restaurant specialising in seafood.
Open all year. **F**

Hôtel Ker-Mor
Plage de Trestraou, 22700 Perros-
Guirec. Tel (96) 23 14 19. Family
hotel in two separate buildings,
with direct access to the beach.
Closed 1 Nov–Easter. **FF**

Hôtel-Restaurant Le Levant
Port de Plaisance, 22700 Perros-
Guirec. Tel (96) 23 20 15. Some
way from the main town and
beaches, this hotel has a panoramic
view over the fishing harbour and
marina. One of the 'Petits Nids de
France' association of hotels. *Closed
mid-Dec–mid-Jan.* V. **FF**

Pléneuf–Val-André   **H   4**

Grand Hôtel du Val-André
80 rue Amiral Charner, 22370
Pléneuf–Val-André. Tel (96) 72 20
56. A large comfortable hotel,
beside the main beach. *Closed mid-
Oct–31 Mar.* A. **FF**

Hôtel de France et du Petit Prince
22370 Pléneuf–Val-André. Tel (96)
72 22 52. In the centre of the
village, this family hotel has a

private garden and is ten minutes'
walk from the beach. A member of
the 'Hôtes Bretons' association.
Open all year. **F**

Hôtel de la Mer
22370 Pléneuf-Val-André. Tel (96)
72 20 44. Only 55yds/50m from the
beach, this is a neat little hotel,
which specialises in seafood and
has its own *vivier* (tank containing
live fish for the table). *Closed mid-
Nov–mid-Mar.* **FF**

Ploumanac'h   **B** 2
Hôtel des Rochers
Le Port, Ploumanac'h, 22700
Perros-Guirec. Tel (96) 23 23 02.
A hotel with a good view over the
harbour. The restaurant serves
such specialities as mussels in
cream and grilled lobster. *Closed
1 Oct–Easter.* Ax. **FF**

Hôtel-Restaurant du Phare
Rue St-Guirec, Ploumanac'h, 22700
Perros-Guirec. Tel (96) 23 23 08.
A moderate-sized hotel, five
minutes' walk from the harbour
and beach. *Closed 1 Oct–Easter.* **FF**

Sables-d'Or-les-Pins   **I** 4
Hôtel Les Ajoncs d'Or
Allée des Acacias, Sables-d'Or-les-
Pins, 22240 Fréhel. Tel (96) 41 42
12. A largish (75-room) hotel, near
beach. *Closed 1 Oct–mid-May.* **FF**

Hôtel au Bon Accueil
Allée des Acacias, Sables-d'Or-les-
Pins, 22240 Fréhel. Tel (96) 41 42
19. An older-style, comfortable
hotel, with a large garden, about
0.5mi/1km from Sables-d'Or's
magnificent beach. *Closed late Sep–
early May (open Easter).* Ax.V. **FF**

Hôtel des Pins
Allée des Acacias, Sables-d'Or-les-
Pins, 22240 Fréhel. Tel (96) 41 42
20. A small family hotel, about
0.5mi/1km from the beach, now
run by the grandson of the founder.
Closed 1 Oct–end Feb. A.V. **F**

St-Brieuc   **G** 5
Hôtel Le Commerce
2 pl Duguesclin, 22000 St-Brieuc.
Tel (96) 33 11 58. A lively hotel,
with a busy bar, overlooking the
square in St-Brieuc's
pedestrianised centre. *Open all
year.* Ax.Dc.V. **FF**

Hôtel Le Covec
Pl de la Poste, 22000 St-Brieuc. Tel
(96) 33 23 18. A small hotel, near

the town centre. *Open all year.*
Ax.Dc.V. **FF**

Hôtel l'Ermitage
9 rue Houvenagle, 22000 St-Brieuc.
Tel (96) 33 28 48. A quiet hotel (no
restaurant, bed and breakfast only)
in the old town, near the cathedral.
Closed 3 wks in Sep. **F**

St-Cast   **J** 4
Hôtel des Dunes
Rue Primauguet, 22380 St-Cast.
Tel (96) 41 80 31. A modern hotel,
set some way back from the beach.
A member of the 'Logis de France'
chain. *Closed 1 Oct–mid-Mar.* **FF**

Hôtel-Restaurant Bon Accueil
19 rue du Port, 22380 St-Cast. Tel
(96) 41 88 08. In a side street about
550yds/500m from the beach. *Open
all year.* Ax. **F**

St-Quay–Portrieux   **F** 4
Hôtel Le Gerbot d'Avoine
Bvd Littoral, 22410 St-Quay-
Portrieux. Tel (96) 70 40 09. This
hotel, on a hill just above the
beach, gets its unusual name
(meaning 'sheaf of oats') from one
of the offshore rocks. It is a
member of the 'Logis de France'
group. *Closed 3 wks in Nov & 2 wks
in Jan.* **FF**

Trébeurden   **B** 2
Family Hôtel
85 rue des Plages, 22560
Trébeurden. Tel (96) 23 50 31. A
traditionally Breton hotel, a short
way from the beach. One of the
'Logis de France' chain. *Closed
1 Oct–end Feb.* Ax.Dc. **FF**

Hôtel des Bains
22560 Trébeurden. Tel (96) 23 50
14. An unpretentious hotel on the
hill road leading down to the Plage
de Postermen. *Closed 1 Oct–
Easter.* **F**

Manoir de Lan Kerellec
Allée de Lan Kerellec, 22560
Trébeurden. Tel (96) 23 50 09. A
luxurious hotel, in the 'Relais et
Châteaux' consortium. From its
gardens there are superb views over
the sea and the rocky offshore
islands. *Closed 1 Nov–mid-Mar.*
Ax. **FFF**

Hôtel Ti Al Lannec
Allée de Mézo-Guen, 22560
Trébeurden. Tel (96) 23 57 26. A
member of the 'Relais du Silence'
chain, this hotel has south-facing

terraces, with private access to the beach. Its specialities include fresh salmon and turbot. *Closed mid-Nov–mid-Mar.* Ax. **FF**

Trégastel   B 2

Grand Hôtel de la Mer et de la Plage
Pl du Coz-Pors, 22730 Trégastel. Tel (96) 23 88 03. A modern hotel by the main beach. *Closed 1 Oct–Easter.* Ax.V. **FF**

Hôtel Armoric
Pl du Coz-Pors, 22730 Trégastel. Tel (96) 23 88 16. The resort's largest hotel, overlooking the beach, with panoramic sea views. *Closed 1 Oct–Whit Sun.* A.Ax. **FF**

Hôtel Beau-Séjour
Pl du Coz-Pors, 22730 Trégastel. Tel (96) 23 88 02. Another hotel on the main beach. Has its own *vivier* (fish-tank for the restaurant). *Closed 1 Nov–Easter.* A. **FF**

Tréguier   D 2

Hôtel-Restaurant Le Saint-Yves
4 rue Colvestre, 22220 Tréguier. Tel (96) 92 33 49. A small hotel, in an old house near the cathedral. *Closed Nov.* A.V. **F**

Hôtel-Restaurant de l'Estuaire
Les Quais, 22220 Tréguier. Tel (96) 92 30 25. By the waterfront, with a terrace restaurant looking across the River Jaudy. *Open all year.* A. **FF**

Restaurants

Unless otherwise stated, all the hotels listed in the previous section have restaurants; they are not listed here.

Dinan   K 6

Grill-Room Duguesclin
9 rue Ste-Claire, 22100 Dinan. Tel (96) 39 22 18. Small restaurant in the old town. *Closed Sat eve & Sun.* **F**

Le Pélican
3 rue Haute Voie, 22100 Dinan. Tel (96) 39 47 05. In the old town, near the Basilica. Dishes cooked in butter by the *patron. Open daily.* **FF**

Le Relais Corsaire
Le Port, 22100 Dinan. Tel (96) 39 40 17. A neat restaurant by the river, below the old town. *Closed Sun eve & Mon.* A.Ax.V. **FF**

Erquy   I 4

Le Triton
Le Port, 22430 Erquy. Tel (96) 72 69. By the harbour, with views over the bay. Specialities include *fruits de mer* and lobster. **FF**

Lamballe   H 6

Bar-Hôtel La Tête Noire
8 rue du Four, 22400 Lamballe. Tel (96) 31 09 93. Bar with rooms. In the centre of old Lamballe, this house was the birthplace of Lamballe's most famous artist, Mathurin Méheut. It gets its name from the black hood worn by the town executioner. *Open all year.* **F**

Grill Les Remparts
Rue Notre-Dame, 22400 Lamballe. Tel (96) 31 02 26. A beamy building in the old part of the town. *Closed Mon.* **F**

Lannion   B 3

La Casa
Venelle des Trois Avocats, 22300 Lannion. Tel (96) 37 74 13. Italian-style pizzeria near the main square. *Closed Sun & Mon.* **F**

L'Entrecôte de la Tour d'Auvergne
Rue de la Tour d'Auvergne, 22300 Lannion. Tel (96) 37 04 73. Comfortable restaurant in an old street near the river. *Closed Tue.* **F**

Paimpol   E 2

Restaurant du Port
17 quai Morand, 22500 Paimpol. Tel (96) 20 82 76. A waterfront restaurant, with a *'salle panoramique'.* Specialises in *fruits de mer. Closed Sun & Mon.* A.V. **FF**

Perros-Guirec   C 2

La Cremaillère
Pl de l'Eglise, 22700 Perros-Guirec. Tel (96) 23 22 08. In an old stone house in the town centre, some way from the beaches. Specialises in charcoal grills. *Closed Mon.* A.Ax.Dc. **F**

L'Homard Bleu
Plage de Trestraou, 22700 Perros-Guirec. Tel (96) 23 24 55. Part of the Grand Hôtel. A comfortable restaurant, with wide views of Trestraou beach. Seafood specialities. *Open daily.* A.Ax.Dc. **FFF**

Ploumanac'h **B 2**

La Buvette St-Guirec
Pl St-Guirec, 22700 Ploumanac'h.
Tel (96) 23 12 82. A bar and
restaurant specialising in seafood. **F**

St-Brieuc **G 5**

Le Porche
9 rue St-Guillaume, 22000 St-
Brieuc. Tel (96) 61 93 77. A crêperie
off the main pedestrianised street in
the old town. *Closed Sun & Mon
lunch.* A.V. **F**

Ty-Bone
16 rue des Trois Frères Le Goff,
22000 St-Brieuc. Tel (96) 61 80 58.
A steakhouse (Ty-Bone equals T-
Bone). *Open eves only. Closed
Mon.* **FF**

Trébeurden **B 2**

La Tourelle
Port de Trozoul, Tresmeur, 22560
Trébeurden. Tel (96) 23 62 73.
Modern restaurant by the sea, with
wide views over the bay and
offshore islands. **F**

Countryside

Cap Fréhel **J 4**
28mi/45km NW of Dinan. On a
clear day this magnificent
headland, 230ft/70m high and one
of the most spectacular landmarks
of northern Brittany, is visible
across the sea from St-Malo, more
than 12.5mi/20km away. On the
eastern side of the cape the mauve-
grey rocks known as the Petite and
Grande Fauconnière form a bird
sanctuary, where gulls, guillemots
and cormorants wheel above the
sea pounding far below, or perch
precariously on their nesting-
ledges. There are two lighthouses:
a small disused tower, dating from
the 17th century; and the modern
lighthouse, built in 1950, which
throws a beam for 63mi/100km
(*open in summer, except in bad
weather,* 09.30–12.00, 14.00–19.00,
charge). On very clear days the
view from the top stretches from
the Cherbourg Peninsula in the
east to the Ile de Bréhat in the
west—about 30mi/50km in each
direction. In the great days of the
St-Malo corsairs, sailors were
absolved from their marriage vows
as soon as their ships had rounded
Cap Fréhel.

Côte d'Eméraude **I–K 4**
The 'Emerald Coast' is a
picturesque and long-established
nickname for the most popular
stretch of holiday seaside in
Brittany, mainly in the Côtes-du-
Nord but partly in Ille-et-Vilaine,
stretching from Pléneuf–Val-André
in the west to Cancale in the east.

Côte de Granit Rose **A–E 2**
The 'Coast of Pink Granite', more
aptly named than most such
imprecise areas, takes in the
northernmost coastline of the
Côtes-du-Nord, from Trébeurden
in the west round to Bréhat in the
east. The rocks attain their most
extraordinary shapes at Trégastel
and Ploumanac'h, where countless
centuries of erosion by the sea have
worn them into strange animal-like
forms, justifying their nicknames
of tortoise, elephant, whale, ram
etc. Further east, round the Pointe
du Château, the rocks have been
ground into fangs jutting out from
the shore, forming a coastline as
inhospitable as a lunar landscape.

*Strange rock formations on the
beach at Trégastel.*

Gorges du Daoulas **D 8**
19mi/30.5km W of Loudéac. A
narrow country road (the D44) runs
through wild countryside beside the
fast-flowing Daoulas River. The
water has cut deeply into the rock,
creating a landscape that can seem
gloomy and depressing on an
overcast day; but when the
summer sun shines the slopes are
bright with broom and gorse,
gleaming yellow among the heather.

Gorges de Toul-Goulic **C 7**
7.5mi/12km NE of Rostrenen. A
romantic wilderness of vast moss-
covered boulders and trees, where
the River Blavet vanishes
underground, rumbling below
one's feet. This stretch of several
hundred metres is called the 'Perte
du Blavet', or 'Disappearance of
the Blavet'. Beside the river the
boulders form huge overhangs,
which look like ideal shelters for
Stone Age man.

Ile de Bréhat

Ile de Bréhat **E 2**

5mi/8km N of Paimpol. Reached by a ten-minute ferry crossing from the Pointe de l'Arcouest, Bréhat is a tiny, away-from-it-all island at the north-east corner of the Côtes-du-Nord. It is a traffic-free haven of bird and plant life, with an almost Mediterranean profusion of trees and shrubs—among them mimosa, figs and oleanders. The little township of Le Bourg has an ancient church, and is an excellent place to sample a wide variety of crêpes washed down with Breton cider. The island's northern coast is exceptionally rugged, made up of a chaotic jumble of the pink rocks from which this coast takes its name (the Côte de Granit Rose). In the Middle Ages Bréhat was famous for the enterprise of its fishermen, who were sailing to the fishing grounds of Newfoundland and Labrador long before Columbus 'discovered' America.

Lac de Guerlédan **DE 8**

12.5mi/20km W of Loudéac. An artificial lake 7.5mi/12km long, created in the 1920s by damming the waters of the River Blavet. The lake is in one of the prettiest and most remote parts of Brittany, and is very popular with small-boat sailors and fishermen. The dam, at the east end of the lake, is 236ft/205m long and 148ft/45m high, and produces hydro-electric power for the region.

Ménez-Bré **C 4**

5mi/8km W of Guingamp. Though less than 1000ft high, at 302m, this is the highest point in North Brittany and dominates the surrounding countryside. The name is really a tautology, as both halves mean 'mountain' (*menez* is

the same as the Welsh *mynydd*, and *bré* is the Scottish *brae*).

On its treeless summit, torn up in summer by motorcycle scramblers, is a small chapel to St-Hervé, a 6thC Breton saint who was a monk, a bard and blind from birth. He is usually shown accompanied by a wolf, as he was believed to have the power to ward off the fear induced by wolves and other wild animals. The chapel was the centre of a ritual known as the *ofern drantel* ('thirtieth mass'), which was considered effective against demons, and had to be conducted by a barefoot priest who recited the words of the Mass backwards.

Montagnes Noires **BC 8**

Like Wales, Brittany has its 'Black Mountains', though they are far less dramatic than their Welsh counterparts. The range is shared between the Côtes-du-Nord, Finistère and Morbihan; its highest summit is the Roc'h Toul-Laeron (410ft/326m), just north of Gourin, near the meeting-point of all three départements. The countryside is far less bleak than that of Brittany's other mountain range, the Monts d'Arrée, to the north, and in recent years it has become a favourite region for retirement. At the beginning of the 20th century many of the inhabitants emigrated to Canada and the USA, as the mountains could no longer provide them with a livelihood.

Pen Guen **J 4**

2mi/3km S of St-Cast. The name of a superb sandy beach, with ample car-parking, a short way down the coast from St-Cast.

Plage Bonaparte **F 3**

2mi/3km NE of Plouha. A stony beach, reached through a tunnel, from which during 1944 the French Resistance smuggled Allied airmen to safety. Over 130 airmen were rescued, in an operation that was given the code name 'Bonaparte'—hence the name for the beach.

Pointe du Château　　D 2
7mi/11km N of Tréguier. A remote northern headland, at the centre of a lunar landscape of shattered and jagged rocks, well worth seeing for its savage beauty.

Les Sept Iles　　B 1
In the Channel. 6mi/9.5km N of Perros-Guirec. The archipelago of the 'Seven Islands' forms one of France's most important sea-bird sanctuaries. As long ago as 1912 a reserve was set up by the LPO (Ligue pour la Protection des Oiseaux), after the birds had been hunted almost to extinction. Species to be seen here include puffins, cormorants, fulmars, guillemots, auks and gannets. From *May–Sep* a regular service of boats takes birdwatchers from Perros-Guirec out to the islands.

Sillon de Talbert　　E 1
9mi/14.5km NE of Tréguier. This long spit of shingle, extending for 2mi/3km from the Pleubian Peninsula, is one of Brittany's most remarkable natural formations. Only 33yds/30m wide, and covered in sea-holly and other marine plants, it protects the estuary of the Trieux from the full force of the north-west gales. It is also of a certain commercial value, as the local farmers collect the seaweed and rot it down to use on their land. During World War II the Germans removed so much shingle and sand, to turn into concrete for the Atlantic Wall, that the ecology of the Sillon was almost destroyed. Today it is rigorously controlled.

Entertainment

Casinos

Casino de la Côte de Granit Rose　　C 2
Plage de Trestraou, 22700 Perros-Guirec. Tel (96) 23 20 51. *Open 1 Apr–30 Sep 22.30–03.00.*

Casino de Pléneuf–Val-André　　H 4
Bvd du Littoral, 22370 Pléneuf–Val-André. Tel (96) 72 20 78. *Open Jul & Aug.*

Casino de St-Cast　　J 4
Bvd de la Plage, 22380 St-Cast-le-Guildo. Tel (96) 41 86 22. *Open Jul & Aug.*

Casino de St-Quay–Portrieux　　F 4
Plage de St-Quay, 22410 St-Quay. Tel (96) 70 40 36. Has disco. *Open 1 Jun–30 Sep 22.00–03.00. Disco closed Mon.*

Discothèques

L'Albatros　　D 2
Plouguiel, 22220 Tréguier. Just N of town. Tel (96) 92 31 20. *Open Jul & Aug, daily 22.00–04.00; out of season, Thur–Sun only.* **Charge**

Bingo Club Géant　　E 3
Plouézec, 22500 Paimpol. 4mi/6.5km SE of Paimpol. Tel (96) 22 76 69. *Open Jul & Aug, daily 22.00–04.00; out of season, Fri–Sun & hols only.* **Charge**

Le New Way　　C 2
Rue de Trébuic, Trestraou, 22700 Perros–Guirec. Tel (96) 23 15 28. **Charge**

Le St-Méen　　C 2
22700 Perros-Guirec. On the Lannion road. Tel (96) 23 18 71. *Open all year, from 22.00.* **Charge**

Leisure activities

Archery

Clubs at:
Etables-sur-Mer　　F 4
Tel (96) 70 41 53. **Charge**
Guingamp　　D 5
Tel (96) 43 96 98. **Charge**
Parc des Sports du Forlach　　B 3
22300 Lannion. Enquiries: tel Syndicat d'Initiative, (96) 37 07 35. **Charge**

Bicycle hire

By day or week from youth hostels (Auberges de Jeunesse) in Dinan, Lannion, Merdrignac, Paimpol and St-Brieuc. Also from individuals in many towns and villages; enquire at the local Syndicat.

For those with own bicycles, local trips are organised on *Suns* by:

Comité Départemental de Cyclo-Tourisme   **G 5**
11bis rue des Cheminots, 22000 St-Brieuc. Tel (96) 33 67 59.

Flying clubs

Aéro-Club de la Côte de Granit Rose   **B 3**
22300 Lannion. Just outside town on D788. Tel (96) 37 47 42. Trips *all year*. **Charge**

Aero-Club de Dinan   **K 6**
Trélivan, 22100 Dinan. 2.5mi/4km W of Dinan on N176. Tel (96) 39 00 25. *Closed Tue.* **Charge**

Aéro-Club de St-Brieuc   **G 5**
22000 St-Brieuc. On W edge of town on N12. Tel (96) 33 15 11. *Closed Tue & Fri.* **Charge**

Golf

Golf des Ajoncs d'Or   **F 4**
Lantic, 22680 Etables-sur-Mer. 4.5mi/7km W of town on D121. Tel (96) 70 48 13. Eighteen holes. **Charge**

Golf de Pen Guen   **J 4**
22380 St-Cast-le-Guildo. Tel (96) 41 03 20. Nine holes. **Charge**

Golf de Sables-d'Or   **I 4**
Clubhouse, Sables-d'Or-les-Pins, 22240 Fréhel. Tel (96) 41 42 57. Nine holes. **Charge**

Golf de St-Samson   **B 2**
22670 Pleumeur-Bodou. Tel (96) 23 87 34. Eighteen holes. **Charge**

Long-distance footpaths

There are almost 530mi/850km of waymarked footpaths in the Côtes-du-Nord. The following Grandes Randonnées run partly through the département: GR 34, estuary of the Rance; GR 341, St-Brieuc to Paimpol by the coast; GR 37, Mur-de-Bretagne towards Carhaix in Finistère.
For shorter walks, apply to the local Syndicat d'Initiative for maps and information.

River fishing

For information on permits etc:

Fédération des Associations de Pêche   **G 5**
6 rue des Buttes, 22004 St-Brieuc. Tel (96) 61 95 00.

Sea angling

For information, apply to:

Fédération de Pêche en Mer   **B 3**
Pont Roux, Le Yaudet, Ploumilliau, 22300 Lannion. Tel (96) 38 31 42.

Seawater cure (thalassothérapie)

Institut de Cure Marine   **C 2**
Plage de Trestraou, 22700 Perros-Guirec. Tel (96) 23 28 97.
Treatments include hot baths in seawater, seaweed and mud applications, and massage. *Open all year. Swimming pool open 11.30–12.30, 17.30–18.30.* **Charge**

Subaqua clubs

Club des Chasseurs Sous-Marins   **G 5**
10 rue des Trois Frères Le Goff, 22000 St-Brieuc. No tel.

Club Inter-Plongée   **B 2**
Plage de Tresmeur, 22560 Trébeurden. Tel (96) 23 56 18.

Le Groupe des Sports Sub-Aquatiques de la Côte de Granit Rose   **B 2**
BP 24, Ploumanac'h, 22700 Perros-Guirec. Tel (96) 23 23 04.

Swimming pools

In the following towns: Dinan, Guingamp, Jugon-les-Lacs, Lamballe, Lannion, Loudéac, Paimpol, Pléneuf–Val-André, St-Brieuc, St-Cast, Tréguier. **Charge**

Excursions

Boat trips

Dinan   **K 6**
Down the Rance to Dinard and St-Malo. *1 May–early Jun, Sun & hols; 1 Jun–mid-Sep daily. Times dependent on tides.*

Ile de Bréhat   **E 2**
Depart from Pointe de l'Arcouest. *Jul & Aug, 08.30–20.30 every half-hour; Jun & early Sep, every hour 08.30–19.30; May & late Sep, regular service 08.30–17.15.*

Mur-de-Bretagne   **E 8**
Boat trips on the Lac de Guerlédan. *1 Jul–mid-Sep, every aft; out of season, by request.*

Radome, Pleumeur-Bodou

Perros-Guirec   **C 2**
Visit to Sept-Iles Bird Reserve.
Three-hour visit, including short
landing on Ile-aux-Moines. *Jun,
14.00–17.00; Jul & Aug,
09.00–12.00, 14.00–17.00.*

St-Cast   **J 4**
Trips to see Fort la Latte and Cap
Fréhel, on Vedettes Vertes (depart
from Dinard). *Daily Jul & Aug.*

Trieux estuary   **E 2**
From Pointe de l'Arcouest, three-
hour trip as far as La Roche-Jagu.
Jul & Aug, depending on tides.

Coach excursions

Dinan   **K 6**
To Cap Fréhel, Bréhat, Mont-St-
Michel in Manche, the Breton
pardons etc. Depart from pl du Clos,
Dinan. Tel (96) 39 21 05.

Festivals

Main *pardons* of the Côtes-du-Nord:

2nd Sun in May   **F 6**
Quintin, Notre-Dame-de-
Délivrance.

Whitsun   **G 7**
Moncontour, St-Mathurin.

Sun nearest May 19   **D 2**
Tréguier, St-Yves.

Last Sun in May   **G 5**
St-Brieuc, Notre-Dame-de-
l'Espérance.

Eve of 1st Sun in Jul   **D 5**
Guingamp, Notre-Dame-de-Bon-
Secours.

Aug 15   **C 2**
Perros-Guirec, Notre-Dame-de-la-
Clarté.

Tours by car

Coast of Pink Granite
A tortuous drive of about 70mi/
110km, centred on Perros-Guirec.
Take coast road west to Ploumanac'h and Trégastel, with their
extraordinary rock formations.

Then to the Space Communications
Centre of Pleumeur-Bodou, to the
resort of Trébeurden, and so to
Lannion. Continue along the coast
road (D786) to Plestin-les-Grèves.
Then inland by minor roads to the
castles of Rosanbo and Tonquédec,
and the Chapel of Kerfons, and so
back via Lannion to Perros.

**Emerald Coast & Valley of the
Rance**
A tour of about 80mi/130km,
beginning and ending at Dinan.
Take D2 to Ploubalay, then north
to Lancieux and back along coast
road (D786). Out to St-Jacut along
peninsula, then via Le Guildo
(ruined castle) to St-Cast. Inland to
Plancoët and Corseul (Gallo-
Roman Temple). To Jugon-les-
Lacs, beside a large inland lake.
Back via Caulnes, either along main
road (D766), or by minor roads
through Guitté and Lehon.

Lamballe to Cap Fréhel
A tour of about 70mi/110km,
beginning at Lamballe. To coastal
resort of Pléneuf-Val-André, on
minor road (D59A), past little
harbour of Dahouët. To Erquy via
Bienassis Château, then out past
resort of Sables-d'Or-les-Pins, to
Cap Fréhel with its lighthouse and
bird sanctuary. Back to Lamballe
through Matignon and Pléven,
past La Hunaudaye Château.

**Paimpol, the coast & inland
villages**
About 62.5mi/100km, first heading
north to the Pointe d'Arcouest,
with boats (ten mins) over to the
Ile de Bréhat. Returning to
Paimpol, take the coast road (D786)
south to the seaside resorts of St-
Quay–Portrieux and Binic, making
diversions to Bréhec and the chapel
of Kermaria-an-Iskuit. After
Binic, take inland road (D4) to
Châtelaudren, then back via the
'Temple' of Lanleff to Paimpol.

Morbihan

The Morbihan is the only one of the Breton départements to have a Breton name. The others are named either after rivers (Loire-Atlantique, Ille-et-Vilaine), or the general landscape (Côtes-du-Nord, Finistère). But the Morbihan takes its name from the most characteristic feature of the whole south coast of Brittany—that gulf, known to the Bretons as '*Mor Bihan*', or 'Little Sea', that lies between Vannes and the Bay of Quiberon, and brings a subtropical mildness to the villages that lie along its fringes, and the islands that stud its lagoon-like surface.

It was round the seaward shores of the Gulf that Neolithic man, from about 3000BC onwards, buried his dead leaders in stone chamber tombs mounded high with soil, and covered the landscape of furze and heath with thousands of standing stones, either singly or in great groups, like the alignments at Carnac that have puzzled archaeologists and fascinated the general public for 200 years or more. No one knows for certain why this limited area was chosen for so sustained an effort of construction, over perhaps 1500 years. All one can conclude is that the Morbihan became a region of the greatest significance to early man, both because of its religious sanctity, and because of the scientific and astronomical knowledge that still lies concealed in the stones, and has so far managed to defy all the efforts of modern astronomy and mathematics to disentangle it. Though many of the stones are now embedded in modern holiday development, they manage to preserve their ancient hold over the imagination, especially when the summer crowds have gone and they can brood once more in silence on their enormous past.

Like the Côtes-du-Nord, the Morbihan is shared between two Brittanies: the Breton-speaking west, looking towards Finistère; and the French-speaking east, looking towards Ille-et-Vilaine and beyond to the wider world of France. In the days of Breton independence the Vannetais, as the country round Vannes was called, held a position of key importance as a point of balance between the two Brittanies. Vannes itself was for a time the seat of the Breton parliament, and it still has far more pride in its past, and far more interest in preserving that past, than most other cities in Brittany.

Though it is possibly the least dramatic region of Brittany, the Morbihan is certainly the most varied. It has the lagoons of the Gulf and the mysterious Rivière d'Etel, and it has a coastline whose resorts, with the exceptions of Quiberon and Carnac-Plage, have hardly grown beyond village size. It has two of the finest castles in Brittany—the ruined Suscinio on the windswept Rhuys Peninsula, and the proudly feudal Josselin, dominating its river. Though it has no religious monuments to compare with the Finistère calvaries, it has an unparalleled wealth of chapels, many of them superbly decorated. In general, it is the least known part of Brittany, and has more to offer in the way of pretty little towns, hidden river valleys and primeval woodland than any other part of the country.

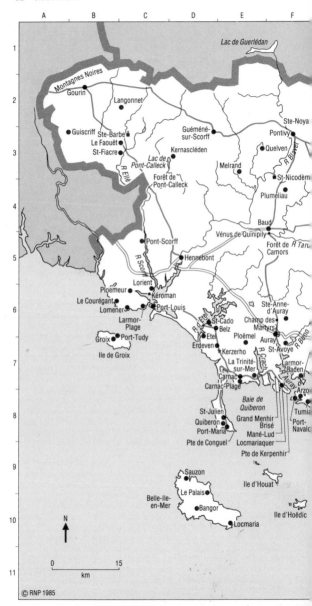

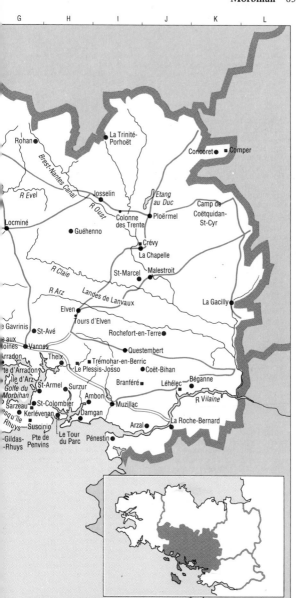

Town's & villages

Arzon   F 8
19mi/30.5km SW of Vannes. Pop:
see Port-Navalo. Village at the centre
of the small peninsula guarding the
eastern side of the entrance to the
Gulf of Morbihan (*see also Port-
Navalo*). Only 2.5mi/4km across,
the Arzon Peninsula has more than
19mi/30.5km of pretty coastline,
with tongues of land jutting north
into the Gulf and south into the
open sea. The climate is
exceptionally mild.
By the hamlet of Tumiac, a tumulus
(burial mound), known as the
Butte de César, is said to be the
vantage point from which Julius
Caesar watched his fleet defeat the
Gaulish navy in 56BC.

Auray   F 6
11.5mi/18.5km W of Vannes. Pop
10,400. MD Fri. An attractive and
sleepy little town, on the Auray
River, Auray is a favourite with
artists and small-boat sailors. The
main shopping and commercial
part of the town is up the hill on
the west bank of the river, while
the picturesque Medieval streets of
St-Goustan are across the ancient
stone bridge on the east bank.
Auray's big 17thC church is right
at the top of the town. The best
viewpoint over the river to St-
Goustan is from the Loch
Ramparts, from which a tree-
shaded zigzag path leads down to
river level. A plaque on one of St-
Goustan's quayside houses records
the visit in 1776 of Benjamin
Franklin, who landed at Auray on
his way to Paris to negotiate a treaty
between France and the fledgling
United States. St-Goustan is largely
pedestrianised, and its little
riverside square is an enjoyable
place to watch the world go by.

In 1364 the Battle of Auray, fought
outside the town, put an end to the
War of Succession, which decided
who was to be duke of Brittany.
Some four centuries later Georges
Cadoudal, the leader of the
Chouans (anti-Revolutionary
Bretons), was born in a suburb of
Auray; he carried on the struggle
long after the Revolution had
triumphed, and was finally
captured and guillotined in 1804.

Baud   F 4
15.5mi/25km N of Auray. Pop
5100. A small country town, at the
heart of a network of rivers (Blavet,
Evel and Tarun) and small streams
that are rich in trout, perch and
many other kinds of fish. The
church is modern, but attached to
it is a 16thC chapel dedicated to
Notre-Dame-de-la-Clarté, much
visited by those suffering from eye
maladies.
Just west of the town, south of the
Lorient road, is Baud's most
famous antiquity, the so-called
'Vénus de Quinipily'. The origins
of this statue have been much
disputed; it has been ascribed to
the Romans, the Gauls and the
ancient Egyptians, and also called
a fake. In earlier centuries the
'Venus' was so revered by the
peasants that a 17thC bishop had
her torn down and thrown in the
river. Fortunately she was retrieved
and placed above a fountain, where
she now stands surveying the Baud
countryside.

Carnac   E 7
7.5mi/12km SW of Auray. Pop
3700. The name of Carnac
nowadays is synonymous with the
endless rows of standing stones
that make it one of the world's most
visited prehistoric sites. But it is
also a pleasant little town in its own

Alignements de Carnac

right, stretching from its old church and main square down to the south-facing sandy beaches of Carnac-Plage.

The name Carnac has nothing to do with the Egyptian Karnak, in spite of attempts to link the two. It derives either from the Breton *karn*, meaning 'horn', or is the same as our 'cairn', meaning a heap of stones on a burial mound. Probably the former is correct, since the patron saint of Carnac is St-Cornély, who is also the patron of all horned animals. Cornély or Cornelius is said to have been a 3rdC pope who was exiled from Rome and pursued north by the emperor's army. When he got to Carnac, he rounded on his pursuers and turned them all to stone—hence the ranks of standing stones outside the town. There is a statue of the saint between two oxen on the outside wall of the church, and each year *in Sep* a cattle festival is held in his honour.

Carnac-Plage　　　　　　**E　7**
Pop: see Carnac. The southerly seaside extension of Carnac, and one of the popular resorts in the Morbihan. Its beaches face south and are protected from the Atlantic rollers by the natural breakwater of the Quiberon Peninsula, which makes them ideal for children, and for windsurfing and other water sports. Near the beach is a centre for *thalassothérapie* (seawater cure).

Damgan　　　　　　　　**H　8**
15.5mi/25km SE of Vannes. Pop 1060. A small seaside resort on a little peninsula, near the estuary of the Vilaine. Its remoteness means that it is far less crowded in summer than resorts like Carnac-Plage. The south-facing sandy beach is 4mi/6.5km long.

Le Faouët　　　　　　　**C　3**
13mi/21km N of Quimperlé. Pop 3200. A small country town, set in peaceful countryside in a landscape of woods and small streams. It gets its name from the Breton *faou*, meaning 'beech tree'. It has a remarkable 16thC covered market, 174ft/53m long by 62ft/19m wide, with massive wooden uprights and a roof supported by gigantic beams. Nearby are two superb

chapels, Ste-Barbe (Barbara) and St-Fiacre (*see Interesting buildings*).

La Gacilly　　　　　　　**K　6**
10mi/16km N of Redon. Pop 2000. This little town, on the borders of Ille-et-Vilaine, has in recent years become a centre of arts and handicrafts of all sorts—sculpture, weaving, pottery, jewellery, perfume-making etc. During summer every window box and hanging basket is full of flowers, making La Gacilly the 'cité fleurie' it claims to be.

Gourin　　　　　　　　**B　2**
24mi/38.5km N of Quimperlé. Pop 5500. The only town of any size in the Montagnes Noires, Gourin was once a centre of slate-quarrying, but with the decline in demand agriculture has taken over. At the end of the 19th century many Bretons from the Black Mountains emigrated to North America, and there is even a town in Alberta called Gourin City.

Guémené-sur-Scorff　　　**D　3**
13mi/21km W of Pontivy. Pop 1400. A remote little town, built beside the fast-flowing Scorff River. It has a 17thC church, and a good many houses in the main square from the same period. It is well known for its *andouilles* (pork sausages).

Hennebont　　　　　　　**D　5**
6.5mi/10.5km NE of Lorient. Pop 12,500. MD Thur. The name of this ancient town derives from the Breton '*Hen Bont*', meaning 'Old Bridge', and it stands at the first point upstream at which the Blavet estuary could be bridged with medieval building methods. It was greatly damaged during World War II and is thus largely new, but the powerful ramparts of the castle survive, as does the church a short way up the hill. Built in the 16th century, it has a massive tower and spire, 213ft/65m high, and is entered through an enormously tall western porch.

During the 14thC War of Succession, which decided the future of the dukedom of Brittany, Hennebont castle was defended by Jeanne of Flanders, the wife of Jean de Montfort, against the French army. One night Jeanne set fire to the French camp, winning for herself the nickname 'Jeanne la Flamme' (in Breton 'Jannedik Flamm'), and a lasting reputation as a Breton patriot.

On the north side of the town is the National Stud (Haras National), built in the grounds of a Medieval abbey in 1857. Many of the stallions are the traditional Breton workhorses, the *Traits Bretons. Guided visits at 09.00, 10.00, 11.00, 14.00, 15.00 & 16.00.*

Josselin   I 4

31.5mi/50km N of Vannes. Pop 3000. MD Sat. The little town of Josselin huddles for protection round the splendid castle of the Rohans, one of the most powerful Breton families during the Middle Ages and later. The castle's three sheer-walled towers, reflected in the waters of the Oust River, must be the most photographed architectural scene in Brittany. But there is plenty to see in the town of Josselin as well—the half-timbered houses that jut across the narrow streets, the superb Gothic church, founded in the 11th century, and the riverside upstream and downstream from the castle. Until about 1100 Josselin was known as Thro, but during the 11th century a Breton lord called Josselin became the *seigneur* of the town and gave it his own name. During the Middle Ages it was attacked on various occasions; and a field a few kilometres away was the setting for one of France's most famous feats of chivalry, the so-called 'Combat des Trente' in 1351 (*see Colonne des Trente*).

Each year on the *2nd Sun in Sep* Josselin celebrates the *pardon* of Notre-Dame-du-Roncier (Our Lady of the Bramble). This gets its name from a miraculous statue of the Virgin, found in a bramble thicket by a peasant during the 9th century. No matter how often the statue was removed from the thicket, it invariably found its way back there; and eventually a chapel was built to house it. The statue was burnt during the Revolution, but a few fragments were saved and are now kept in a reliquary. The *pardon* was also known as the '*pardon des aboyeuses*'—the 'barking women' or epileptics who hoped for a cure from kissing the holy relics.

Larmor-Plage   C 6

3mi/5km S of Lorient. Pop 6500. A seaside resort, facing east across the Blavet estuary to the walls of Port-Louis, and popular with day-trippers from Lorient. The 16thC church has two fine altar-pieces, and a chapel dedicated to the Jews. By French naval tradition, warships leaving Lorient harbour fire a salute when passing Larmor church, while the church bells ring in reply. West from Larmor, the coast road gives magnificent views out to sea towards the Island of Groix, and passes a string of tiny seaside resorts.

Locmariaquer   F 7

8mi/13km S of Auray. Pop 1300. A pretty little fishing village, from which it is possible to take a boat across to Port-Navalo on the other side of the channel into the Gulf of Morbihan. Apart from its oysters, it is best known for the megalithic remains in the countryside round about, of which the main ones are the dolmen of Mané-Lud, the Grand Menhir, and the Table des Marchands (for all these, *see Interesting buildings*).

Locminé   G 4

17.5mi/28km N of Vannes. Pop 3600. MD Thur. An attractive small market town in the heart of the Morbihan countryside, built on the little Tarun River. An abbey was founded here by monks in the 7th century (the town's name means 'City of the Monks' in Breton). The 17thC church has an extraordinary modern annexe on the north side, looking like a vast lean-to, constructed of wood and slate, and lit by huge windows. In the town centre there are several restored 16thC houses.

Lorient   C 6

33mi/53km W of Vannes. Pop 72,000. One of the chief harbours of Brittany and a major fishing port, Lorient stands on a magnificent site on the west side of an estuary, at the junction of the Scorff and Blavet rivers. It was founded as recently as 1666, by order of Louis XIV, under the name of l'Orient, as the home port of the Compagnie des Indes Orientales, the French equivalent of the East India Company. In 1770 the French Navy took over from the Compagnie, and Lorient has remained a naval base ever since. During World War II the Germans built a huge submarine base at Kéroman, on the south side of Lorient, and in 1944, after the Allied invasion of France, the town was largely destroyed. Like Brest in Finistère and St-Nazaire in Loire-Atlantique, which were fiercely defended by the Germans and suffered the same fate, Lorient has been almost entirely rebuilt in a faceless modern style. A few old buildings from the time of the Compagnie des Indes survive in the quai des Indes, at the heart of the town.

There is a permanent exhibition of Lorient's seafaring history in the Town Hall (Hôtel de Ville). Modern Lorient is an important centre of the Breton revival, and each *Aug* it is host to a major festival of bagpipe music (Festival Interceltique des Cornemuses).

Malestroit   **J 5**
22mi/35km NE of Vannes. Pop 2500. Malestroit is one of the most delightful old towns of the Morbihan, beautifully sited by the Oust River, which here forms part of the Canal de Nantes à Brest. The town's name derives from poor communications in medieval times, '*mala strata*' (Latin for 'bad road') becoming 'Malestroit'. The town has plenty of Medieval houses, many of them slate-hung, and several of them recently well restored. By the main square is the timber-framed 'Maison de la Truie qui File' ('House of the Spinning Sow'), so called from one of the humorous painted statues on the beam ends. The splendid church is basically 12thC Romanesque, greatly enlarged in the 16th century

Maison de la Truie qui File, Malestroit

by the addition of a second nave. The side doorway into the church is exceptionally fine; on either side are animal statues, notably an ox and a lion.

Malestroit prides itself on being the home town of Roger Plisson, who sailed round the world single-handed in a boat he constructed himself.

Ploërmel   **J 4**
29mi/46.5km NE of Vannes. Pop 7100. MD Mon & Fri. This small country town gets its name from St Armel, a 6thC monk from Britain (Plou-Armel, altered down the years to Ploërmel). Armel built himself a forest hermitage, where he was confronted by a dragon; fortunately he succeeded in taming it, and led it around by his stole. The town was fortified in the Middle Ages and was for a time occupied by the English. The magnificent church, in Flamboyant Gothic, is mainly 16thC; the spire was destroyed by a shell in World War II and has not been rebuilt. There is a very fine stained-glass window, on the 'Tree of Jesse' theme, and some 15thC glass illustrating the life of St Armel. Ploërmel's chief curiosity is an astronomical clock, in a courtyard in the town centre. Built by a monk in the 1850s, it is a superb piece of craftsmanship, with ten dials giving the time both local and worldwide, the positions of the moon, earth and sun, and a view of the heavens as seen from Ploërmel.

On the west side of the town is a large lake, the Etang au Duc, popular with fishermen, dinghy-sailors and windsurfers.

Pontivy   **F 3**
Pop 14,325. 33mi/52km N of Vannes. In the heartland of Brittany, at the junction of a number of important roads and commanding the Nantes–Brest Canal, the position of Pontivy was well appreciated by Napoleon, who greatly enlarged it and renamed it Napoléonville. The new name did not last long, though it re-emerged briefly in the Second Empire (1852–70).

Pontivy is said to have been founded in the 6th century by St Yvi, a monk from Wales, who built the first bridge across the

Château des Ducs de Rohan, Pontivy

river—hence the town's name. At its centre is the large church, in 16thC Flamboyant Gothic, with a few old houses round it in an irregular pattern of streets contrasting with the grid of Napoleon's town. Nearby are the massive walls and slate-capped towers of Pontivy's castle, built by the powerful Rohan family at the end of the 15th century. Recently restored, it is now used as an exhibition centre. There are attractive walks along the Blavet River and the Nantes–Brest Canal.

Pont-Scorff   C 5
7mi/11km W of Hennebont. Pop 2300. A small town on the main road, above the picturesque valley of the Scorff. It is worth a stop here to look at the mairie, which is a fine Renaissance town house.

Port-Louis   C 6
7.5mi/12km S of Hennebont. Pop 3700. Built in the 17th century to guard the entrance to the estuary of the Blavet and the Scorff, Port-Louis was the predecessor of Lorient as the headquarters of the Compagnie des Indes. Its citadel, with triangular granite bastions jutting into the sea, was built mainly in the first half of the 17th century, under Cardinal Richelieu; and the little fishing port of Blavet, enlarged and strengthened, was renamed Port-Louis in honour of Louis XIII. With the growth of Lorient in the second half of the 17th century, Port-Louis declined, and nowadays its citadel and strong curtain wall seem far too large and impressive for so small a place. The citadel is now a museum (the Musée de l'Atlantique), and the wide esplanade in front of it is used for open-air concerts and shows.

Port-Navalo   F 8
20mi/32km SW of Vannes. Pop 2700. Port-Navalo is a small

harbour and resort, at the western extremity of the Rhuys Peninsula, guarding the entrance to the Gulf of Morbihan. From the point, there are wide views out to sea to the islands of Houat and Hoëdic, and to the Quiberon Peninsula. Port-Navalo is the starting point for boat trips round the Gulf, and across to Locmariaquer on the west side of the water.

Questembert   I 7
17mi/27km E of Vannes. Pop 4900. A quiet little town, surrounded by wooded countryside. Its name comes from the Breton *kistin*, meaning a chestnut tree. Questembert has a magnificent 16thC market building, open at the sides and with a slate roof supported by enormous beams. In AD888 Duke Alan of Brittany won a resounding victory over Norman invaders at Coët-Bihan, 4mi/6.5km SE of Questembert. Out of 15,000 Normans, only 400 are said to have survived.

Quiberon   E 8
17.5mi/28km SW of Auray. Pop 4800. Apart from the Côte Sauvage along its western side, most of the Quiberon Peninsula is built up to a greater or lesser degree, and there is no real feeling of a town centre. Quiberon itself is at the southern end of the peninsula. From its small protected harbour (Port-Maria) there are regular boat services to Belle-Ile and the smaller islands of Houat and Hoëdic. Near the harbour is Quiberon's main beach (the Grande Plage), and there are a number of smaller beaches round the Pointe de Conguel, at the south-east tip of the peninsula. Quiberon has a large centre for seawater cure (*thalassothérapie*), sailing schools and marinas, and a small aerodrome.

La Roche-Bernard   J 8
25mi/40km SE of Vannes. Pop 1050. MD Thur. La Roche-Bernard stands on a hill overlooking the valley of the Vilaine, here beginning to widen into an estuary. It gets its name from a 10thC Norseman called Bernhardt, who sailed up the Vilaine in his longship, took possession of a rocky hill, and built his fortress on it.

The town centre still has a number of timber-framed 15th and 16thC houses, built when La Roche-Bernard was a major shipbuilding centre. During the Revolution the town was taken over by the Royalists, and the Republican mayor, called Sauveur, was ordered to shout 'Vive le roi!'. When he refused, he was shot dead on the spot. In honour of his heroism, the town was briefly renamed La Roche-Sauveur by the revolutionaries.

Just upstream from the town the Vilaine is spanned by a splendid new suspension bridge, while 4mi/5.5km downstream the Barrage d'Arzal has turned the lower waters of the river into a reservoir.

Rochefort-en-Terre   J 6

21.5mi/34km E of Vannes. Pop 600. A little jewel of an old town, on a hilly site, with steps leading from one level to another. In summer Rochefort is a true 'cité fleurie', festooned with geraniums. The 13thC château is in ruins, but the town's granite 17thC houses have been well restored, and are largely occupied by antique and curio shops. The church (12thC, much altered and enlarged in the 16th and 17th centuries) is dedicated to Notre-Dame-de-la-Tronchaye, a *tronchaye* being a cluster of tree-trunks, where a miraculous statue of the Virgin was discovered in the 12th century, hidden there for 300 years since the Norman invasions of Brittany. Rochefort is a centre of trout-fishing, in the Arz, Claie and Oust rivers nearby.

St-Gildas-de-Rhuys   G 8

17.5mi/28km SW of Vannes. Pop 1000. A village on the Rhuys Peninsula, not far from the sea, St-Gildas owes its origins to a Welsh monk, Gildas or Gweltaz, who founded a monastery here in the 6th century. The present 17thC church still has its 11thC Romanesque choir and apse, with the tomb of Gildas behind the high altar. The monastery became famous in the Middle Ages for its connection with Peter Abelard, the great 12thC teacher and philosopher. Abelard fell in love with Heloïse, one of his pupils, had a child by her, and was brutally castrated by her uncle.

Taking refuge from the world, Abelard was appointed abbot of St-Gildas, then one of the wildest and most remote places in the whole of France. Here he fell foul of the monks, who tried to poison him. After several miserable years in Brittany, he returned to Paris and resumed his successful teaching career, dying in 1142. His letters to Heloise give a masterly picture of his life and tragic love.

St-Gildas has a small harbour 0.5mi/1km down the hill, and there are several good beaches nearby.

Sarzeau   G 8

14mi/22km SW of Vannes. Pop 4100. MD Thur. The small 'capital' of the Rhuys Peninsula. In the town centre are some good 17thC houses, with carved window frames. A portrait bust in the main square commemorates Alain-René Lesage, one of the most successful French writers of the early 18th century and the author of the novel 'Gil Blas'.

La Trinité-sur-Mer   E 7

8mi/13km S of Auray. Pop 1530. MD Tue & Fri. La Trinité is a fishing village and holiday resort, at the top of a slope above the Crach estuary. The tidal flats below are excellent for oyster cultivation, and the harbour is popular with small-boat sailors.

Vannes   G 7

66mi/106km SW of Rennes. Pop 45,000. MD Wed & Sat. The capital of the Morbihan, Vannes is an attractive city currently engaged in a major programme of restoration. Arriving at Vannes, you are at once struck by the superb Medieval ramparts, of which about a third of the original circuit survives. The moat is filled with flowerbeds laid out in the most elaborately formal French style, while nearby a group of restored wash-houses bring back the flavour of the Middle Ages. Though Vannes is so far from the sea, its harbour comes right to the old city and is still busy, used by yachtsmen from the Gulf of Morbihan, and by boats taking trippers to explore the islands and fishing ports round about.

Vannes gets its name from the Veneti, a powerful Gaulish tribe

City walls and cathedral, Vannes

conquered by Julius Caesar in 56BC. Under the Romans, it was the starting point for a network of roads radiating all over Brittany; and in the 9th century Nominoë, the first ruler of Brittany, proclaimed his country's independence here. Almost exactly 700 years later Breton independence died at Vannes, when in 1532 the States (parliament) of Brittany declared their wish to unite with France.

The Medieval town behind the ramparts has now been largely pedestrianised, and can be explored on foot without worrying about the traffic. Round the Gothic cathedral is a warren of narrow streets of half-timbered houses and small squares, full of antique shops, boutiques and restaurants. The administrative buildings, mainly 19thC, are west of the old town, across the wide rue Thiers. East of the ramparts is a fine public garden, the Jardins de la Garenne; and the harbour area, south of the pl Gambetta, is well worth seeing.

Interesting buildings

This section includes the prehistoric stone remains of the Morbihan which, though not buildings in the strict sense of the word, were planned constructions, carried out with the full technological and human resources of their epoch. The stones themselves are in two categories: the *dolmens*, consisting of two uprights with a horizontal laid across them (from the Breton *dol*, table, and *men*, stone); and the *menhirs*, or standing stones (from

men, stone, and *hir*, long). Originally the dolmens would have had earth piled over them, to form a tumulus or burial mound. The menhirs may be found singly, arranged in circles, or in rows (alignments), like the astonishing rows at Carnac.

Churches and other ecclesiastical buildings are normally *open 10.00–12.00, 14.00–17.00 (18.00 in summer)*.

Abbaye de Langonnet   C
7.5mi/11km NE of Le Faouët. Standing in quiet countryside above the Ellé River, Langonnet is a 12thC Cistercian monastery, mainly rebuilt in the 17th and 18th centuries, and still in full monastic use. *Open by request.*

Alignements de Carnac   E
7.5mi/12km SW of Auray. Just north of the little town of Carnac, endless lines of stones, like armies on parade, stride into the distance across the gorse and wiry grass of the heathland. Along with Stonehenge and Avebury in England, the Carnac stones rank as the largest and most impressive constructions of Stone Age man. Archaeologists and scholars still cannot agree on their significance, apart from linking them in some undefined way with the observation of the stars and the seasons by a priestly caste, who used their knowledge to instruct their peoples when they should sow and harvest.

The stones were probably set in place about 2000BC, at the same time as Avebury and Stonehenge, and as part of the same culture that covered the western fringe of

Europe. In the main alignments and in the countryside nearby there are about 5000 menhirs, together with a number of dolmens large and small. Such constructive activity, no doubt over several centuries, argues great powers of organisation on the part of the rulers of the time—to be compared with the amount of organisation needed to build the Egyptian pyramids. There are three main alignments, running roughly from south west to north east: Ménec, about 0.5mi/1km long by 110yds/100m wide; Kermario, covering much the same extent; and Kerlescan, slightly shorter and correspondingly wider. The road (D196) runs right alongside them, and in summer there are so many crawling cars that it is much better to walk. The Stone Age artefacts found in the neighbourhood are kept in the Miln-Le Rouzic Museum, in Carnac (*see* Museums).

Cathédrale de St-Pierre   **G 7**
Vannes. In old walled town. Dedicated to St Peter, Vannes cathedral is in a number of architectural styles, from the 13thC Romanesque bell-tower at the north-west corner, to the curious circular Renaissance tower on the north side, built in the 1530s in Italian style, and thus a rarity in Brittany. In the round tower is a chapel containing the tomb and relics of St Vincent Ferrier, a Spanish missionary who died at Vannes in 1419, and is recalled elsewhere in the city by the Porte St-Vincent at the southern end of the Medieval town, and in the pl Valencia at its centre. Round the walls of the chapel are tapestries, woven in 1615, showing St Vincent's miracles. The cathedral has a treasury with a number of rare objects, of which the finest is a small wooden marriage casket, painted in brilliant colours with scenes of court life in the 12th century. It was later turned into a reliquary.

Chapelle de St-Avoye   **F 7**
2mi/3km SE of Auray. A dainty 16thC Renaissance chapel, with a fine carved rood-screen. Avoye was a 6thC Irishman, said to have sailed over to Brittany in a stone drinking trough. St-Avoye itself is

an attractive little hamlet, near the Bono River.

Chapelle de St-Cado   **D 6**
10mi/16km W of Auray. St-Cado is one of the most mysteriously beautiful places in the Morbihan, on an island in the Rivière d'Etel, linked to the mainland by a narrow causeway. St Cado (Catwg in Welsh) was a Glamorgan prince who made his way by devious means to this corner of Brittany; a poem in ancient script round the walls of the chapel gives the story of his travels. Cado is said to have outwitted the Devil, who had agreed to build a bridge from the island to the mainland in exchange for the soul of the first creature across it. St Cado, being a wily Welshman, sent a cat across, thus foiling the Devil's plan.
Outside the chapel is a stone crucifix approached by a triple flight of stairs, used by the St-Cado fishermen to dry their nets.

Chapelle de St-Fiacre   **C 3**
Le Faouët. 1.5mi/2.5km S of the town. Inside this 15thC chapel is one of the finest painted rood-screens in Brittany. Carved about 1480 in Flamboyant style, it is an intricate piece of work, covered with a variety of figures, from the emaciated Christ on the Cross to Adam and Eve, and grotesque carvings illustrating the Deadly Sins, including a Breton playing the bagpipes (symbolising laziness).

Chapelle de St-Nicodème   **F 4**
Pluméliau. 9mi/14.5km S of Pontivy. Dedicated to St Nicodemus, this chapel (2.5mi/4km NW of the village) is a fine example of Flamboyant Gothic, built about 1530, with a pinnacled bell-tower surmounted by a graceful spire. Inside there is a good 17thC stone reredos on the high altar; but the most unusual feature of the church is the number of statues, which include, besides Nicodemus himself, St-Cornély the patron saint of cattle. There is a *pardon* in honour of Nicodemus on the *1st Sun in Aug.*

Chapelle Ste-Barbe   **C 3**
Le Faouët. 13mi/21km N of Quimperlé. St Barbara's chapel, built in Flamboyant Gothic style about 1500, is 1.5mi/2.5km E of

the town, perched high above the valley of the Ellé River. Some of the chapel windows illustrate the life of St Barbara, who was believed to be able to ward off lightning. Outside is a bell, rung by pilgrims in search of heavenly favours. A fountain down by the river was much used by local girls hoping for husbands: if a girl's hairpin floated, she would be married within the year.

Chapelle de Ste-Noyale   **F 3**
4mi/6.5km NE of Pontivy.
Surrounded by trees in a hamlet near Pontivy, this chapel, built in Flamboyant style, is decorated with frescoes illustrating the life of Ste-Noyale (Nolwen in Breton). Outside is a large 19thC calvary.

Château de Branféré   **I 7**
23mi/37km SE of Vannes. Tel (97) 41 69 21. There have been several castles at Branféré: the 14thC château was rebuilt in the 17th century, almost entirely destroyed at the Revolution and restored in the 19th century. Round the château is a 85-acre/35-hectare open-air zoo, with over 200 animal species. Exhibitions of works by wildlife painters are sometimes shown in the castle. *Open 1 Apr–mid-Sep 09.00–12.00, 14.00–18.30; mid-Sep–mid-Nov, 09.00–12.00, 14.00–17.30.* **Charge**

Château de Comper

Château de Comper   **K 3**
12.5mi/20km NE of Ploërmel. The gabled château (*private*) is reflected in the calm waters of a large lake, on the edge of the Forest of Paimpont (*see Ille-et-Vilaine*). The whole region is permeated with the legends of King Arthur and the Round Table, and it was from Comper's lake that Sir Lancelot took the name Lancelot du Lac. The original castle is said to have been built by Diana the Huntress (even more remote in time than the Round Table); but the present building is a large 19thC farmhouse.

Château du Crévy   **I**
La Chapelle. 5mi/8km S of Ploërmel. A turreted château, built in the 18th and 19th centuries on the foundations of a 14thC fortress, dominating the Oust Valley. Inside is a display of Breton costume from the 18th century to 1930. *Open Jul & Aug, daily 10.00–12.00, 14.00–18.00; Jun, daily 14.00–18.00; Easter–31 May & 1 Sep–31 Oct, Wed, Sat & Sun 14.00–18.00.*

Château des Ducs de Rohan G
Pontivy. In centre of town. Tel (9) 25 12 93. Built in the late 15th century by Jean de Rohan, this massive castle, with walls 10ft/3m thick and 59ft/18m high, dominates the town and the Blavet River. It is surrounded by a moat, and still has its complete circuit of walls. Recently restored, it is now mainly used for exhibitions. *Open mid-Apr–mid-Oct 10.00–12.00, 14.00–18.00, closed Mon; mid-Oct–mid-Apr 10.00–12.00, 14.00–16.00.* **Charge**

Château de Josselin   **I**
Josselin. In centre of town. Tel (9) 22 22 50. Josselin's granite castle, with its three conical-roofed towers rising from the living rock, is the quintessence of feudal grandeur. Though hackneyed from being reproduced in every tourist brochure for Brittany, it remains enormously impressive, both on its own account and for the contrast with the pretty little town that clusters around it.
The first castle, built in the 11th century, was attacked by the English in the 1160s and largely destroyed. The present fortifications were built by Olivier de Clisson towards the end of the 14th century. Known as the 'Butcher of the English', from his savagery in the Hundred Years' War, Clisson was appointed commander of the French armed forces in 1380. When first built, Josselin's mighty walls rose sheer from the river, not from the road as they do today. Clisson's successors, the powerful Rohan family, built the internal *corps-de-logis* dwelling, whose fanciful

Gothic pinnacles, gables and balustrades form a delightful contrast to the grim military appearance of the outer walls. The Rohan motto '*A plus*' ('Even more') is carved into the stonework, along with the initial A for Duchess Anne of Brittany, in whose reign (about 1500) the *corps-de-logis* was built. The Rohans still own the château, and live there for much of the time. The sumptuous ground-floor rooms, restored and redecorated in the 19th century, are on view to the public. *Open 1 Jun–mid-Sep, daily 14.00–18.00; Apr & May, Wed & Sun 14.00–18.00.* **Charge**

Château de Suscinio

Château de Kerlévenan　G 8

11.5mi/18.5km S of Vannes. Tel (97) 26 41 10. An 18thC château, near Sarzeau in the Rhuys Peninsula. It is built in Italianate style, with portico and rows of columns, and is in white stone from Touraine instead of the usual Breton granite. During the 19th century it was much visited by artists, including JMW Turner. *Open 1 Jul–mid-Sep, by request.*

Château de Largoët　*See Tours d'Elven*

Château de Léhélec　J 7

11.5mi/18.5km W of Redon. Tel (99) 91 81 14. Near the village of Béganne, on the north side of the Vilaine River, Léhélec is a 17thC château, in sober Classical style, built of grey granite and pink schist rock. At the end of the 18th century it was a refuge for the Chouans (anti-Revolutionary and pro-Royalist Bretons). Inside there is a good collection of old furniture, and occasional concerts are given. *Open Jul & Aug 14.00–19.00, closed Tue; mid-May–30 Jun, Sun & hols only 14.00–19.00.* **Charge**

Château Le Plessis-Josso　H 7

9.5mi/15km SE of Vannes, near village of Theix. Tel (97) 43 16 16. A large and imposing fortified manor house, built between the 14th and 16th centuries, and linking the Middle Ages and the Renaissance in its building styles. A wing was added in the 17th century. House, watermill, lake and woodland form an attractive unity. *Open Jul & Aug 14.00–19.00.* **Charge**

Château de Suscinio　G 8

14mi/22.5km S of Vannes. Built between the 13th and 16th centuries, Suscinio is a warlike fortress, standing so near the shore of the Rhuys Peninsula that when it was built the moat used to fill and empty with the tides, though the sea has now retreated. During the Middle Ages it was one of the residences of the dukes of Brittany, which accounts for the contrast (as at Josselin) between the strength of the outer walls and the comfort of the interior accommodation. Each surviving bedroom has a window seat, fireplace and lavatory. In 1373 the great French general Bertrand du Guesclin recaptured the château from the English, destroying a stretch of wall later rebuilt in different stone. During the Revolution, Suscinio was used as a stone quarry; but today it is undergoing a long process of restoration. *Open 1 Apr–30 Sep, daily 10.00–12.00, 14.00–18.00; 1 Oct–31 Mar, Thur, Sat & Sun, 10.00–12.00, 14.00–17.00.* **Charge**

Château de Trémohar-en-Berric　H 7

10mi/16km E of Vannes. Tel (97) 43 03 24. Built in the 14th and 15th centuries the fortifications were largely destroyed at the end of the 16th, during the Wars of the League. The château was rebuilt in Classical style early in the 18th century. *Open 1 Jul–mid-Sep 09.00–12.00, 14.30–18.00.* **Charge**

La Cohue　G 7

Rue des Halles, Vannes. A covered market, dating from the 12th–14th century, and restored in the 1970s. Known as La Cohue ('Hubbub'), it has stalls selling everything from jewellery to pancakes. *Open daily.*

Colonne des Trente   **I 4**

On 'island' in dual carriageway, 4mi/6.5km E of Josselin. This monument commemorates a famous feat of arms that took place in 1351, during the War of Succession over the dukedom of Brittany. The garrison at Josselin was commanded by the Breton, Jean de Beaumanoir, while English mercenaries under Robert Bemborough held Ploërmel. The commanders agreed to meet at an oak tree half-way between the two towns, to battle it out with 30 knights each. The two sides fought all day, until the English knights were routed. The survivors were taken back to Josselin and ransomed. In the course of the battle, Beaumanoir, who had been wounded and lost a lot of blood, called out for a drink. One of his men answered: "Drink your blood, Beaumanoir, your thirst will pass"—a reply that has become proverbial.

Eglise de Ste-Anne-d'Auray   F 6

10mi/16km W of Vannes. The sanctuary of Ste-Anne-d'Auray is the most important religious centre in Brittany, and owes its existence to the vast *pardon* held there each year on *25–26 Jul.* Everything is on the largest scale: an enormous basilica, a huge open space for the crowds to gather, and a gigantic war memorial to 250,000 Bretons killed in World War I. Ste-Anne's fame is due to a miraculous statue of Anne, the mother of the Virgin Mary, discovered in 1625 by a local farmer, Yves Nicolazic. A chapel was built on the site in the 17th century, succeeded by the present vast church in the 1860s. Ste-Anne is honoured not only as the mother of the Virgin but as the patron saint of the whole of Brittany. According to one story, she was a Breton who made her way to Palestine, gave birth to Mary there, and eventually returned to Brittany.

Gavrinis, tumulus   **F 7**

9mi/14.5km SE of Auray. On the tiny island of Gavrinis, in the Gulf of Morbihan, is a magnificent tumulus (burial mound) dating from about 2000BC, at the height of the Neolithic Age. Inside the mound, which is about 98ft/30m across and 26ft/8m high, is a passageway 46ft/14m long, made of horizontal slabs laid across uprights, and leading to a burial chamber, which was probably a royal tomb. Many of the stones are carved with snakes, axes and other symbolic designs.
Gavrinis is reached by boat from Larmor-Baden in about 15 minutes; regular service *in summer.*

Grand Menhir Brisé   **F 7**

Just N of Locmariaquer. The biggest menhir known, now lying on the ground in four pieces, which weigh an estimated 350 tons/356 tonnes. Before the stone was broken it would have stood about 66ft/20m high. It is thought that it may have been the main element in some kind of Neolithic observatory.

Guéhenno, calvary   **H 4**

7mi/11km SW of Josselin. One of the few elaborate calvaries in the Morbihan, put up about 1550. It was smashed to pieces in the Revolution, but the locals collected the fragments and in the 1850s the rector of Guéhenno and his assistant put them together again, carving any missing pieces themselves. Now, after 130 years, only experts can tell the difference. In front of the calvary is a column with a cock on the top, in reference to St Peter's denial of Christ.

Mané-Lud, dolmen   **F 7**

0.5mi/1km N of Locmariaquer. A large and impressive dolmen in the form of an underground chamber. Inside there are a number of symbolic carvings on the stones.

Melrand, calvary   **E 3**

10mi/16km SW of Pontivy. This village has three calvaries, of which the best, carved in the early 19th century, is a little north of the village, on the D142 towards Guéméné.

Notre-Dame-de-Kernascléden   **D 3**

21.5mi/34.5km W of Pontivy. The interior of this chapel, built in the mid-15th century in Flamboyant

Gothic style, is one of the most remarkable in the whole of Brittany. Much of the original wall painting has survived, including scenes from the lives of Mary and Jesus, and vivid paintings of the Dance of Death and Hell, with the souls of the damned suffering a variety of unpleasant tortures. Art historians have compared them with the paintings of Hieronymus Bosch.

Notre-Dame-du-Loc   **G 6**
St-Avé. 2.5mi/4km NE of Vannes. The 15thC chapel, restored in the 20th century, has some remarkable wood carving, including the wall plates (*sablières*) and a wooden calvary carved about 1500. The high altar is embellished with six alabaster statues of biblical figures, carved in England in the 15th century.

Notre-Dame-de-Quelven   **E 3**
7mi/11km SW of Pontivy. A country chapel, mainly 15thC with a tower restored in the 19th. Inside, its chief treasure is a statue of the Virgin, which opens to reveal 12 little panels depicting Christ's Passion.

Table des Marchands   **F 7**
550yds/500m N of Locmariaquer. A massive chamber tomb, with a capstone 20ft/6m long by 13ft/4m wide. Some of the stones are carved with symbolic designs (crosses, axes etc).

Tours d'Elven   **H 6**
9.5mi/15km NE of Vannes. The 'Elven Towers', together with the remains of curtain walls, are the twin towers of the once-mighty castle of Largoët, destroyed by a French army that invaded Brittany in 1488. The 15thC round tower has been restored, but the tall octagonal keep is in a state of ruin. *Son-et-lumière* shows are held at Largoët *in summer. Open all year 09.00–18.00. Charge*

Tumulus St-Michel   **E 7**
Carnac. NE of town centre. This is a massive burial mound, 410ft/125m long by 197ft/60m wide, made of two layers of stones with an earth layer between. The lower level contained burial chambers, whose contents are now in the Carnac museum. On top of the mound is

a small chapel dedicated to St Michael, and from the platform on which it stands there are wide views over the whole megalith area, and far out to sea. In earlier centuries the locals believed that Julius Caesar was buried under the mound, in a golden coffin.

Vannes, old buildings   **G 7**
Much of the Medieval city is now pedestrianised. There are half-timbered 15th and 16thC houses in all the ancient streets, such as the rue St-Salomon, rue des Orfèvres, and the rue des Halles. In the rue Noë is the Château Gaillard, a dignified 15thC stone townhouse which from 1456–1532 was the seat of the Breton Etats (States, or parliament). Nearby, on a beam end, are the famous carved figures of a plump bourgeois couple, nicknamed 'Vannes and his Wife'. The southern and eastern sides of the town wall are complete, and there is a walk along much of the ramparts. Two of the town gates (the Medieval Porte Prison and the Renaissance Porte St-Vincent) lead into the town, and half-way along the wall is the mighty 15thC Tour du Connétable (Constable's Tower). Just outside the walls, at their south-eastern end, are the slate-roofed washing-places (*lavoirs*), where the washerwomen of Vannes used to scrub the city's laundry in the stream.

Museums & galleries

Atlantique, Musée de l'   **C 6**
La Citadelle, 56290 Port-Louis. Tel (97) 21 14 01. The barrack buildings and bastions of Port-Louis's 17thC citadel have been transformed into a museum illustrating French maritime history, both naval and domestic, with documents, ship models, figureheads and photographs. *Open 10.00–12.00, 14.00–19.00. Closed Tue. Charge*

La Compagnie des Indes, Exposition de   **C 6**
Hôtel de Ville, 56100 Lorient. Tel (97) 21 20 51. An exhibition on the history of the Compagnie des Indes (the French equivalent of the East India Company) and its connections with Lorient. *Open summer only,*

10.00–12.00, 15.00–18.00. Closed Tue. **Charge**

Miln–Le Rouzic, Musée   E 7
Rue du Tumulus, 56340 Carnac.
No tel. Named after its founder,
the Scottish archaeologist James
Miln, and its first curator, Zacharie
Le Rouzic, this small museum
gathers under one roof the carved
stones, arrowheads, axes and other
artefacts found in the Carnac
region during the past century.
*Open Easter–30 Sep 10.00–12.00,
14.00–17.00.* **Charge**

Préhistoire, Musée de   G 7
Château Gaillard, 2 rue Noë, 56000
Vannes. No tel. The museum of the
Société Polymathique du
Morbihan, in a magnificent
Medieval townhouse, displaying
archaeological finds from the whole
of the Morbihan. *Open summer only,
09.30–12.00, 14.00–18.00. Closed
Sun.* **Charge**

**Sciences Naturelles,
Musée de**   G 7
Hôtel de Roscanvec, rue des Halles,
56000 Vannes. Tel (97) 42 59 80.
This museum, in a mansion in the
Medieval centre of Vannes,
includes collections of ornithology,
the minerals of Brittany, shells and
fossils. *Open summer only,
09.30–12.00, 14.00–18.00. Closed
Sun.* **Charge**

Accommodation

Campsites

Prices at campsites vary according
to the facilities available but
seldom exceed ten francs per person
at present. There will usually also
be a charge for the car and for the
site.

Arradon   G 7
Municipal Parc Priol
56610 Arradon. Tel (97) 26 70 49.
A fairly small site, grassy but with
some stones, south-west of the
village. *Open mid-Jun–mid-Sep.*

Arzon   F 8
Le Tindio
56640 Arzon. Tel (97) 41 25 59.
This grassy site is a little north-
east of the village, on the Gulf
of Morbihan by the sea. *Open
all year.*

Baud   F 4
Municipal de Bot Kermarec
56150 Baud. Tel (97) 51 02 29. A
quiet site, grassy and tree-shaded
but on the small side, south-west of
the town. *Open mid-Jun–mid-Sep.*

Belle-Ile-en-Mer   DE 9–10
Bordenéo
56360 Belle-Ile. Tel (97) 31 88 96.
A flat, grassy site, 550yds/500m
from the sea and 1.5mi/2.5km
NW of Le Palais, Belle-Ile's little
capital. *Open 1 Jun–mid-Sep.*

Municipal de Bangor
Bangor, 56360 Belle-Ile. Tel (97) 31
84 06. A small, grassy site, with few
facilities but quiet, in Bangor
village. *Open 1 May–30 Sep.*

Belz   E 6
St-Cado
56550 Belz. Tel (97) 55 33 54. A
grassy site, by the beautiful lagoon
known as the Rivière d'Etel and
near the little chapel of St-Cado.
Open mid-Jun–mid-Sep.

Carnac   E 7
La Grande Métairie
56340 Carnac. Tel (97) 55 71 47.
This large and well-equipped site is
about 2mi/3km from the sea, with
many facilities, including a
common-room and heated
swimming pool. It is also near many
of the prehistoric standing stones.
Open mid-May–mid-Sep.

Rosnual
56340 Carnac. Tel (97) 52 14 57. A
grassy, smallish site near the
alignements of standing stones. *Open
1 Jun–mid-Sep.*

Carnac-Plage   E 7
Les Druides
56340 Carnac-Plage. Tel (97) 52 08
18. A small site, east of the village
and about 550yds/500m from the
sea. *Open Easter & mid-May–
mid-Sep.*

Damgan   H 8
Kerlan
56750 Damgan. Tel (97) 41 11 64.
A flat, grassy site, 0.5mi/1km E of
the village and 325yds/300m from
the sea. *Open mid-May–mid-Sep.*

Oasis
56750 Damgan. Tel (97) 41 10 52.
About 1.5mi/2.5km E of the
village, this grassy site is only

10yds/100m from the sea. *Open
May–30 Sep.*

rdeven E 7

e Kerzerho
6410 Etel. Tel (97) 55 37 35. A
airly large and well equipped site,
.5mi/1km SE of the village. The
Kerzerho standing stones are
nly 220yds/200m away. *Open
aster–mid-Sep.*

e Faouët C 3

eg er Roch
6320 Le Faouët. Tel (97) 23 15 11.
quiet site, 1.5mi/2.5km SE of the
wn beside the Ellé River. *Open
id-Mar–mid-Sep.*

ourin B 2

ont Min
6110 Gourin. Tel (97) 23 42 74. A
mall site, not far from the town
entre. *Open all year.*

e de Groix B/C 7

es Sables Rouges
6590 Groix. Tel (97) 05 81 32. A
te with a fine outlook, by the sea
mi/3km SE of Port-Tudy, the
land's harbour. *Open Easter–
0 Sep.*

osselin I 4

as de la Lande
6120 Josselin. Tel (97) 22 22 20.
grassy and partly terraced site,
5yds/50m from the banks of the
ust, 1.5mi/2.5km W of the town
ong the Lorient road. *Open all
ar.*

armor-Plage C 6

u Phare
6260 Larmor-Plage. Tel (97) 65 53
2. A fairly large site, near the sea
d looking across the estuary of
e Blavet. *Open 1 Jun–mid-Sep.*

ocmariaquer F 7

ann Brick
6740 Locmariaquer. Tel (97) 57 32
9. A flat, grassy site, 1.5mi/2.5km
W of the village and 220yds/200m
om the sea. Near some of the
nest prehistoric remains. *Open
id-Jun–mid-Sep.*

ocminé G 4

unicipal de Beaulieu
6500 Locminé. Tel (97) 60 02 16.
n attractive small site, 1mi/1.5km
E of the town along the Josselin
ad, and beside a small lake. *Open
id-Jun–mid-Sep.*

Malestroit J 5

La Daufresne
56140 Malestroit. Tel (97) 75 13 33.
A small site near the Oust River,
with swimming and water sports
close by. *Open mid-May–mid-Oct.*

Muzillac I 8

Le Relais de l'Océan
56190 Muzillac. Tel (97) 41 66 48.
A grassy site, with games room,
1.5mi/2.5km W of the town in the
direction of Ambon. *Open mid-
Jun–mid-Sep.*

Pénestin I 8

Inly
56760 Pénestin. Tel (97) 90 35 09.
A large, quiet site, 1.5mi/2.5km
SE of the village beside a small
lake. It has a large number of
facilities, including snack bar and
common-room. *Open Easter–
mid-Sep.*

Ploemeur C 6

Les Pins
Lomener, 56270 Ploemeur. Tel (97)
82 93 75. At the little resort of
Lomener, 2.5mi/4km S of the
village, a grassy, tree-shaded site.
Open all year.

St-Jude
Le Courégant, 56270 Ploemeur. Tel
(97) 05 99 81. At the resort of Le
Courégant, 3mi/5km SW of the
village. A flat and grassy site, with
some sand, near the sea. *Open mid-
Jun–31 Aug.*

Ploërmel J 4

Les Belles Rives
56800 Ploërmel. Tel (97) 74 01 22.
A fairly large, grassy site, by the
lake known as the Etang au Duc,
1.5mi/2.5km NW of the town.
Good opportunities for water
sports. *Open 1 Apr–31 Oct.*

Port-Louis C 6

Les Remparts
56290 Port-Louis. Tel (97) 82 47
16. A municipal site, on the
outskirts of the town and 550yds/
500m from the sea. *Open mid-
Jun–mid-Sep.*

Questembert I 7

Moulin de Célac
56230 Questembert. Tel (97) 26 11
24. A slightly sloping site, beside
a lake 0.5mi/1km from the town.
Open mid-Jun–mid-Sep.

Quiberon   E 8

Do-Mi-Si-La-Mi
56170 Quiberon. Tel (97) 50 22 52.
A musically named site, only 55yds/
50m from the sea near St-Julien, on
the sheltered east side of the
Quiberon Peninsula. *Open mid-
Mar–31 Oct.*

Les Joncs du Roc'h
56170 Quiberon. Tel (97) 50 24 37.
A flat, grassy site, 1.5mi/2.5km SE
of Quiberon town, south of the
airport. *Open Easter–mid-Oct.*

La Roche-Bernard   J 8

Le Pâtis
56130 La Roche-Bernard. Tel (99)
90 60 13. A small site, on the south-
west side of the town, beside the
Vilaine. *Open mid-Jun–mid-Sep.*

St-Gildas-de-Rhuys   G 8

Le Menhir
56730 St-Gildas-de-Rhuys. Tel (97)
53 42 88. A grassy site, quiet and
with games room among the
facilities. *Open 1 Jun–mid-Sep.*

Ste-Anne-d'Auray   F 6

Municipal du Motten
Ste-Anne-d'Auray, 56400 Auray.
Tel (97) 57 60 27. A small site,
0.5mi/1km SW of the village, off
the Auray road. *Open mid-
Jun–mid-Sep.*

Sarzeau   G 8

La Madone
56370 Sarzeau. Tel (97) 41 70 64.
A large site with many facilities,
5.5mi/9km SE of the town on the
way to the Pointe de Penvins. *Open
1 Apr–mid-Sep.*

La Trinité-sur-Mer   E 7

Kervilor
56470 La Trinité-sur-Mer. Tel (97)
55 76 75. A quiet, grassy site, with
limited facilities, 1mi/1.5km N
of the village. *Open mid-Jun–
mid-Sep.*

La Plage
56470 La Trinité-sur-Mer. 0.5mi/
1km S of village. Tel (97) 55 73 28.
This site is part grassy and part
sandy, and has direct access to the
beach. *Open 1 Jun–mid-Sep.*

Vannes   G 7

Conleau
Conleau, 56000 Vannes. Tel (97) 63
13 88. Within easy reach of the Gulf
of Morbihan, this is a three-star sit
at Conleau, a village just south of
Vannes. *Open all year.*

Hotels

Auray   F

Hôtel L'Armoric
56400 Auray. Tel (97) 24 10 36. B
the river, in the Medieval quarter o
St-Goustan. *Closed Jan. Restaurant
closed Tue.* A.Ax.V. **F**

Hôtel Le Belvédère
2 rue du Belvédère, 56400 Auray.
Tel (97) 24 03 48. Friendly small
hotel, without restaurant, near the
rampart gardens. *Closed 1 Nov–en
Feb.* **F**

Hôtel de la Mairie
24–26 pl de la Mairie, 56400 Auray
Tel (97) 24 04 65. A 'Logis de
France' hotel in the town centre.
Closed 18 Sep–5 Nov. **FF**

Belle-Ile-en-Mer   DE 9–1

Hôtel Castel Clara
Le Palais, 56360 Belle-Ile-en-Mer.
Tel (97) 31 84 21. A modern luxur
hotel on a picturesque fjord on the
island's south coast. Heated
swimming pool and two tennis
courts. *Closed 1 Nov–31 Mar.*
A.Ax.V. **FFF**

Carnac   E

Hôtel L'Armoric
53 av Poste, 56340 Carnac. Tel (97
52 13 47. A modern hotel some
way from the sea, overlooking
oyster beds. The restaurant
specialises in seafood including,
appropriately, oysters. *Closed 15
Sep–Whit Sun.* **FF**

Carnac-Plage   E

Hôtel Diana
21 bvd de la Plage, 56340 Carnac.
Tel (97) 52 05 38. A comfortable
hotel on the seafront. *Closed mid-
Sep–30 Apr.* A.V. **FF**

Ker Ihuel
59 bvd de la Plage, 56340 Carnac.
Tel (97) 52 11 38. Seafront hotel
with a fine view, which is
particularly dramatic at sunset.
Closed 1 Oct–Whit Sun. **FF**

La Gacilly   K

Hôtel France
15 rue du Montauban, 56200 La
Gacilly. Tel (97) 08 11 15. Small
hotel in an enchanting little town.
Open all year. **F**

Hennebont D 5

Château de Locguénolé
56700 Hennebont. Tel (97) 76 29
04. A luxury hotel in the
'prestigious 'Relais et Châteaux'
chain, 3mi/5km S of Hennebont on
the Port-Louis road. The 18thC
classical château is in a park above
the Blavet River. *Closed 1 Dec–end
Feb.* Ax.Dc.V. FFF

Hôtel de la Poste
4 pl Maréchal Foch, 56700
Hennebont. Tel (97) 36 22 19. An
older-style hotel in the town centre.
Open all year. F

Ile de Groix B/C 7

Hôtel Ty Mad
56590 Groix. Tel (97) 05 80 19.
Small hotel near Port-Tudy harbour. *Closed 1 Nov–end Feb.* V. F

Josselin I 4

Hôtel du Château
rue Général-de-Gaulle, 56120
Josselin. Tel (97) 22 20 11. A roomy,
white-painted hotel, with a
magnificent view across the river
to the château. A 'Destination
Bretagne' hotel. *Closed Feb.*
A.V. FF

Hôtel de France
1 Notre-Dame, 56120 Josselin. Tel
(97) 22 23 06. Hotel in the main
square, opposite the church. *Open
all year.* FF

Larmor-Plage C 6

Hôtel Beau Rivage
Plage de Toulhars, 56260 Larmor-
Plage. Tel (97) 65 50 11. A small
seaside hotel, with a fine view.
Closed Nov. A.Ax.Dc.V. FF

Locmariaquer F 7

Hôtel L'Escale
56740 Locmariaquer. Tel (97) 57 32
01. Small hotel near the harbour,
and within walking distance of
some of the finest prehistoric
remains. *Closed mid-Sep–mid-May.*
A.V. F

Locminé G 4

Hôtel de l'Argoat
Rte Vannes, 56500 Locminé. Tel
(97) 60 01 02. Quiet hotel near the
own centre. *Closed mid-Dec–31
Jan.* F

Lorient C 6

Hôtel Richelieu
1 pl Jules Ferry, 56100 Lorient.

Tel (97) 21 35 73. A luxury hotel
close to the harbour and town
centre. *Open all year.* A.Ax.Dc.
V. FFF

Hôtel Le Victor Hugo
36 rue Lazare Carnot, 56100
Lorient. Tel (97) 21 16 24.
Medium-sized hotel, without
restaurant, not far from the
harbour. *Open all year.*
A.Ax.Dc.V. F

Ploërmel J 4

Relais du Val d'Oust
La Chapelle, 56800 Ploërmel. Tel
(97) 74 94 33. Small hotel in the
village of La Chapelle, 5mi/8km
S of the town. *Closed Jan &
Feb.* V. F

Pontivy F 3

Hôtel Porhoët
41 av Général-de-Gaulle, 56300
Pontivy. Tel (97) 25 34 88. Hotel on
the main street near the castle.
Closed Jan. A. F

Quiberon E 8

Hôtel Beau Rivage
Rue Port-Maria, 56170 Quiberon.
Tel (97) 50 08 39. Medium-sized
hotel near the harbour and main
beach. *Closed 1 Oct–31 Mar.* V. FF

Hôtel Hoche
Pl Hoche, 56170 Quiberon. Tel (97)
50 07 73. In the main square and
near the sea. *Closed 1 Oct–31 Jan.*
A.V. FF

Sofitel
Bvd Goviro, 56170 Quiberon. Tel
(97) 50 20 20. Luxury hotel
incorporating a centre for seawater
treatment (*thalassothérapie*). *Closed
Jan.* A.Ax.Dc.V. FFF

La Roche-Bernard J 8

Hôtel de Bretagne
Rue Crespel de Latouche, 56130 La
Roche-Bernard. Tel (97) 90 60 65.
Small hotel with a fine view across
the Vilaine River. *Closed mid-
Jan–end Feb.* F

Ste-Anne-d'Auray F 6

Hôtel de la Paix
Rue Vannes, Ste-Anne-d'Auray,
56400 Auray. Tel (97) 57 65 08.
Small hotel near the vast sanctuary
of Ste-Anne. *Closed 1 Oct–Easter.* F

Sarzeau G 8

Hôtel Le Sage
Pl de l'Eglise, 56370 Sarzeau. Tel

(97) 41 85 85. Medium-sized hotel in the town's main square. *Closed Jan.* FF

Vannes   G 7

Hôtel de Bretagne
34 rue du Mené, 56000 Vannes. Tel (97) 47 20 21. A small hotel, without restaurant, in the Medieval walled town, not far from the cathedral. *Closed Jan & Feb.* F

Hôtel La Marébaudière
4 rue Aristide-Briand, 56000 Vannes. Tel (97) 47 34 29. A medium-sized hotel, a short way east of the walled town. *Closed 17 Dec–2 Jan.* A.Ax.Dc.V. FF

Hôtel Richemont
24 av Favrel et Lincy, 56000 Vannes. Tel (97) 66 12 95. A medium-sized hotel near the station. The restaurant specialises in meat dishes. *Closed Jan.* A. FF

Restaurants

Auray   F 6

L'Abbaye
56400 Auray. Tel (97) 24 10 85. A 17thC half-timbered building by the river, in the Medieval quarter of St-Goustan. *Closed Thur.* FF

Brasserie Le Rétro
23 rue Barré, 56400 Auray. Tel (97) 56 44 12. An ultra-modern tea-room and snackbar in the main part of town. *Closed Sat lunch & Sun.* F

Carnac   E 7

Lann Roz
35 av de la Poste, 56340 Carnac. Tel (97) 52 10 48. Restaurant, with rooms, specialising in lobster, mussels and fish soup. *Closed Mon & 15 Nov–15 Dec.* FF

Carnac-Plage   E 7

Le Celtic
17 rue de Kermario, 56340 Carnac-Plage. Tel (97) 52 11 49. A short walk from the sea, specialising in fish and grills. *Closed 1 Oct–30 Apr.* FF

Hennebont   D 5

Pizzeria Del Castello
Rue Maréchal Joffre, 56700 Hennebont. Tel (97) 36 12 59. A quick-food restaurant near the castle. *Closed Sun lunch & Mon.* F

Josselin   I

À La Bonne Crêpe
8 rue du Canal, 56120 Josselin. Tel (97) 22 21 98. A bar and crêperie overlooking the river and almost next door to the château. *Closed Mon.* F

La Duchesse Anne
8 pl de la Duchesse Anne, 56120 Josselin. Tel (97) 22 22 37. A dignified 17thC building, on the edge of the old town. *Closed Mon & Feb.* FF

Lorient   C

Cornouaille
13 bvd Franchet d'Espérey, 56100 Lorient. Tel (97) 21 23 05. A modestly priced restaurant, a little way from the town centre. *Closed Mon.* Ax.V. F

Le Poisson d'Or
1 rue Maître Esvelin, 56100 Lorient. Tel (97) 21 57 06. A top-quality restaurant, specialising in fish. *Closed Sat lunch, Sun, Nov & Feb.* A.Ax.Dc.V. FF

Ploërmel   J

Crêperie de la Tour
1 pl d'Armes, 56800 Ploërmel. Tel (97) 74 05 40. Crêperie and snackbar by the church in the town centre.

Quiberon   E

Le Continental
21 pl Hoche, 56170 Quiberon. Tel (97) 50 15 50. In the main square not far from the sea, this restaurant specialises in *fruits de mer.* *Closed Mon.* A.Dc.V. FF

La Roche-Bernard   J

Auberge Bretonne
Pl du Guesclin, 56130 La Roche-Bernard. Tel (99) 90 60 28. Small friendly restaurant, with country specialities. *Closed Thur.* A.Ax.Dc.V. FF

Rochefort-en-Terre   J

Auberge du Vieux Logis
56220 Rochefort-en-Terre. Tel (97) 43 31 71. A 17thC stone-built house in the old town. *Open daily* A.V. FF

Hostellerie du Lion d'Or
Rue du Pélican, 56220 Rochefort-en-Terre. Tel (97) 43 32 80. A 16thC stone building in the flower-filled centre of this little town. *Closed Tue.* Ax. FF

Ste-Anne-d'Auray   **F 6**

L'Auberge
56 rte Vannes, Ste-Anne-d'Auray, 56400 Auray. Tel (97) 57 61 55. Restaurant, with some rooms, near the sanctuary of Ste-Anne. *Closed Mon.* **F**

Vannes   **G 7**

La Benjamine
7 rue des Halles, 56000 Vannes. Tel (97) 54 08 34. Restaurant full of atmosphere, in the heart of the pedestrianised section of the medieval city. *Closed Wed.* A.V. **FF**

Crêperie Charleston
Rue de la Fontaine, 56000 Vannes. Tel (97) 54 05 00. Restaurant and crêperie near the cathedral, specialising in fish soup and sea-food. *Closed Sun lunch & Mon.* **F**

Le Lys
1 rue Maréchal Leclerc, 56000 Vannes. Tel (97) 47 29 30. Restaurant near the Préfecture, specialising in *cuisine nouvelle.* *Open daily.* **FF**

Countryside

Belle-Ile-en-Mer   **DE 9–10**
9mi/14.5km S of Quiberon. Pop 5300. The largest of Brittany's offshore islands, Belle-Ile is 10.5mi/7km long and 5.5mi/9km across at its widest point. Its 50mi/80km of coastline, contrasting rocky headlands with small beaches and creeks, makes it a favourite with both holidaymakers and artists. Monet, Derain and Matisse came to paint, while among writers Dumas, Flaubert and Proust visited the island.

The ferry trip from Quiberon to Le Palais, Belle-Ile's little capital, takes about 45 minutes. Apart from Le Palais, there are only three other places of any size: Bangor, which shares its name with the Welsh city; Locmaria; and Sauzon, whose name is Breton for 'Saxon' or 'English'. The English connection became reality in 1761, when British troops conquered Belle-Ile and occupied it for two years, exchanging it in 1763 for Canada by the Treaty of Paris. During this short period the English succeeded in introducing the potato to the island, but apart from that their influence was minimal.

The citadel that dominates Le Palais was built in the 16th century and strengthened in the 17th by Vauban, Louis XIV's great military architect. The *landes* (moors) outside the villages are dotted with menhirs and other megalithic remains. According to legend, a pair of stones on the south side of the island, known as Jean and Jeanne de Runello, were once human lovers. But Jeanne was a peasant girl while Jean was a bard and hence a member of the ruling class; when he refused to give her up, his fellow Druids turned them both into stone.

For many years the famous 19thC actress Sarah Bernhardt owned an old fortress on Belle-Ile, where she spent the summer shooting seagulls and looking after a household menagerie that included a wildcat and a boa constrictor.

Camp de Coëtquidan-St-Cyr   **K 4**
9.5mi/15km E of Ploërmel. A huge plateau of heathland, 13,500 acres/5470 hectares in extent, is now the training ground for officers of the French army. Except when manoeuvres are actually taking place, it is possible to take the minor roads over the heath, which give wide views over the surrounding wild countryside. The military academy can also be driven past, and there is a small museum devoted to French military glories.

Champ des Martyrs   **F 6**
1mi//2km N of Auray. The 'Field of the Martyrs', consisting of a grassy rectangle with a small temple at one end, commemorates an atrocity that took place in the later stages of the French Revolution, when Royalists from Brittany and the Vendée (known as Chouans) were fighting the revolutionary forces. In 1795, after the Chouans had been defeated at Quiberon, over 900 of them were taken to this field and summarily shot without trial.

Côte Sauvage   **D 8**
On Quiberon Peninsula. The west coast of the Quiberon Peninsula, facing into the full force of the Atlantic wind and waves, has been pounded and fretted by the

elements into a rocky landscape of rugged majesty. From the coast road some of the strange rock formations can be visited, among them the Old Woman (La Vieille) and the Bull's Cave (Grottes du Taureau).

Forêt de Camors   **F 5**
2.5mi/4km S of Baud. A splendid stretch of woodland about 4mi/6.5km square, consisting largely of beech trees. At its heart are the remains of a Roman camp.

Forêt de Pont-Calleck   **CD 3–4**
15.5mi/25km N of Lorient. A small but highly picturesque forest, by the upper waters of the Scorff River. Just to the north is a 19thC château, looking across Pont-Calleck lake.

Golfe du Morbihan   **G 7–8**
S & SW of Vannes. In Breton, '*Mor Bihan*' means the 'Little Sea', in contrast to the '*Mor Braz*' or 'Great Sea' around the shores of the country. Linked by a single channel to the open waters of Quiberon Bay, the Gulf is an enormous lagoon, 7.5mi/12km across, dotted with islands large and small, a place of open skies and spectacular sunsets. All round are the standing stones and tumuli of men of the Stone Age, to whom Morbihan seems to have had some special religious significance. Fortunately for the peace and tranquillity of the people who live round the Gulf, the narrow channel between the Pointe de Kerpenhir and Port-Navalo has never been bridged. This means that to get from one side to the other—a distance of only 220yds/200m or so—you have to drive 40.5mi/65km via Auray and Vannes, going round the complete circumference in the process.
With its 125mi/200km of coast and muddy creeks, and its dozens of islands (tradition says there are 365, one for every day of the year), the Gulf is a paradise for the small-boat sailor, the birdwatcher, and the lover of open air and the changing moods of sea, land and sky.

Ile d'Arz   **G 7**
5mi/8km S of Vannes. An island in the Gulf of Morbihan, reached by boat from Vannes. Its village church is Romanesque in part, and

there are several menhirs. '*Arz*' is Breton for 'bear', dating from a time when the wild life was fiercer than it is today.

Ile de Groix   **BC 7**
4mi/6.5km SW of Lorient. Pop 2700. About 5mi/8km long and 1.5mi/2.5km wide, Groix is largely surrounded by tall cliffs. The boat trip from Lorient takes about 45 minutes. In former times, Groix was a centre of tunny-fishing, but this occupation has now given way to small-boat fishing and pleasure trips out to sea.

Ile d'Hoëdic   **F 10**
10mi/16km E of Belle-Ile. Pop 100. This tiny island, 1.5mi/2.5km by 0.5mi/1km, forms a pair with Houat (*see below*) and is about 30 minutes from it by boat. Archaeological evidence shows that it has been inhabited since prehistoric times.

Ile d'Houat   **F 9**
7.5mi/12km NE of Belle-Ile. Pop 400. Slightly larger than Hoëdic (3mi/5km long by 1mi/1.5km wide), Houat likewise has prehistoric remains. There is a small sandy beach. The boat trip from Quiberon takes about an hour.

Ile aux Moines   **G 7**
6.5mi/10.5km SW of Vannes. The largest of the islands that dot the Gulf of Morbihan, the 'Monks' Island' is about 4mi/6.5km long and is famous for the mildness of its climate, which allows subtropical flowers and plants to flourish. It gets its name from the monks who were given it in the 9th century by the king of Brittany, and curiously enough is shaped like an irregular cross. There are a number of megalithic monuments on the island, notably the Penhap dolmen at the southern end. A regular ferry service across the narrow channel operates from Port Blanc, on the mainland.

Lac de Guerlédan   **EF 4**
10mi/16km NW of Pontivy. The southern side of the lake forms the boundary between Morbihan and Côtes-du-Nord. (*See Côtes-du-Nord.*)

Landes de Lanvaux   **H–J 6**
10mi/16km inland from Vannes. The Lanvaux heathlands are the

eroded remains of a mountain ridge, about 32mi/51km long by 3mi/5km broad, running roughly from Baud in the west to Rochefort-en-Terre in the east. Until the last century the region was a barren wilderness, but it is now largely tamed, with chestnuts and conifers, and agricultural crops of all sorts.

Towards the end of World War II, at the time of the Allied invasion of France in June 1944, the Landes saw a heroic operation against the Germans by a combined force of French paratroopers and members of the Breton resistance. A full-scale pitched battle took place near the village of St-Marcel, just west of Malestroit, commemorated by a memorial deep in the countryside.

Montagnes Noires, near Gourin

Montagnes Noires **AB 2–3**
In the north-west corner of the Morbihan. Though the Black Mountains are mainly in the Côtes-du-Nord and Finistère, owing to the irregular nature of boundaries they also intrude into the Morbihan. One Morbihan town, Gourin, can be described as belonging properly to this range of hills. (*See also Côtes-du-Nord.*)

Pointe d'Arradon **G 7**
4mi/6.5km SW of Vannes. A headland in the Gulf of Morbihan. The view across the water and islands large and small is spectacular, especially early in the morning.

Pointe de Conguel **E 8**
2.5mi/4km E of Quiberon. This headland, at the southern tip of the Quiberon Peninsula, gives wide panoramas across the sea to Belle-Ile (south) and the small island of Houat (south-east).

Pointe de Kerpenhir **F 8**
9mi/14.5km S of Auray. Facing across the narrow entrance of the Gulf of Morbihan to the Rhuys Peninsula, this promontory is an excellent vantage point for watching the yachts on a fine summer day. At the end of the promontory, a German World War II blockhouse and a statue of the Virgin make an incongruous pair.

Presqu'Ile de Quiberon **E 8**
15.5mi/25km SW of Auray. Until comparatively recent times, the Quiberon Peninsula was a separate island, and it is still only joined to the mainland by a narrow sandy isthmus. The western side is rocky and inhospitable (*see Côte Sauvage, above*), while on the east there are the long sandy beaches of Quiberon Bay, deservedly popular with tourists in summer.

Quiberon Bay has seen important battles on three separate occasions. In 56BC Julius Caesar defeated the Gauls in these waters as a prelude to his conquest of Brittany; in 1759 the English fleet defeated the French during the Seven Years' War; and in 1795 the Revolutionary army, under General Hoche, routed a combined Anglo-French expeditionary force, allied with the Breton Royalists known as Chouans. After the battle many of the Royalists were rounded up and shot (*see Champ des Martyrs*). If possible, avoid the single main road down the peninsula on summer weekends, as it is liable to be solid with traffic.

Presqu'Ile de Rhuys **G 8**
Across the Gulf of Morbihan from Vannes. The Rhuys Peninsula forms the southern side of the Gulf of Morbihan. Its climate is very mild, and at one time it was famous for its wine, though vines are no longer grown here. At its western end, Port-Navalo faces the Pointe de Kerpenhir across the narrow channel between Quiberon Bay and the Gulf of Morbihan.

Rivière d'Auray **F 6**
S & N from Auray. Some of the prettiest and gentlest countryside in the Morbihan lies round this river, which runs into the Gulf of Morbihan. Its many creeks are very popular with small-boat sailors.

Islet off St-Cado, Rivière d'Etel

Rivière d'Etel   **D 6**
Between Lorient & Auray. The
Rivière d'Etel is not really a river at
all, but an inland lagoon, studded
with islets and latticed with tiny
peninsulas, like a smaller version of
the Gulf of Morbihan. The
entrance to the Etel, south of the
village of the same name, is
blocked by a sandbank, the Barre
d'Etel, which can cause difficulties
to yachtsmen as the tide falls.

Entertainment

Casino de Quiberon   **E 8**
2 bvd de la Mer, 56170 Quiberon.
Tel (97) 50 23 57. This casino has a
disco ('Le Squal-Club') and pizzeria
as well as gaming-rooms. *Open
nightly in summer.*

Discothèques

Le Bilboquet   **E 8**
14 rue de Kervozès, 56170
Quiberon. Tel (97) 50 13 88. *Open
nightly in summer to 04.00.* **Charge**

Cap 3000   **D 5**
56700 Hennebont. Tel (97) 65 26
46. Club and disco. *Open Sat &
Sun only.* **Charge**

Les Chandelles   **E 7**
56340 Carnac-Plage. Tel (97) 52 13
80. Night club and disco. *Open
nightly in summer 16.30–04.00.*
Charge

Le Suroît   **E 8**
29 rue de Port-Maria, 56170
Quiberon. Tel (97) 50 10 67. Disco
and night club. *Open to 04.00.*
Charge

Leisure activities

Golf

Golf de St-Laurent   **E 7**
Ploëmel, 56400 Auray. 7mi/11km
SW of Auray. Tel (97) 24 31 72.
An 18-hole course, in the St-
Laurent Leisure Park. *Open all year
09.00–18.00.*

Sailing

Club Nautique St-Jacques   **G 8**
Port St-Jacques, 56370 Sarzeau. Tel
(97) 41 84 69.

**Ecole de Croisière Jacques
Riguidel**   **E 8**
40 rue de Port-Maria, 56170
Quiberon. Tel (97) 50 19 64.

Société Nautique   **E 8**
Port de Plaisance, 56170 Quiberon.
Tel (97) 50 17 45. In the marina.

Seawater cure

Centre de Thalassothérapie   **E 7**
BP 83, 56340 Carnac. Tel (97) 52
04 44. Cures for rheumatic
complaints, also for stress caused
by city living. *Open all year.*

Institut de Thalassothérapie **E 8**
BP 170, 56170 Quiberon. Tel (97)
50 20 00. Everything from mud
baths to radiography in this ultra-
modern health centre. Heated
swimming pool. *Closed Jan.*

Excursions

Boat trips

Les Vedettes Vertes   **G 8**
La Rabine, 56000 Vannes. Tel (97)
47 10 78. Excursions all round the
Gulf are run by the Vedettes
Vertes. They operate from Vannes
with departures from there and
from Auray, Locmariaquer and
Port-Navalo, to the islands of the
Gulf (Ile d'Arz, Ile aux Moines,
Gavrinis), along the Auray River,
and out to sea to Belle-Ile, Houat
and Hoëdic. Regular services
1 Mar–30 Sep.

Coach trips

Quiberon Voyages   E 8
21 pl Hoche, 56170 Quiberon. Tel
(97) 50 15 30. A luxury coach service
to beaches and inland sites, to the
major *pardons*; also links to boat
services to the offshore islands.

Festivals

Main *pardons* of the Morbihan:

Last Sun in Jun   C 3
Le Faouët, Ste-Barbe (Barbara).

Jul 25–26   F 6
Ste-Anne-d'Auray.

Aug 15   E 3
Quelven, Notre-Dame.

2nd Sun in Sep   E 7
Carnac, St-Cornély.

2nd Sun in Sep   I 4
Josselin, Notre-Dame-du-Roncier.

Last Sun in Sep   D 5
Hennebont, Notre-Dame-du-Voeu.

Tours by car

These routes are between
63mi/100km and 94mi/150km, and
can be comfortably done in
a day.

Around Josselin
From Josselin, take the Baud road
west, then the D778 to Guéhenno
with its superb calvary. To
Locminé and Baud, see the Vénus
de Quinipily a short way along the
Hennebont road (N24). To
Pontivy via the Chapel of St-
Nicodème (1.5mi/2.5km W of
N168). From Pontivy, take the D2

east to Rohan, then to La Trinité-
Porhoët and from there south east
to Ploërmel (fine country town).
From Ploërmel, back to Josselin by
way of the Colonne des Trente,
scene of a famous medieval battle
between 30 Breton and 30 English
knights.

Auray, Carnac & the coast
Beginning from Auray, head north
east to Ste-Anne-d'Auray, with its
enormous pilgrim church and
concourse. Then south to the little
Chapel of St-Avoye, and back
through Auray to Locmariaquer
with its stone remains (Table des
Marchands, Grand Menhir Brisé).
Out to the Pointe de Kerpenhir.
Then over the Crach estuary to La
Trinité-sur-Mer (yachting centre),
follow the coast road to Carnac-
Plage, then inland to Carnac
(prehistory museum). Explore the
alignments of standing stones, then
climb tumulus of St-Michel for
view of whole area. Through
Erdeven to beautiful St-Cado
Chapel, in Etel lagoon. Back to
Auray by D22.

**Gulf of Morbihan & Rhuys
Peninsula**
A circuit in two sections, with
Vannes as the central point. From
Vannes, head south west to the
Pointe d'Arradon, with spectacular
views over the Gulf. To Port-Blanc
(possibility of short boat trip over to
Ile aux Moines). Down to Larmor-
Baden, then take D101 which
crosses Bono River by high bridge,

Château de Josselin

with fine views of oyster beds.
Back via Ste-Anne-d'Auray.
For the Rhuys Peninsula, head
south east from Vannes along
N165, then south along D780. Take
minor parallel road where possible
(St-Armel–St-Colombier). To
Sarzeau (nice old town), past Butte
de César (where Caesar watched his
fleet defeat the Gauls), through
Arzon to Port-Navalo at west end
of peninsula. To St-Gildas-de-
Rhuys, then magnificent Suscinio
Château, one of the finest in Mor-
bihan. Follow winding coast road
to Le Tour du Parc, then inland to
Surzur and back to Vannes.

Hills & valleys of the interior
(Owing to the irregular boundary
between Morbihan and Finistère,
this route starts at Quimperlé, over
the Finistère border.) From
Quimperlé, head north to Le
Faouët, with its two superb chapels
(St-Fiacre and Ste-Barbe) and its
impressive 16thC market building.
To Gourin in the Montagnes
Noires, heading west towards Scaër
(in Finistère), then north through
Guiscriff. East of Gourin, follow
winding D128 to Langonnet and
12thC Langonnet Abbey. Back
to Quimperlé along picturesque
D790.

Ille-et-Vilaine

This département gets its name from its two main rivers, and rightly so, as they have largely shaped its history. The two meet at Rennes, which is the capital both of Ille-et-Vilaine and of Brittany. From Rennes the Ille flows north, joining the Rance just south of Dinan in the Côtes-du-Nord; it is navigable to St-Malo as the Ille et Rance Canal. The Vilaine meanders southwards to Redon, where it crosses the Brest–Nantes Canal before reaching the sea near the Gulf of Morbihan. In earlier centuries the rivers were of far greater commercial importance than they are today, but they still serve a useful purpose as waterways for a growing army of pleasure craft, bringing unspoilt countryside to people tired of the eternal battle with road traffic.

In character, Ille-et-Vilaine is the least Breton of all the Brittany départements. It has always been a French-speaking rather than a Breton-speaking region, and it has none of the religious *pardons* or the typical Breton calvaries that become more frequent the further west you go. In earlier times it formed a buffer between France and the independent Duchy of Brittany—a status typified by the mighty frontier castles of Fougères and Vitré, guarding the eastern approaches to Rennes and frequently besieged during the endless wars of the Middle Ages.

If Ille-et-Vilaine seems more French than Breton, it has two claims to uniqueness that do not belong to either side. On its extreme western edge, where its frontier dovetails into the Morbihan with a jigsaw-like lack of regularity, is the Forest of Paimpont, once part of the vast Forest of Brocéliande. Here the Druids had their university, undergoing a long apprenticeship of 20 years or so; and here, even more than in our own West Country, is the centre for the survival of King Arthur and the knights of the Round Table, who live on in legend and place names, haunting the lakes and woodland with memories of Lancelot and Guinevere, Merlin and Arthur himself. In contrast to this imprecise region of magic and fantasy, the sturdy walls of St-Malo away to the north are solidly planted on the edge of the sea. No other town in Brittany had St-Malo's combination of adventurousness and independence, typified by the corsairs who scoured the seas for 200 years, and it is fitting that it should still be most visitors' first introduction to Brittany.

As a place for a seaside holiday, Ille-et-Vilaine cannot compare with the other Breton départements, though it has in Dinard the earliest of Brittany's resorts, where tourists have been flocking for well over a century. So it tends to be a region that people rush through on their way south to the Loire valley and the warmer parts of France, or west to the Côtes-du-Nord and Finistère. But anyone who stops in Ille-et-Vilaine to explore its quiet byways will be well rewarded by its contrasts of secluded river valleys and stretches of woodland, and by the dozens of sleepy towns and hidden villages that the tourist boom has so far passed by.

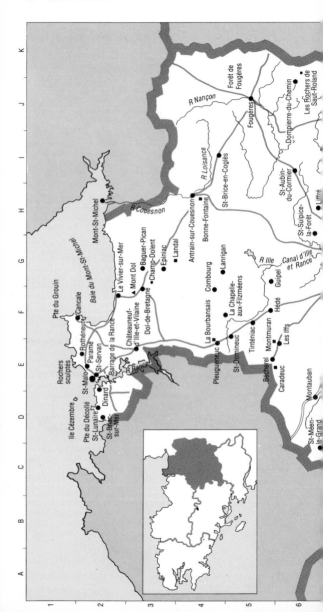

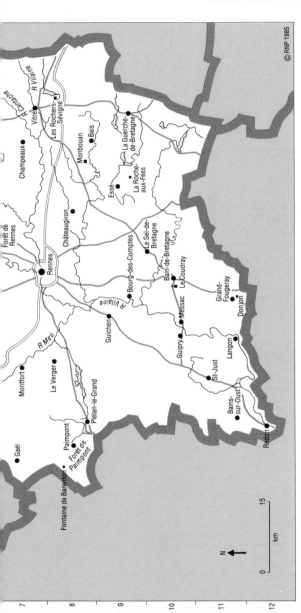

© RNP 1985

Towns & villages

Antrain-sur-Couesnon   **H 4**
28mi/45km N of Rennes. Pop 1500.
A small country town near the
Normandy border, at the junction
of the Couesnon and the Loisance.
The church is 12thC Romanesque
in part, and there are a few 15th
and 16thC houses in the town.
The Château de Bonne-Fontaine is
just outside the town.

Bain-de-Bretagne   **G 10**
18mi/29km S of Rennes. Pop 5100.
A crossroads town on the main road
between Rennes and Nantes,
usually choked with traffic. It is
worth stopping to see the peaceful
little lake on the south-west side of
the town, which has an attractive
lakeside walk and is popular with
local fishermen. About 0.5mi/1km
W of the town is the 17thC Chapel
of Le Coudray. Inside is a stone
with a small cavity, the size of a
child's foot, into which mothers
used to place the feet of children
with walking problems.

Bains-sur-Oust   **D 11**
4mi/6.5km N of Redon. Pop 800.
The origins of this village go back
to the time of the Romans, who
called it 'Aquae Rothonae' ('Redon
Waters'), and presumably had a
bath complex here. In AD845 a
historic battle was fought just
outside Bains, when the Frankish
king Charles the Bald was defeated
by the Breton Nominoë, who
thereupon declared Brittany an
independent dukedom. A statue of
Nominoë stands in front of the
village church.

Bécherel   **E 5**
19.5mi/31km NW of Rennes. Pop
875. A village in a fine situation,
with wide views to the north in the
direction of Dol-de-Bretagne. A
few old houses still survive, but the
Medieval castle has vanished. In
feudal times the lord of Bécherel
had an unusual right over his
vassals. On Easter Monday he
would burn any flax or hemp that
had not been got ready for weaving,
to teach the women of Bécherel not
to be lazy.

Cancale   **F 2**
9mi/14.5km E of St-Malo. Pop
4900. This picturesque fishing port
faces east across the Bay of Mont-
St-Michel, and is famous for the
quality and size of its oysters, which
grow to perfection in the rich silt
of the bay. The modern church and
large shops are in the upper town,
from which a steep hill leads down
to the harbour, and the quayside
lined with bars, restaurants, and old
ladies selling oysters from open-air
stalls. At low tide the stone-built
oyster tanks become visible; here
the oysters are kept to get rid of
their impurities in mud-free water.
Offshore are the *parcs* where the
oysters grow in the mud, and are
regularly visited when the tide is
right by the growers, who chug out
to them in their flat-bottomed boats
(*chalands*). There are three main
types of oyster: the giant oysters,
weighing up to 1.1lb/500gms,
known as *pieds de cheval* (horses'
hooves); flat oysters (*plates*), called
Bélons, originating from the Bélon
River in Finistère; and *creuses*
(hollow oysters), also called
Portugaises, but now largely bred
from Japanese stock. Long before
the Revolution, Cancale oysters
were so highly esteemed that Louis
XIV used to have convoys of them
sent to him twice a week at
Versailles.
Smaller than St-Malo, Cancale
makes a good centre for exploring
the Emerald Coast, the Bay of
Mont-St-Michel, and the quiet
inland scenery of Ille-et-Vilaine.

Châteaugiron   **H 8**
10mi/16km SE of Rennes. Pop
3300. This compact little town,
built round a Medieval castle, still
has a good many of its ancient
houses. First built in the 11th
century, the castle was often
besieged, and was repaired and
altered until the 18th century.
During the Middle Ages the
seigneur of Châteaugiron had the
right, on Easter Monday, of
throwing into the water of the moat
any fishmongers who had
overcharged during the previous
year—a custom known as the
'fishmongers' leap' ('*saut des
poissonniers*').

Châteauneuf-d'Ille-et-Vilaine   **E 3**
9mi/14.5km S of St-Malo. Pop
1200. A small town of no particular
interest, with one ruined tower
surviving from its Medieval
château. Its park is said to be

haunted by the ghost of Renée de Rieux, mistress of Henri III of France, born in the château in 1550 and known as 'la Belle de Châteauneuf'.

Combourg   **F 4**
23mi/37km N of Rennes. Pop 4700. MD Mon. The pretty little town of Combourg clusters tightly round its château, and is best seen from across the lake on its south side, with the castle's pointed turrets, surrounded by tall trees, reflected in the water. When the English agricultural writer Arthur Young visited Combourg in 1788, he called it 'one of the most brutal filthy places that can be seen'. Fortunately it has been repaired and cleaned up in the past 200 years, and is now justifiably classified as a 'Petite Cité de Caractère'.
Combourg is best known today as the town where the great 19thC writer Chateaubriand spent his childhood shortly before the Revolution (*see Château de Combourg*). Apart from the château, there are one or two streets of old houses in its immediate neighbourhood that are well worth seeing. The church is 19thC.

Dinard   **E 2**
14mi/22.5km N of Dinan. Pop 9600. MD Tue, Thur & Sat. Apart from La Baule away to the south, Dinard is the only resort in Brittany to rival the sophistication of Deauville or Le Touquet. It has superb beaches, a casino, a small aerodrome, and a wide choice of hotels. Because of its nearness to St-Malo, until the 1950s it was the favourite Breton resort with British holidaymakers.
Until the 1850s, Dinard was nothing more than a small fishing village attached to St-Enogat, a short way to the west. At about that time wealthy visitors from England started spending their summers here, in rented cottages; and it was really put on the map as a resort by an American called Coppinger, who built a château here and launched a building wave. Its period of greatest growth came between the wars, and Dinard, with its old-fashioned hotels and genteel atmosphere, seems to have remained in that idyllic pre-1939

period ever since.
Apart from its own attractions, Dinard is a good centre for excursions inland up the Rance to Dinan and beyond, to St-Malo across the Rance barrage, and to St-Cast and the other resorts of the Emerald Coast.

Cathedral, Dol-de-Bretagne

Dol-de-Bretagne   **F 3**
15mi/24km SE of St-Malo. Pop 5100. This ancient and very attractive town is the first place of any consequence in Brittany reached by visitors driving from Cherbourg or the Pas de Calais. The name Dol is Breton for 'table' (as in dolmen, 'table stone'), and it probably derives from the flat-topped Mont Dol just north of the town. For centuries the seat of a bishopric, Dol has a strangely arresting cathedral, and one of the finest Medieval town streets in Brittany.
In AD848 the first duke of an independent Brittany, Nominoë, was crowned at Dol, and during the Middle Ages and later centuries the town was much fought over. In 1075 William the Conqueror besieged it unsuccessfully; in 1164 Henry II captured it; and six centuries later, in 1758, the English took it in the course of the Seven Years' War and destroyed the fortifications. In 1795 the last bishop of Dol was captured at Quiberon with the Chouans (anti-Revolutionary Bretons) and shot (*see also Champ des Martyrs, Morbihan*).
Nowadays Dol is an agricultural centre, specialising in sheep reared on the nearby salt meadows (*moutons de pré salé*). An important fair is held here at the end of *Oct*.

Epiniac   **G 3**
4mi/6.5km SE of Dol-de-Bretagne. Pop 500. An undistinguished village

with a modern church, and the source of a typical Breton legend. This concerns the 'washerwomen of the night' (*lavandières de la nuit*)—women of Epiniac who were so idle during the week that they had to catch up with their work on Sunday. As the penalty for their sins, they spend eternity washing clothes by night, lit by the flames of ghostly candles. If anyone comes by and sees them at work, they ask him to help with wringing out their linen; but if he lends a hand, his death is sure to follow.

Fougères J 5
30mi/48km N of Rennes. Pop 27,700. MD Fri. For centuries one of the main frontier towns between Brittany and the rest of France, Fougères has a superb Medieval castle excellently preserved. The town is in two parts: the upper, more recent half, with the main shops and administrative buildings, and the lower Medieval town, consisting of the castle, the ancient church of St-Sulpice, and jumbled streets of old houses.

Château, Fougères

Its key strategic position meant that Fougères was much fought over during the Middle Ages. Its most famous *seigneur* was the 12thC Raoul de Fougères, who made the castle one of the most powerful in Europe. Fougères was the birthplace in the 18th century of the Marquis de la Rouërie, the chief instigator of the rebellion against the Revolution among Royalists in Brittany and the Vendée. La Rouërie himself died in 1793; but the revolt continued spasmodically until 1804. Balzac's novel 'Les Chouans', which tells the story of the rebellion, is set largely in and around Fougères.
For more than a century Fougères has been a centre of shoe

manufacture, and still keeps up the tradition. During the summer, *son-et-lumière* shows are given in the courtyard of the castle.

La Guerche-de-Bretagne J 9
14mi/22.5km S of Vitré. Pop 3900. MD Tue. A small country town with a central square of fine old houses, and a 13thC church enlarged and rebuilt at various periods. The curious name is said to derive from a Frankish word '*werki*', meaning a fortified hill. A number of the oldest houses have their upper storeys supported on massive wooden pillars. In recent years La Guerche has become something of a craft centre. On *15 Aug* each year the town holds a grand festival, when a 17thC statue of the Virgin is carried in solemn procession through the streets.

Guipry–Messac F 10
25mi/40km SW of Rennes. Pop 2415. Guipry and Messac are two villages separated by the Vilaine River, but they share a joint waterfront half-way between them. Guipry-Messac is central to the navigable waterway system of Brittany. From its canal basin or quayside, boating enthusiasts can head north up the Vilaine to Rennes and there link up with the Canal d'Ille et Rance, navigable to Dinan and St-Malo; or south to join the Nantes–Brest Canal at Redon. The Guipry–Messac waterfront is the ideal place for watching the boating world go by.

Hédé F 5
14mi/22.5km N of Rennes. Pop 550. An attractive small hilltop town, above the Ille et Rance Canal. The Romanesque church with its tall spire dates from the 12th century, and some fragments survive of its 11thC castle, demolished at the end of the 16th century. At Hédé, the canal falls 89ft/27m through a dramatic flight of 11 stepwise locks ('Les Onze Ecluses'), and both the canal and the lakes round about are popular with fishermen. Since 1974 Hédé has been the headquarters of a Paris-trained ballet-theatre company, who put on a week-long festival each *Aug*, with dance, jazz and classical concerts, and a 'pocket theatre'.

Montfort   E 7

14mi/22.5km W of Rennes. Pop
4500. A small town on the Meu
River, with some remains of its
Medieval fortifications. For
hundreds of years it was known as
Montfort-la-Cane (Montfort-the-
Duck), after a legendary event that
took place in 1386. One day a
beautiful girl came to the castle,
bringing some food to her father,
who was working on the walls.
Unfortunately the evil baron of
Montfort saw her, seized her and
locked her up in one of his castle
towers until he could have his
wicked way with her. The girl
called upon St Nicholas to help her,
was immediately transformed into
a duck, and flew out of the tower
window to a nearby lake. And for
350 years afterwards, on the
anniversary of the transformation, a
duck, followed by a dozen
ducklings, would waddle up to the
church and attend Mass in
Montfort's Church of St Nicholas.

Paimpont   C 8

25mi/40km W of Rennes. Pop
1600. An unusual little town, with a
single main street entered through
an ancient gate, leading to a large
Medieval abbey. The abbey was
founded in the 7th century; the
present large abbey church was
built in the 13th century and much
altered in the 15th and 17th. Part
of the monastic buildings is now
the town hall. The surroundings of
Paimpont, beside a lake and in the
middle of the ancient Forest of
Brocéliande, are exceptionally
beautiful.

Paramé   E 2

1.5mi/2.5km W of St-Malo. MD
Wed & Sat. Pop: see St-Malo. Now
swallowed up by St-Malo, Paramé
is a resort in its own right, quite
distinct from its grand neighbour.
In the countryside on the western
outskirts of Paramé are some fine
Malouinières—country houses built
in the 17th and 18th centuries by
wealthy shipowners and corsairs.

Redon   D 12

40mi/64km SW of Rennes. Pop
11,000. A small market town,
which stands at the crossing-point
of the Vilaine River and the
Nantes–Brest Canal. A Benedictine
monastery was founded here in

AD832, destroyed soon after by the
Norsemen, but rebuilt on the
grandest scale. The Basilica of St-
Sauveur, with a tower that is the
finest example of Romanesque
architecture in the whole of
Brittany, was originally the abbey
church. A few old houses survive
in the Grande rue, behind the
church. The railway runs at the
very foot of the church, which
means that drivers often have to
wait for the level crossing to open
before they can reach it.
Redon has had a good deal of recent
industrial expansion. It is best
known for its chestnuts, which are
made into *marrons glacés*.

Rennes   G 7

216mi/345km W of Paris. Pop
206,000. MD Sat. The capital both
of Ille-et-Vilaine and of the whole
of Brittany, Rennes is a major city
in its own right. It has a solidly
prosperous business and shopping
centre, and a rapidly expanding
suburbia of industry and high-rise
flats. The Vilaine runs across it
from east to west, either between
embankments or driven
underground in the interests of
parking space, with a regular grid
pattern of streets north and south
of the river. The main buildings
along the Vilaine are in sober
Classical 19thC style; but the city is
saved from visual dullness by its
plantings of flowers, which enliven
every open space.
Rennes (called Roazon in Breton)
gets its name from the Redones,
one of the Celtic tribes conquered
by Caesar. In Roman times it was
a strongly fortified town, at the
confluence of the Ille and Vilaine
rivers and the junction of three
main Roman roads. A glance at the
map will show that Rennes today is
still at the centre of the Breton road
network, with ten major roads
radiating from it to all parts of the
country. The Roman town was
almost certainly where Medieval
Rennes was built, in the area just
north of the river round the
cathedral. This is virtually the only
part of the city to preserve any
aspect of ancient Rennes, since
most of it was burnt down in a
disastrous fire in 1720. The fire
meant that the Rennais could
rebuild more or less from scratch,

on a classical grid pattern rather than using the haphazard medieval street plan. This 'new' 18thC quarter, of shops and houses built of granite to a sober and uniform design, is now carefully preserved. Rennes' grandest building is the 17thC Palais de Justice, not far from the river. Once the seat of the Breton parliament, it links the city with Brittany's troubled history. Between 1554 and the Revolution, the parliament (Etats) at Rennes had a semi-independence under the overall rule of France; but after 1790, when France was divided into départements, Brittany disappeared as a separate entity, and Rennes reverted to being a provincial capital.

Apart from its administrative buildings, central Rennes has one of the finest public gardens in France, the 25-acre/10-hectare Jardin du Thabor, once the garden of a Benedictine monastery. Modern architecture is exemplified by the graceful twin blocks of flats, 30 storeys high, known as Les Jumelles ('The Twins'); and the new university complex is one of the world's most up-to-date centres of electronic teaching. Since 1980, the old centre of Rennes has held a festival in the *2nd wk in Jul*. Called 'La Tombée de la Nuit' ('Nightfall'), it is largely a street festival devoted to all aspects of contemporary Breton culture.

Rothéneuf   E   2
4mi/6.5km NE of St-Malo. Pop: *see St-Malo*. Though officially classified as part of St-Malo, Rothéneuf is far enough away to have kept its own identity, with streets of small 19thC villas, and a single good beach. Rothéneuf is best known for its 'Rochers Sculptés'—a surrealist group of rock carvings above the sea, where earlier this century an eccentric recluse, the Abbé Fouré, spent 25 years of his life carving grotesque figures of corsairs, peasants, devils and sea monsters. As the years go by they are getting steadily worn back to the rock from which they were carved, and soon there will be little of them left.

St-Aubin-du-Cormier   I   6
12.5mi/20km SW of Fougères. Pop 1500. The ruined castle of St-Aubin,

once an important frontier town but now hardly more than a village, stands on a rock above the Couesnon River. In July 1488 St-Aubin was the scene of a decisive battle between the French and the Bretons, in which the Bretons were routed, and many of the survivors massacred. The battle was followed by a humiliating treaty for the Bretons, in which Duke François II of Brittany signed over various Breton rights to King Charles VIII of France. This treaty (the Traité du Verger) marked the beginning of the end of Breton independence.

St-Briac-sur-Mer   D   2
5.5mi/9km W of Dinard. Pop 1600. A quiet little seaside resort on the borders of Ille-et-Vilaine and the Côtes-du-Nord. It has good beaches, a small boating and fishing harbour, and spectacular views west towards St-Cast. In the 1920s members of the exiled imperial Russian family settled in St-Briac.

St-Brice-en-Coglès   I   4
9.5mi/15km NW of Fougères. Pop 1100. A long, straggling village, and a centre of granite-quarrying, St-Brice was famous for sorcery and witchcraft until quite recently. Known as '*faïnoux*', the sorcerers would cast spells on crops, animals and human beings; while others could call up hordes of rats, induce lightning, or prevent a neighbour's cow from giving milk. The region was also known for the goblins and other spirits that haunted its roads by night, among them '*loups garous*', or werewolves, and a terrifying witch known as 'Bête Martine'.

St-Lunaire   D   2
3mi/5km W of Dinard. Pop 1600. A small seaside resort, built along the sides of a peninsula, with two good beaches, one facing north east, the other north west. There are fine views along the Emerald Coast from the Pointe du Décollé, at the end of the peninsula. A tomb said to be that of St-Lunaire, who came to Brittany from Ireland in the 6th century, is kept in the village church.

St-Malo   E   2
39mi/62.5km N of Rennes. Pop 46,300. MD Tue & Fri. The pride of the inhabitants of St-Malo in

their wave-beaten town is summed up by their motto, "*Malouin d'abord, breton peut-être, français s'il en reste*" ("A St-Malo man first, a Breton perhaps, a Frenchman if there's anything left over"). The ideal way to come to Brittany is across the sea to St-Malo, preferably in the early morning, when the grey shape of the little town appears through its protecting cluster of rocky islets like a ship at anchor. Though the present St-Malo is largely a reconstruction, made necessary by the immense damage the town suffered in World War II, the restoration has been so well done that a 17thC corsair returned from the dead would have no difficulty in finding his way to the quayside, and then through the gates into the streets of the ancient town that has seen little change in the past 300 years.

St-Malo's origins go back to the 6th century, when a Welsh monk, St Maclou or Malo, landed on the peninsula of Aleth (now St-Servan), to convert the Romanised Gauls living there. During the centuries of attacks by the Norsemen, the people of Aleth took refuge on an uninhabited island—the site of St-Malo, which only became attached to the mainland in the 18th century by a build-up of sand. The bishopric of Aleth was transferred to the island in the 12th century, and the town of St-Malo was born.

From the outset it was of great strategic importance during the everlasting wars with the English, through its position at the mouth of the Rance, guarding access to the heartland of Brittany. The Malouins became some of the most skilled sailors in the whole of France, producing explorers like Jacques Cartier, the discoverer of the St Lawrence River, and the thousands of corsairs who, under captains like Duguay-Trouin and Surcouf, harried the oceans for 200 years or more. During the 17th century St-Malo was the leading port of France, trading all over the world; and though after 1700 it lost something of its prominence, it has remained an important harbour from that time until the present day.

There are two distinct St-Malos: 'Intra-Muros', the old town within the walls, and 'Extra-Muros', the resort part outside the walls, now far larger in area and taking in St-Servan, Paramé and Rothéneuf. It is the part within the walls that tourists come in their hundreds of thousands to see. With its complete circuit of ramparts, its ancient cathedral, its superb granite houses built by the shipowners (*armateurs*) in the 17th and 18th centuries, its frowning castle, and its shops and restaurants, it well deserves its popularity. It even has its own sandy beach, below the ramparts. The car-ferry terminal opened by Brittany Ferries in the 1970s has brought a new lease of life to the harbour. But besides the ferryboats, there is an enormous amount of cargo loaded and unloaded in the harbour's inner basins, while the marina beneath the walls is so crammed in summer that there is hardly an empty berth to be seen. Apart from the cross-Channel ships, there are regular services by boat and hydrofoil to the Channel Islands, and trips up the Rance to Dinan. St-Malo is also a good centre for car and coach trips along the Emerald Coast, to Mont-St-Michel, and inland to Rennes and the country round about.

St-Servan   E 2

0.5mi/1km S of St-Malo. MD Tue & Fri. Pop: *see St-Malo*. In pre-Roman times the St-Servan Peninsula, known as Aleth, was the capital of the Gaulish people called the Curiosolites, and it kept its importance through Roman and early Christian times until the bishopric of Aleth was moved to the new town of St-Malo in the 12th century. St-Servan is now one of the resorts attached to St-Malo, but it is a distinct place in its own right, separated from St-Malo by the harbour, and offering a far more open layout, with wide squares and gardens. The Tour Solidor, an imposing tower guarding St-Servan's own small harbour, was built in the 1380s, probably on Roman foundations, and is now a museum of the ships that once plied the trade routes round Cape Horn.

Vitré   **J 7**
22.5mi/36km E of Rennes. Pop
13,000. MD Mon. A frontier town
between Brittany and the rest of
France, Vitré, like Fougères a
short way to the north, has a
magnificent Medieval castle and
well preserved streets of half-
timbered houses. The town grew
up in the early Middle Ages outside
the walls of a primitive castle; the
present majestic fortress was built
mainly in the 15th century. In the
17th century the Breton parliament
met at Vitré from time to time, and
Mme de Sévigné had a townhouse
here (see *Château des Rochers-
Sévigné*). When the railway was
built in the mid-19th century, it
cut a swathe through the buildings
of old Vitré; what remains of the
medieval town now forms a '*secteur
sauvegardé*' (protected area).
Near the château is the spiky Notre-
Dame church, in 15thC
Flamboyant Gothic, with an
unusually large number of gables. In
the 16th century Vitré became a
centre for Huguenots following the
new Protestant religion. The best of
the Medieval buildings are
between the church and the
château, in the rue Baudrairie and
the streets leading off it.

Interesting buildings

Churches and other ecclesiastical
buildings are normally *open
10.00–12.00, 14.00–17.00 (18.00 in
summer)*.

Abbaye de Mont-St-Michel **H 2**
32.5mi/52km E of St-Malo. Though
Mont-St-Michel is officially in
Normandy, it is an essential part of
anyone's visit to the north-east
corner of Brittany, and so is
included here.
Seen at a distance from the road
below Avranches, or from the coast
road south of Cancale, with its spire
rising through the haze from its
bastion of rock, the abbey is still a
place of mystery and magic, in
spite of its over-exposure on tourist
brochures and posters. Getting to
and from the abbey is less of a
problem than it was before the
causeway from the mainland was
built, when visitors were warned
that they might be cut off by a tide

'as fast as a galloping horse'.
Nowadays, in high summer at least,
the tide is a human one, struggling
for a place in the overcrowded car
parks, or plodding up the steep
street to the abbey steps.
The abbey is one of the marvels of
Medieval architecture, and indeed
the finest ensemble of its Gothic
buildings is called simply that—La
Merveille, or The Marvel.
Originally Mont-St-Michel, like
Mont Dol a short way inland, was
a rocky outcrop rising from the
Forest of Scissy. But some time
between the 4th and 8th centuries
the sea swept in, drowning the
forest, and leaving the outcrop
(then known as Mont Tombe) cut
off except at low tide. As early as
the 6th century there were hermits
on the rock, and the abbey's
beginnings go back to the 8th
century, when an oratory
dedicated to St Michael was built
here. In the 9th and 10th centuries
the rock was a refuge from
marauding Norsemen; the first
abbey dates from about this time,
followed by a splendid 11th–12thC
Romanesque abbey.
What we see today is mainly the
Gothic abbey, built between the
13th and 16th centuries. Its main
feature is the astonishing Merveille
complex, on the north side, built
1210–1228 and consisting of three
levels: the monks' refectory and
cloister above; the guests' hall and
knights' hall below this; and on the
lowest level the cellar and almonry.
The abbey church was built over
many years and is a combination
of different styles. The nave is in
the severe Romanesque of the 11th
century, while the choir and east
end are in the most elaborate and
fanciful Flamboyant Gothic of the
15th and 16th centuries.
After its heyday in the Middle Ages
the abbey gradually declined, and
in the 18th century was degraded to
a prison. In 1874 it was taken over
by the State as a national
monument, and has been restored
and beautified for the past century.
The slender spire, which has an
authentically Medieval look and
completes the picture of the abbey
from a distance, in fact was added
as recently as 1897. *Open 16 Mar–
30 Sep, 09.00–11.30, 13.30–18.00
(16.00 1 Oct–15 Mar)*. **Charge**

Barrage de la Rance   E 2
3mi/5km S of St-Malo. Tel (99) 46
21 81. Though hardly a building,
this is a major construction work,
which provides a roadway across
the mouth of the Rance between St-
Malo and Dinard, and is also a
source of electrical power.
Completed in 1967, the 'Usine
Marémotrice' generates electricity
through turbines driven by the
force of the tides. A movable bridge
allows boats to enter and leave the
river.

Basilique de St-Sauveur   D 12
Redon. In town centre. Above the
central crossing of the Basilica of St-
Sauveur rises a low arcaded tower,
dating from the 12th century and
one of the finest examples of
Romanesque architecture in
Brittany. Built in a mixture of grey
granite and dark red sandstone,
with open arcading, it looks almost
as if hewn from living rock. The
nave of the basilica, originally the
church of a 9thC Benedictine
abbey, is also Romanesque, the
chancel is 13thC Gothic, and the
high altar is 17thC Baroque.
Separate from the main church is the
tall Gothic bell-tower, which has
stood isolated since much of the
nave was destroyed by fire in 1780.
On the south side is a college,
housed in abbey buildings rebuilt
in the 18th century.

Cathédrale de St-Pierre   G 7
Rennes. In city centre. Dedicated
to St Peter, and built as recently as
1787–1844, this is an austere
building, incorporating elements
of an earlier church. The interior
has ponderous columns and is
heavily gilded. Its main treasure is
a 16thC Flemish altarpiece,
illustrating scenes from the life of
the Virgin.

Cathédrale de St-Samson   F 3
Dol-de-Bretagne. In town centre.
Built mainly in the 13th century,
Dol's cathedral is a nobly
impressive church on the largest
scale. It has an oddly asymmetrical
west front, with two towers, one of
them only rising to just above roof
level; this was begun in the 16th
century but never completed. The
huge south porch, built in the
14th–15th century, is very fine.
Inside, the cathedral creates an
overwhelming effect, with its lofty
vaulting rising to 66ft/20m and its
length of 262ft/80m. The great east
window is 13thC, subsequently
restored. The 80 oak choir stalls are
15thC, and carved with foliage and
human heads.
Dol cathedral is dedicated to St-
Samson, whose life is one of the
best documented of all Brittany's
thousands of saints, as his
biography was written down early
in the 7th century, soon after his
death. He was born in Wales, and
went first to Ireland and then to
Cornwall, where there is still a St
Samson village. Around the mid-
6th century he crossed from
Cornwall to Brittany and founded
a monastery at Dol, eventually
becoming the town's first bishop.
In 1799 the bishopric of Dol was
abolished by the revolutionaries.

Cathédrale de St-Vincent   E 2
St-Malo. In town centre. Dedicated
to St-Vincent, this church (no longer
a cathedral) was built at various
times from the 12th century on,
and has been much restored. The
vaulted nave dates from this early
period, while the chancel, well lit
and with slender columns, is from
a century later. Outside there is
part of a small cloister against the
wall.

Château de Bonne-Fontaine   H 4
1mi/1.5km S of Antrain-sur-
Couesnon. A combination of castle
and country house, built mainly in
the mid-16th century. The end
tower, with its rounded walls and
conical roof, is especially fine.
Duchess Anne of Brittany is said to
have administered justice in the
park, sitting under an oak tree.
Park open in summer, 14.00–18.00.

Château de la Bourbansais

Château de la Bourbansais   E 4
Pleugueneuc. 8mi/13km W of
Combourg. Tel (99) 45 20 42. A
château built in various styles, from
the 16th to the 18th century, with

a main central block flanked by pavilions. Inside there is fine 18thC panelling, and the gardens are laid out in the formal French style. During the 18th century, La Bourbansais was an official residence of members of the Breton parliament. It is now much visited for the small open-air zoo laid out in its grounds. *Gardens and zoo open daily 10.00–12.00, 14.00–18.00. House open 1 Jun–30 Sep 14.00–18.00.* **Charge**

Château de Caradeuc   **E 6**
Nr Bécherel, 19.5mi/31km NW of Rennes. Tel (99) 66 77 76. Known as the 'Versailles of Brittany' because of the Classical symmetry of its building and the formal elegance of its park, Caradeuc was built in the 1720s by Anne-Nicolas de Caradeuc, a prominent Breton politician. His son, La Chalotais, was a fanatical defender of the Breton right to independence, and Caradeuc still belongs to his descendants. The north terrace gives wide views over the valley of the Rance. *Open (park & gardens only) all year, dawn to dusk.*

Château de Combourg   **F 4**
Combourg. In centre of town. Tel (99) 73 04 83. Combourg's turrets with their pointed roofs, rising above the trees, make an attractive picture from the far side of the lake on the south side of the town. The original château was built by the bishop of Dol in the 11th century, but the present castle is mainly 15thC. In the 18th century it belonged to the family of François-René de Chateaubriand, who spent much of his childhood here in the years before the Revolution, and wrote about it in his autobiography. Visitors are shown Chateaubriand's bedroom, in a tower called the 'Tour du Chat', from a cat's skeleton discovered under the stairs. The tower was said to be haunted by the ghost of one of the counts of Combourg, who had a wooden leg and would stump about the château with the cat at his heels. *Open Easter–30 Sep 14.00–18.00. Closed Tue.* **Charge**

Château de Fougères   **J 5**
Fougères. In centre of town. Tel (99) 99 18 98. Built on a rocky spur almost entirely surrounded by a loop in the Nançon River, Fougères breathes an atmosphere of feudal military pride. In summer, pennons flutter from its turrets, and its strong walls, now with gardens at their foot, still look capable of keeping invading armies at bay, as they did for hundreds of years. The plan of the castle is mainly due to Baron Raoul II of Fougères, who rebuilt it in 1173 after it had been destroyed by Henry II of England. The 13 superb towers (among them the Tours Raoul, Surienne and Mélusine, the tallest of all) were added in the 14th–15th century, making Fougères one of the most powerful castles in the whole of Europe. The main keep was dismantled in 1626, on the orders of Richelieu.
The full extent of the layout, with its irregular walls following the contour of the rock, is best appreciated from the ramparts that lead to the upper town. *Son-et-lumière* shows are held in the courtyard during the summer, and there is a small museum devoted to footwear (the town's chief industry) in the Tour Raoul. *Open mid-Apr–mid-Sep, daily 09.00–12.00, 14.00–18.00; Mar, early Apr, late Sep & Oct, until 17.00; Nov & Feb, Sat & Sun only. Closed Dec & Jan.* **Charge**

Château de Landal   **G 3**
6.5mi/10.5km SE of Dol-de-Bretagne. The ruins of the 15thC castle of Landal, surrounded by a romantic park and with a lake at their foot, are well worth hunting out for their peaceful remoteness.

Château de Lanrigan   **G 4**
3mi/5km E of Combourg. This château, built in the 15th and 16th centuries, is a fortified manor house with flanking turrets and an imposing Renaissance façade. The castle itself is *closed to visitors*, but the exterior can be seen from the park. *Park open 1 Jun–30 Sep 09.00–12.00, 14.00–19.00.*

Château de Monbouan   **I 8**
11.5mi/18.5km SW of Vitré. Tel (99) 49 01 51. An 18thC château in Classical style, surrounded by a fine garden and park. The gardens are laid out in French formal style, and look across a small lake. Monbouan has belonged to the

same family since it was built. *Open mid-Jul–31 Aug 09.00–12.00, 14.00–18.00.* **Charge**

Château de Montauban D 6
Montauban. 19.5mi/31km W of Rennes. Tel (99) 09 40 21. The ruins of this imposing castle are just north of Montauban village, across the N12. The Montaubans were a powerful local family in the Middle Ages; one of them, Bertrand de Montauban, was killed at Agincourt in 1415. Built in the middle of an artificial lake, now partly dry, Montauban was largely destroyed by the invading French army in 1487. The impressive fortified gateway still survives, as do the lower stages of the keep. *Open in summer 09.00–12.00, 14.00–18.00. Closed Mon.* **Charge**

Château de Montmuran E 5
4mi/6.5km W of Hédé. Tel (99) 45 88 61. This fine château stands on a rocky promontory at the end of a tunnel-like avenue of huge trees. Founded in the 12th century by the lords of Tinténiac, it still has its powerful 14thC gate-tower and corner tower, linked by a 17thC central block in Classical style. The drawbridge is still in working order. Montmuran has links with the great 14thC soldier Bertrand du Guesclin, who was knighted and married in the chapel of the castle. The main tower has a curious medieval back-boiler system for hot water. *Open Easter–31 Oct 14.00–19.00, 1 Nov–Easter 14.00–16.00.* **Charge**

Château des Rochers-Sévigné

Château des Rochers-Sévigné J 8
4mi/6.5km SE of Vitré. Tel (99) 96 61 96. A château of more literary than architectural interest, since it was the home of Mme de Sévigné, whose letters give an unrivalled picture of 17thC life both at the court of Louis XIV, and in the Breton countryside at Les Rochers. The turreted château

dates mainly from the early 16th century; Mme de Sévigné added a chapel in the 1670s. Though most of the château is *private*, her workroom can be visited, as can the delightful park and gardens, which were her pride and joy. *Open all year 09.00–12.00, 14.00–18.00.* **Charge**

Château de St-Malo E 2
St-Malo. Tel (99) 56 41 36. At east corner of walled town. St-Malo's magnificent 15thC castle was built not to enable the Malouins to defend themselves, but so that the dukes of Brittany could keep a check on their independence and power. One of the towers (the Grand Donjon) is now used as the town museum, while another, the Quic-en-Groigne, houses a collection of waxwork tableaux. The latter tower was built by Duchess Anne about 1500, and when the Malouins complained about its strength, she added the inscription: "*Qui qu'en groigne, ainsi sera: tel est mon bon plaisir*" ("Complain as much as you like, that is how it will be: such is my desire"). The town hall is also in the castle. (*For opening times see Museums section, Histoire de la Ville and Quic-en-Groigne.*)

Château de Vitré J 7
Vitré. In town centre. Tel (99) 75 04 54. A magnificent feudal castle, compact and impregnable with its curtain walling and imposing cluster of towers. The best long-distance view of it is from the hill called Les Tertres Noirs, across the Vilaine. The first castle was built here in the 11th century, followed by the present stronghold in the 15th. Its plan is triangular, due to the shape of the plateau on which it is built, making the central courtyard a good deal more cramped than that of a conventional square or rectangular castle. Early in the 20th century the interior was not improved by the addition of a pseudo-Gothic town hall. There is a small museum in one of the towers (*see Château, Museé du*). *Open 1 Jul–30 Sep, daily 09.30–12.30, 14.00–18.00; 1 Oct–30 Jun 14.00–17.30, closed Tue.* **Charge**

Les Demoiselles de Langon E 11
Langon. 14mi/22.5km NE of

Redon. The 'Young Ladies of Langon' are a group of about 30 standing stones, scattered about on the open ground just outside Langon village. According to legend, they were girls of the neighbourhood, turned into blocks of stone for dancing on Sunday instead of going to church.

Eglise des Iffs   **E 6**
Les Iffs. 4mi/6.5km W of Hédé. One of the finest churches of the region, built in rich Flamboyant Gothic style in the 14th and 15th centuries by the Laval family, *seigneurs* of the Château de Montmuran nearby (*see above*). Like the Eglise St-Mars at Bais (*see below*), it has a large porch built so that lepers could take part in the Mass. The church is famous for its stained glass: nine windows of 16thC Breton glass, inspired by Flemish work, and showing the Passion, Last Judgement, and biblical scenes such as Susannah and the Elders. *If* is French for yew tree, and the name Les Iffs comes from the yews planted in the graveyard.

Eglise St-Germain   **G 7**
Pl St-Germain, Rennes. A fine church from about 1500, in Flamboyant Gothic style, which escaped the great fire of 1720. It has a splendid east window, and a spectacular 18thC baldacchino (canopy), white-painted and gilded, above the altar.

Eglise St-Mars   **I 8**
Bais, 10mi/16km SW of Vitré. This 16thC church, greatly restored in the 19th century, has a remarkable gabled entrance-porch. Known as the Porche-aux-Lépreux, it was built for the local leper community who were not allowed into the body of the church. An elaborate doorway, carved with Renaissance motifs mixing Christian and pagan themes, leads from the porch into the church.

Eglise St-Pierre et
Chapelle Ste-Agathe   **E 11**
Langon. 14mi/22.5km NE of Redon. On the border between Ille-et-Vilaine and Loire-Atlantique, Langon is a pretty village on the west side of the Vilaine. The 12thC Romanesque Church of St Peter, enlarged in the

Gothic period, has a remarkable tower with a spire surrounded by 12 pointed spirelets. Just opposite is the far older Chapel of St Agatha, at present being restored, and Gallo-Roman in origin. It is thought that the chapel (probably 4th or 5thC) was once a temple dedicated to Venus, since until the 17th century it was known as the Eglise St-Vener, and the vaulting is decorated with a fresco that is thought to show a nude goddess rising from the waves. In the 18th century the dedication was changed to St Agatha, martyred in Sicily in the 3rd century, and the patron saint of women with breast disorders.

Eglise St-Sulpice   **J 5**
Fougères. Near castle. The graceful Church of St-Sulpice, built in the 15thC in Flamboyant Gothic style, has an unusually tall and slender tower and spire, entirely covered in slates. Inside is a miracle-working 12thC statue of the Virgin suckling the infant Jesus; thrown into the moat by the English, it was recovered in the 14th century and later placed in the church.

Eglise Ste-Barbe   **I 7**
Champeaux. 4.5mi/7km W of Vitré. This 15thC church contains some remarkable examples of 16thC Renaissance art and craftsmanship, notably a vast monument to Guy d'Espinay (died 1553) and his wife, finely carved canopied oak stalls, and a stained-glass window of the Crucifixion. Outside in the square is an unusual well, protected by a neatly shingled roof.

Eglise de Tinténiac   **F 5**
17mi/27km NW of Rennes. An enormous church for so small a town, built in 1908 in Byzantine style. It incorporates fragments from the former church, including part of a 16thC Renaissance doorway. Inside the church is a Romanesque holy water stoup nicknamed the 'Devil of Tinténiac'.

Fort National   **E 2**
St-Malo. Just north east of walled town. Built by Louis XIV's military architect Vauban in 1689, the fort is linked to the mainland by a causeway that is flooded for four hours at high

tide. *Open during summer when the tide allows.*

Grand Bé   E 2
St-Malo. Just noth of walled town. The tomb of Chateaubriand (*see Famous people*) is on this small island, facing out to sea. The word '*Bé*' is Celtic for tomb, so the island makes a fitting burial place. It is linked to the mainland by a causeway and cut off at high tide.

Jardin du Thabor   G 7
Rennes. On east side of city centre. A superb public garden, once the garden of the Benedictine monastery of St-Melaine, whose church is on its west side. The monks named it after the biblical Mount Tabor. Apart from its formal beds laid out in the elaborate French style, it includes a botanic garden, and a rose garden with dozens of named varieties. *Open dawn to dusk.*

Mégalithes de St-Just   E 11
12mi/19km NE of Redon. Though of little interest in itself, the village of St-Just is in a wild landscape scattered with menhirs singly and in groups, with dolmens, and other remains of Stone Age Man. The curiously named heath called the Lande de Cojoux derives its name from the Latin '*Collis Jovis*', 'Hill of Jove'.

Menhir du Champ-Dolent   G 3
0.5mi/1km S of Dol-de-Bretagne. One of the most impressive standing stones of Brittany, 31ft/9.5m high. Legend says that it is sinking into the earth at the rate of an inch a century, and that when it finally disappears, the world will come to an end. The name, meaning 'Field of Grief', refers to

a battle fought here between two brothers and their armies in the remote past.

Palais de Justice   G 7
Pl du Palais, Rennes. Tel (99) 79 40 22. A large and imposing building, in sober Classical style, built in the first half of the 17th century as the seat of the Breton parliament (Etats). The symmetrical façade, with its high mansard roof, was designed by the Paris architect Salomon de Brosse. The main rooms are open to the public, and include the magnificent Grande Chambre du Parlement de Bretagne, painted, gilded and hung with tapestries. Guided tours, lasting 45 minutes. Groups should telephone in advance. *Open 10.00–12.00, 14.00–18.00.* **Charge**

Rennes, old streets   G 7
A few Medieval streets, mainly round the cathedral, escaped the fire that burnt most of the inner city in 1720. Among them are the rue de la Monnaie, where the Rennes mint once stood, the rue des Dames, and the rue St-Guillaume. The pl des Lices, now largely covered by the glass-roofed meat market, was the tiltyard ('*Lices*' means 'Lists') where du Guesclin and other knights tried out their skill in the tournament. Behind the cathedral is the little rue de la Psalette, so called from the room where the cathedral choir used to practise singing the psalms.

La Roche-aux-Fées   I 9
Near Essé. 19.5mi/31km SE of Rennes. The 'Fairies' Rock' is one of the most important megalithic monuments in the whole of France: a covered way (*allée*

La Roche-aux-Fées

couverte) made of huge stone blocks, probably around 2000BC. There are over 40 blocks, some of them weighing more than 40 tons/ 40.5 tonnes; they are of red schist, and had to be man-handled across country for 2.5mi/4km from their place of origin. The locals used to say that it was impossible to count them exactly, as the fairies were in league with the Devil, who was notoriously deceitful. In the old days, before a couple got married, the man would walk clockwise round the stones while the woman went anticlockwise, both counting the stones as they went. If they came up with the same number, the marriage went ahead; but if the numbers were different, the wedding was off.

St-Malo, ramparts   E 2
Every visitor to St-Malo should make the circuit of the town walls, both for the views out to sea, and for the constantly changing perspectives of streets and houses, dominated by the spire of the cathedral. The walls survived World War II virtually intact, unlike the houses, 80% of which were destroyed or badly damaged. *En route* there are statues of the explorer Jacques Cartier, and the corsairs Surcouf and Duguay-Trouin.

Tour du Grand-Fougeray   F 11
27mi/43km S of Rennes. The tall 14thC *donjon* or keep is all that survives of the castle of Le Grand-Fougeray, one of the major strongholds of the Hundred Years' War. In 1356 it was captured from the English by Bertrand du Guesclin in one of his most daring exploits. Disguised as a woodcutter, he talked his way into the castle accompanied by 30 soldiers carrying firewood. Once inside, they threw down their bundles, drew their swords and butchered the garrison. The tower is kept locked.

Museums & galleries

Aquarium Malouin   E 2
Pl Vauban, 35400 St-Malo. Tel (99) 81 64 34. Near the castle of St-Malo and right under the ramparts, this is a well presented little aquarium with specimens from all over the world. *Open 1 Jul-30 Sep, daily 09.00-23.00; 1 Oct-30 Jun 09.00-12.00, 14.00-19.00.* **Charge**

Beaux-Arts, Musée des   G 7
20 quai Emile Zola, 35000 Rennes. Tel (99) 30 83 87. Housed in a dignified 19thC building known as the Palais des Musées, on the south side of the Vilaine, this is an important collection of paintings of all periods, together with a section of Egyptian and Græco-Roman antiquities. Among the best of the earlier paintings is a 'Nativity' by the 17thC French artist Georges de la Tour, and there are several works by artists of the 19thC Pont-Aven school, who painted in Finistère. *Open 10.00-12.00, 14.00-18.00. Closed Tue & hols.* **Charge**

Bretagne, Musée de   G 7
20 quai Emile Zola, 35000 Rennes. Tel (99) 30 83 87. In the same building as the Beaux-Arts (*see above*), this is Brittany's most comprehensive museum of Breton life and culture. There is a historical survey from prehistoric times, through the Gauls, the Romans and the dukedom of Brittany to the present day; collections of traditional furniture and costumes; and an audio-visual room with slide shows on Brittany today. *Open 10.00-12.00, 14.00-18.00. Closed Tue & hols.* **Charge**

Château, Musée du   J 7
Château, 35500 Vitré. Devoted to the history of Vitré, with documents, old engravings and exhibits illustrating the cloth trade on which the town's prosperity was built. *Open 1 Jul-30 Sep, daily 09.30-12.30, 14.00-18.00; 1 Oct-30 Jun, 14.00-17.30, closed Tue.* **Charge**

Chaussure, Musée de la   J 5
Château, 35300 Fougères. For this footwear museum, *see Château de Fougères in Interesting buildings section.*

**Histoire de la Ville,
Musée de l'**   E 2
Château, 35400 St-Malo. Tel (99) 56 41 36. This museum, in the great tower (Grand Donjon) of the castle, tells the seafaring story of St-Malo, from the earliest medieval

days of the town, through its period of greatest prosperity in the 17th and 18th centuries, when its shipowners traded all over the world, to World War II and the present day. *Open daily 09.30–12.00, 14.00–18.00.* **Charge**

Long-Cours et des Cap-Horniers, Musée du   **E 2**
Tour Solidor, St-Servan, 35400 St-Malo. Tel (99) 56 26 68. This tall 14thC tower, guarding the old harbour on the west side of the St-Servan Peninsula, now houses a fascinating small museum devoted to the 19thC sailing ships that traded round the world, via Cape Horn. There are exhibits on the vessels themselves, and on the discoveries they made. *Guided tours in summer at 10.15, 11.15, 13.15, 15.00, 16.15, 17.10. Less frequently in winter.* **Charge**

Quic-en-Groigne   **E 2**
Château, 35400 St-Malo. Tel (99) 56 41 36. An exhibition of waxwork tableaux, mainly on the theme of the exploits of the St-Malo corsairs, displayed in one of the towers of the castle. (For explanation of name, *see under Château de St-Malo in Interesting buildings section.*) *Open Easter–mid-Sep, daily 09.00–12.00, 14.00–17.45.* **Charge**

Accommodation

Campsites
Prices at campsites vary according to the facilities available but seldom exceed ten francs per person at present. There will usually also be a charge for the car and for the site.

Bain-de-Bretagne   **G 10**
Municipal du Lac
35470 Bain-de-Bretagne. Tel (99) 43 70 24. A quiet site, flat and grassy, and with lakeside walks, on the south-east side of this little town. *Open 1 Apr–31 Oct.*

Bains-sur-Oust   **D 11**
L'Ile aux Pies
35600 Redon. Tel (99) 91 71 41. A quiet site near the Oust River, 2mi/3km NW of Bains in the direction

of Gacilly; grassy and tree-shaded. *Open Jul & Aug.*

Bourg-des-Comptes   **F 9**
La Courbe
35580 Guichen. 12.5mi/20km S of Rennes. Tel (99) 57 41 08. Only 55yds/50m from the banks of the Vilaine, this is a small country site. *Open all year.*

Cancale   **F 2**
Notre-Dame-du-Verger
Le Verger, 35260 Cancale. Tel (99) 89 72 84. Terraced site 2mi/3km NW of the town, at the hamlet of Le Verger. *Open 1 Apr–30 Sep.*

Pointe de Grouin
35260 Cancale. Tel (99) 89 63 17. A municipal site with good facilities, near the spectacular Grouin headland. *Open 1 Apr–30 Sep.*

La Chapelle-aux-Filzméens   **F 5**
Camping du Château
St-Domineuc, 35190 Tinténiac. Tel (99) 45 21 55. A peaceful site with many facilities, in the heart of the countryside between St-Domineuc and Combourg. In the parkland of a 17thC château and one of the 'Castels et Camping' association. *Open mid-May–mid-Sep.*

Combourg   **F 4**
Municipal du Vieux Chatel
35270 Combourg. Tel (99) 73 07 03. A flat, grassy site, with some gravel, beside the lake 0.5mi/1km S of the town. *Open 1 Jun–mid-Sep.*

Dinard   **E 2**
Municipal du Port Blanc
35800 Dinard. Tel (99) 46 10 74. A large site by the sea, partly terraced, with some sand, 1mi/1.5km W of the town in the direction of St-Lunaire. *Open 1 Apr–30 Sep.*

Le Prieuré
35800 Dinard. Tel (99) 46 20 04. A grassy site, partly terraced, 220yds/200m from the sea, with a games room and many other amenities. *Open 1 Mar–mid-Nov.*

Dol-de-Bretagne   **F 3**
Château des Ormes
35120 Dol-de-Bretagne. Tel (99) 48 10 19. A very well appointed site, with restaurant, boating, swimming pool and other facilities. It is one of the 'Castels et Camping' chain,

in the park of a château that once belonged to the bishops of Dol, about 5mi/8km S of Dol, off the Combourg road. *Open mid-May–mid-Sep.*

Du Vieux Chêne
35120 Dol-de-Bretagne. Tel (99) 48 09 55. An attractive site, with plenty of trees, and a small lake, near Baguer-Pican, 3mi/5km E of Dol. *Open mid-May–30 Sep.*

Fougères   J 5

Municipal de Paron
35300 Fougères. Tel (99) 99 40 81. A quiet site, 1mi/1.5km E of the town, grassy and mainly flat. *Open all year.*

Guipel   G 5

La Plousière
35440 Guipel. Tel (99) 45 72 32. A grassy site with plenty of trees, 1.5mi/2.5km N of the village near the Ille et Rance Canal. *Open 1 May–mid-Sep.*

Montfort   E 7

Municipal
35160 Montfort. Tel (99) 09 00 17. A small, grassy site, beside a stream near the centre of this old town. *Open 1 Apr–mid-Oct.*

Paimpont   C 8

Municipal
Paimpont, 35380 Plélan-le-Grand. Tel (99) 06 84 62. A small site in this woodland area, with boating facilities nearby. *Open all year.*

Paramé   E 2

Municipal Le Nicet
Paramé, 35400 St-Malo. Tel (99) 58 26 32. A seaside site, partly terraced, with limited facilities, beside a good beach. *Open 1 Apr–mid-Sep.*

Rennes   G 7

Municipal des Gayeulles
35000 Rennes. Tel (99) 36 91 22. A quiet site beside a small lake, off the av des Gayeulles on the north-east side of the city, in the direction of Fougères. *Open Easter–31 Oct.*

St-Aubin-du-Cormier   I 6

Municipal
35140 St-Aubin-du-Cormier. Enquiries: tel Mairie, (99) 55 10 42. A small site beside a lake on the south side of the village. *Open 1 Apr–mid-Oct.*

St-Briac-sur-Mer   D 2

Eméraude
St-Briac-sur-Mer, 35800 Dinard. Tel (99) 88 34 55. A flat, grassy site on the edge of the village and near the sea. Facilities include a games room. *Open Easter–mid-Sep.*

St-Lunaire   D 2

Le Longchamp
St-Lunaire, 35800 Dinard. Tel (99) 46 31 84. On the west side of St-Lunaire, 220yds/200m from the sea. A tree-shaded site with grass and sand. *Open mid-Jun–mid-Sep.*

St-Servan   E 2

Municipal le Grand Domaine
St-Servan, 35400 St-Malo. Tel (99) 81 35 92. A fairly large site, flat and grassy, on the south side of the town in the direction of Dinard. *Open late Jun–early Sep.*

Tinténiac   F 5

Les Peupliers
35190 Tinténiac. Tel (99) 45 49 75. A flat, grassy and tree-shaded site, 1.5mi/2.5km SE of the village, beside some small lakes. *Open all year.*

Le Vivier-sur-Mer   F 2

Municipal
35960 Le Vivier-sur-Mer. Tel (99) 48 91 92. A fairly small site, by the sea looking across the wide bay of Mont-St-Michel. *Open 1 Jun–30 Sep.*

Hotels

Bain-de-Bretagne   G 10

Hôtel des Quatre Vents
Rte Rennes, 35470 Bain-de-Bretagne. Tel (99) 43 71 49. A small 'Logis de France' hotel on the Rennes road. *Closed Feb.* A. F

Cancale   F 2

Hôtel La Bisquine
4 quai Gambetta, 35260 Cancale. Tel (99) 89 61 30. Hotel overlooking the harbour and the oyster tanks. A *bisquine* was a small fishing-boat. *Open all year.* A. F

Hôtel Le Continental
Quai Thomas, 35260 Cancale. Tel (99) 89 60 16. A 'Logis de France' hotel, near the port. The restaurant specialises in oysters and other seafood. *Closed mid-Nov–31 Mar.* A.V. FF

Combourg   F 4

Hôtel du Château
Pl Chateaubriand, 35270
Combourg. Tel (99) 73 00 38. A
'Logis de France' hotel, near the
château. *Closed mid-Dec–31 Jan.*
A.Ax.Dc. **FF**

Dinard   E 2

Grand Hôtel
46 av George V, 35800 Dinard. Tel
(99) 46 10 28. A large and
luxurious hotel on the grandest
scale, not far from the marina, and
with its own garden. *Closed 1 Nov–
31 Mar.* Ax.Dc.V. **FFF**

Hôtel Eméraude-Plage
1 bvd Albert 1er, 35800 Dinard. Tel
(99) 46 15 79. One of the earliest
hotels in Dinard, built in 1898.
Near the casino and 55yds/50m
from the beach. The restaurant
serves Breton specialities. *Closed
mid-Sep–Easter.* **FF**

Hôtel de la Plage
3 bvd Féart, 35800 Dinard. Tel (99)
46 14 87. A 'Logis de France' hotel
with a sea view, near the main
beach. The restaurant specialises
in *fruits de mer. Closed mid-Oct–early
Mar.* **FF**

Dol-de-Bretagne   F 3

Logis de la Bresche-Arthur
36 bvd Deminiac, 35120 Dol-de-
Bretagne. Tel (99) 48 01 44. A
'Logis de France' hotel a short way
from the town centre. The name
refers to a mythical siege of Dol by
King Arthur, who made a breach
(*bresche*) in its walls. *Closed Nov.*
A.Ax.Dc.V. **FF**

Fougères   J 5

Hôtel Balzac
15 rue Nationale, 35300 Fougères.
Tel (99) 99 42 46. A fine stone
18thC building in the centre of the
old town. No restaurant. *Open all
year.* **FF**

La Guerche-de-Bretagne   J 9

Hôtel La Calèche
Av Général-Leclerc, 35130 La
Guerche-de-Bretagne. Tel (99) 96 20
36. A quiet and unpretentious hotel
near the centre of this small town.
Closed late Sep–early Oct. A.V. **F**

Paimpont   C 8

Relais de Brocéliande
Paimpont, 35380 Plélan-le-Grand.
On D773. Tel (99) 06 80 03. Hotel

with a large garden, opposite the
old town gate of Paimpont. *Open
all year.* Ax.V. **FF**

Paramé   E 2

Grand Hôtel de Courtoisville
69 bvd Hébert, 35400 St-Malo. Tel
(99) 40 83 83. A quiet hotel, set well
back from the beach, with a
country-like atmosphere. *Closed
mid-Nov–end Feb.* A. **FF**

Hôtel Rochebonne
15 bvd Chateaubriand, 35400 St-
Malo. Tel (99) 56 01 72. A
comfortable hotel with a good
restaurant, built at the turn of the
century. *Closed Wed 15 Oct–1 May.*
A.V. **FF**

Hôtel des Thermes
100 bvd Hébert, 35400 St-Malo.
Tel (99) 56 02 56. A luxurious,
château-like hotel overlooking the
sea, one of the 'Best Western'
group. A water-cure centre is
attached, and there is an outdoor
swimming pool. The restaurant
('Le Cap Horn') specialises in
seafood and oysters. *Closed Jan.*
Ax.Dc.V. **FFF**

Pointe du Grouin   F 2

Hôtel Pointe du Grouin
35260 Cancale. Tel (99) 89 60 55.
Comfortable hotel with fine views
over seabird-covered rocks, and out
to sea. The restaurant specialises
in lobster and other seafood. *Closed
1 Oct–Easter.* V. **FF**

Redon   D 12

Hôtel La France
30 rue Duguesclin, 35600 Redon.
Tel (99) 71 06 11. Moderate-sized
hotel without restaurant, a short
way from the Vilaine. *Closed late
Dec–early Jan.* **F**

Rennes   G 7

Hôtel Angelina
1 quai Lamennais, 35000 Rennes.
Tel (99) 79 29 66. A small hotel
without restaurant, right in the city
centre. *Open all year.* A.V. **FF**

Hôtel Le Cheval d'Or
6 pl de la Gare, 35000 Rennes. Tel
(99) 30 25 80. Moderate-sized hotel,
without restaurant, a short way
south of the city centre. *Closed last
2 wks in Dec.* **FF**

Hôtel Frantel
Pl du Colombier, 35000 Rennes.
Tel (99) 79 54 54. A luxury hotel

with first-class restaurant ('La Table Ronde'), south of the city centre. *Restaurant closed Sat lunch & Sun.* A.Ax.Dc.V. **FFF**

St-Malo E 2

Hôtel France et Chateaubriand
Pl Chateaubriand, 35400 St-Malo. Tel (99) 56 66 52. Hotel in the heart of the walled city, near the sea and looking towards the château. The famous author Chateaubriand was born in this house, which has an attractive courtyard. *Closed 1 Dec–Easter.* Ax.Dc.V. **F**

Hôtel de la Porte St-Pierre
2 pl du Guet, 35400 St-Malo. Tel (99) 40 91 27. This hotel, below the ramparts on the seaward side of the town, is named after one of the Medieval fortified gateways. Its restaurant specialises in seafood. *Closed mid-Dec.* **F**

Vitré J 7

Hôtel Le Chêne Vert
Pl de la Gare, 35500 Vitré. Tel (99) 75 00 58. A modest hotel, near the château and Medieval town. *Closed mid-Sep–mid-Oct.* **F**

Restaurants

Bain-de-Bretagne G 10

La Croix Verte
Pl Henri IV, 35470 Bain-de-Bretagne. Tel (99) 43 71 55. Small restaurant in the town centre, with a few rooms attached. *Closed Sat eve, Sun & hols.* **F**

Cancale F 2

L'Armada
La Houle, 35260 Cancale. Tel (99) 89 60 02. Restaurant overlooking the oyster tanks and bay, specialising in grilled lobster and other seafood. *Closed Jan.* A.Ax.Dc. **F**

À L'Escale
2 quai Gambetta, 35260 Cancale. Tel (99) 89 62 56. Friendly waterfront restaurant with seafood specialities. *Closed 1 Dec–end Feb.* **F**

Ty Breiz
Quai Gambetta, 35260 Cancale. Tel (99) 89 60 26. Restaurant on the quayside and overlooking the harbour, specialising in oysters and other seafood. *Closed mid-Nov–end Feb & Tue out of season.* V. **FF**

Combourg F 4

La Charrette
1 pl de l'Eglise, 35270 Combourg. Tel (99) 73 00 60. A restaurant with some rooms, about five minutes' walk from the château and town centre. **F**

Dinard E 2

Dragon d'Eméraude
54 bvd Féart, 35800 Dinard. Tel (99) 46 94 29. A restaurant serving Chinese and Vietnamese food, for these who feel like a little variety. *Closed Wed.* **FF**

Le Sporting
66 bvd Albert-Lacroix, 35800 Dinard. Tel (99) 46 16 44. In St-Enogat, on the west side of Dinard. Specialises in *fruits de mer* and oysters. *Open all year.* **FF**

Fougères J 5

Des Voyageurs
10 pl Gambetta, 35300 Fougères. Tel (99) 99 14 17. Restaurant on the edge of the Medieval town centre, not far from the château. *Closed last 2 wks in Aug, Sat & Sun eve.* Ax.V. **FF**

Hédé F 5

La Vieille Auberge
35630 Hédé. On N137. Tel (99) 45 46 25. On the outskirts of the town, with a garden and pond. Seafood can be selected fresh from a water-tank in the restaurant. *Closed Sun eve & Mon.* **FF**

Paimpont C 8

Auberge Le Pont du Secret
Paimpont, 35380 Plélan-le-Grand. Tel (99) 06 82 54. The bridge is so called because it was here that Queen Guinevere confessed her love for Sir Lancelot. The restaurant specialises in eel, frogs' legs and salmon soufflé. *Open all year.* **F**

Redon D 12

La Bogue
3 rue des Etats, 35600 Redon. Tel (99) 71 12 95. A restaurant near the main market, specialising in seafood. *Closed Tue eve & Wed.* A.V. **FF**

La Vieille Auberge
62 Grande rue, 35600 Redon. Tel (99) 71 25 71. Restaurant near the Romanesque church and old harbour. *Closed Tue eve.* Ax. **F**

Rennes   **G 7**

Auberge St-Sauveur
6 rue St-Sauveur, 35000 Rennes.
Tel (99) 30 42 69. In a timber-
framed 15thC house in the old
part of the city, with traditional
Breton cooking. *Closed mid-Aug &
Sun.* V. **FFF**

Le Palais
7 pl du Palais, 35000 Rennes. Tel
(99) 30 21 19. Centrally placed
near the Palais de Justice, this
restaurant serves food fresh from
the market. *Closed Aug, Sun eve &
Mon.* Ax.V. **FFF**

Ti Koz
3 rue St-Guillaume, 35000 Rennes.
Tel (99) 30 52 98. 'Ti Koz' means
'old house' in Breton, and this half-
timbered house near the castle is
said to have belonged to du
Guesclin. The restaurant
specialises in seafood. *Closed early
Aug & Sun.* A.Dc.V. **FFF**

La Villa d'Este
4 rue de la Psalette, 35000 Rennes.
Tel (99) 30 42 07. Italian restaurant
in the old city near the cathedral.
Closed Sun. **F**

St-Malo   **E 2**

À la Duchesse Anne
Porte St-Vincent, 35400 St-Malo.
Tel (99) 40 85 33. By the main gate
and below the town walls,
specialising in seafood of all sorts.
*Closed Dec, Jan & Wed out of
season.* **FF**

La Bisquine
21 rue Jacques-Cartier, 35400 St-
Malo. Tel (99) 40 97 40. A
restaurant under the ramparts,
serving lobster fresh from the tank.
Closed Thur out of season. **FF**

Le Faisan Doré
Rue de l'Orme, 35400 St-Malo. Tel
(99) 40 91 70. A quiet, friendly
restaurant in the centre of the
walled town. **FF**

Les Iles
5 rue de la Corne de Cerf, 35400
St-Malo. Tel (99) 40 98 68. In the
middle of the old town, quiet and
specialising in seafood. **FF**

Vitré   **J 7**

La Belle Oseille
40 Rue d'Embas, 35500 Vitré. Tel
(99) 74 64 54. In a Medieval
building in the old town, specialising in *fruits de mer.* **FF**

Countryside

Côte d'Eméraude   **BCD 1**
The 'Emerald Coast' is mainly in
the Côtes-du-Nord; but its eastern
section, roughly from Cancale
round to St-Briac, is in Ille-et-
Vilaine.

Fontaine de Barenton   **C 8**
4mi/6.5km W of Paimpont. A
spring on the edge of the Forest of
Paimpont, with legendary
associations going back to the time
of the Druids. Barenton was a
centre of Druidic teaching, and the
fountain may have been used in
some kind of initiation ritual. In
former times the water was said to
be good for mental disorders.
Beside the spring is a square stone
called the *'Perron de Merlin'*
('Merlin's Threshold'). This had
the magical power of summoning
up a thunderstorm when water was
sprinkled on it from the spring;
after the storm the sun would
come out, and flocks of singing
birds would fill the air above
the spring.

Forêt de Brocéliande
25mi/40km W of Rennes.
Brocéliande was the medieval
name for the vast woodland that
once covered much of central
Brittany, of which part still survives
in the Forêt de Paimpont (*see
below*). Arthur and Guinevere,
Lancelot and Sir Galahad still
haunt its paths and glades, as do
the legends of the Druids, who
were ousted by the coming of
Christianity in the 5th and 6th
centuries.

Forêt de Fougères   **JK 5**
Immediately north east of the town.
This magnificent stretch of state-
owned woodland, consisting largely
of beech trees, spreads on either
side of the D177 between Fougères
and Landéan. With its paths and
rides, and its prehistoric standing
stones, it is a popular area for
summer walks and picnics.

Forêt de Paimpont   **C 8**
25mi/40km W of Rennes. The
Forêt de Paimpont, covering about
16,000 acres/6480 hectares, is all
that survives of the vast
Brocéliande forest (*see above*),
which once extended over much of

central Brittany. Many of the names have associations with King Arthur, since Brocéliande was one of the places where he is said to have held sway, and where his memory still lingers. With its glades, paths and hidden pools, the forest is one of the prettiest and most evocative places in the whole of Brittany.

Forêt de Rennes   **G 7**
6.5mi/10.5km NE of the city. This fine area of woodland, 7000 acres/2835 hectares in extent, stretches along either side of the N12, and is one of the main country 'lungs' for the people of Rennes. On its northern side, at St-Sulpice-la-Forêt, are the ruins of a 12thC Benedictine abbey.

Ile Cézembre   **E 2**
2.5mi/4km NW of St-Malo. A small island guarding the estuary of the Rance and commanding the approaches to St-Malo. It was fortified in the 17th century by Vauban, Louis XIV's military architect.

Marais de Dol   **F 3–H 2**
Immediately north of Dol-de-Bretagne. The 'marshland of Dol', stretching from Dol to the shore of Mont-St-Michel Bay, is no longer marshland but rich farmland, reclaimed after centuries of irrigation work. Until some time between the 4th and 8th century, the Marais and the bay beyond were covered by a vast forest, the Forêt de Scissy. Then the sea swept in, flooding the low-lying areas and isolating the rocky mound on which Mont-St-Michel was later built. Ancient tree-trunks from Scissy are still found from time to time buried in the soil. Reclamation of the marshland began in the Middle Ages, and the work is still going on in the direction of Mont-St-Michel, where the reclaimed areas are called by the Dutch name of *polders*.

Mont Dol   **F 3**
2mi/3km N of Dol-de-Bretagne. The table-top of this hill is a landmark in the flat landscape south of the Bay of Mont-St-Michel. An isolated granite outcrop, it once rose above the vanished Forest of Scissy and is said to have been a Celtic holy place. Early Christians

established their hermitages on it, and both St Michael and the Devil left their footprints in its rocks. The tower on top of it, now a chapel, was built as a naval telegraph station at the end of the 18th century—one of a chain built between Brest and Paris, which transmitted messages by a semaphore system of pivoting wooden arms.

Pointe du Grouin   **F 1**
2.5mi/4km N of Cancale. A rocky headland that gives panoramic views east to Mont-St-Michel and the Cherbourg Peninsula, and west beyond St-Malo to Cap Fréhel. Across a narrow sound on the east side of the point is a small island designated as a nature reserve and seabird sanctuary.

Rochers du Saut-Roland   **K 6**
Near Dompierre. 7.5mi/12km S of Fougères. Rocky outcrops above a ravine, named after the 8thC hero of the medieval poem 'Le Chanson de Roland'. Though Roland is traditionally said to have died fighting the Saracens at Roncesvalles in the Pyrenees, the Bretons tell another story. According to this, Roland survived Roncesvalles and became the governor of Brittany. One day he was exercising his horse, and decided to jump it across the ravine of the Cantache River. He succeeded twice; but the third time his horse slipped and he was thrown into the ravine, with fatal result—hence the name, 'Roland's Leap'.

Entertainment

Casinos

Casino de Dinard   **E 2**
Palais d'Eméraude, 4 bvd Wilson, 35800 Dinard. Tel (99) 46 15 71. An entertainment centre as well as a casino, with tea room, restaurant with a panoramic view, and disco. *Closed Jan & Feb.*

Casino de St-Malo   **E 2**
Esplanade du Casino, 35400 St-Malo. Tel (99) 56 00 05. St-Malo's casino is just outside the main gate of the old walled town. Apart from the gaming rooms, it has a restaurant and two discos. *Casino*

*open Jul & Aug, nightly from 17.00;
Sat & Sun only out of season.*

Discothèques

Disco Club 2000   **F 4**
35270 Combourg. Tel (99) 73 03
47. *Disco by the lake. Open Sat &
Sun in summer & hols.* **Charge**

L'Espace   **G 7**
43 bvd de la Tour d'Auvergne,
35000 Rennes. Tel (99) 30 21 95.
*Disco and nightclub. Open nightly
from 22.30.* **Charge**

Safari Club   **F 5**
Québriac, 35190 Tinténiac. Tel (99)
00 03 50. In Québriac village, 2mi/
3km N of Tinténiac. *Open
22.00–03.00. Closed Mon & Tue.*
Charge

Leisure activities

Golf

Golf de Dinard   **E 2**
35800 Dinard. Tel (99) 88 32 07. *A
seaside 18-hole course, on the west
side of the resort. Open all year.*
Charge

**Golf de St-Jacques
de la Lande**   **G 7**
35100 Rennes. Tel (99) 64 24 18. *A
9-hole course, 5mi/8km SW of the
city. Open all year.* **Charge**

Horseriding

**Centre Equestre de la Côte
d'Eméraude**   **E 2**
35800 Dinard. Tel (99) 46 23 57.
Horses for hire all year. **Charge**

Sailing
Sailing and windsurfing schools at
Dinard and Paramé.

Sea angling
At Cancale, Dinard and Paramé.

Seawater cure
(thalassothérapie)

Les Thermes Marins   **E 2**
100 bvd Hébert, 35400 St-Malo.
Tel (99) 56 02 56. *Attached to the
Hôtel des Thermes, beside the
Grande Plage. Water cures of all
sorts for rheumatic complaints;
seaweed and ultrasonic treatments
etc. Open mid-Jan–mid-Dec.*
Charge

Excursions

Boat trips

St-Malo–Dinan   **E 2**
Cale de Dinan, 35400 St-Malo. Tel
(99) 56 63 21. *Regular trips up the
Rance, via Dinard.*

St-Malo–Jersey   **E 2**
Esplanade St-Vincent, 35400 St-
Malo. Tel (99) 40 88 59. *By
catamaran, hydrofoil or ship.
Regular daily services throughout
spring & summer. Catamaran
crossing time 70 mins.*

St-Malo–Iles Chausey   **E 2**
Cale de Dinan, 35400 St-Malo. Tel
(99) 56 63 21. *Trips in summer to
these small islands, opposite
Granville on the Cherbourg
Peninsula.*

Vilaine River cruises   **D 12**
Office du Tourisme, 35600 Redon.
Tel (99) 71 06 04. *From Redon,
mainly at weekends.*

Coach trips

Cars Rouge et Blanc   **E 2**
Esplanade St-Vincent, 35400 St-
Malo. Tel (99) 40 85 96. *Excursions
all over Brittany and to Mont-St-
Michel and the Normandy
beaches.*

Tours by car

From Rennes

Frontier castles
From Rennes, take N12 north east
through Rennes Forest. Through
St-Aubin-du-Cormier (ruined
castle), where in 1488 the French
defeated the Bretons. To Fougères,
which has one of most magnificent
Medieval castles in Brittany. Head
south along D178 to Vitré, another
Medieval town with superb castle.
Then south 6mi/9.5km to Les
Rochers-Sévigné, home of Mme de
Sévigné, famous 17thC letter-
writer. Back to Rennes by La
Guerche-de-Bretagne, old town.

King Arthur's country
Head west from Rennes to
Montfort (Medieval town). Then
north west to Montauban (castle),
west to St-Méen-le-Grand, and
south through Gael into Forêt de
Paimpont. Past Château de
Comper (in Morbihan) to
Paimpont, centre for exploring

Château de Combourg

forest, with its memories of King
Arthur and the Druids (Fontaine
de Barenton, Pont-du-Secret etc).
Back to Rennes through Plélan-le-
Grand.

River Vilaine
Though the ideal way to see the
Vilaine is from a boat, or from the
train between Rennes and Redon,
it is possible to keep fairly close to
it by using the most minor roads
marked on the Michelin 1cm:2km
map. A good target for a day's trip
from Rennes would be
Guipry–Messac, which, though
only 19mi/30.5km from Rennes as
the crow flies, is probably double
that as the tiny roads meander. An
alternative would be to take the
main road to Redon (D177),
returning to Rennes by as much of
the minor road system as there is
time for.

From St-Malo

Inland tour
From St-Malo, go west across the
Barrage de la Rance to Dinard,
sophisticated resort. Due south to
Dinan (in Côtes-du-Nord),

beautiful Medieval town on the
Rance. South to Bécherel and
Caradeuc Château (the 'Versailles
of Brittany'), then west to Les Iffs
(fine Gothic church) and
Montmuran Château. Through
Hédé to Combourg, old town and
château made famous by author
Chateaubriand. Back via Dol, or
straight up D73 to St-Malo.

Mont-St-Michel
Though Mont-St-Michel is just
over the Normandy border, it is a
trip well worth making.
From St-Malo, head east along
coast via Rothéneuf (strange
Rochers Sculptés) to the Pointe du
Grouin, with its magnificent views
out to sea. Then south down the
coast to Cancale, to try the oysters
either in a restaurant or from one
of the stalls. Along shore of Bay of
Mont-St-Michel, and then north along causeway to the
Mont—a marvel of Medieval
architecture. Back to St-Malo
through Dol-de-Bretagne, superb
old town with cathedral, making a
detour up Mont Dol.

Loire-Atlantique

The noblest and most historic of all French rivers, the Loire reaches deep into the heartland of France. From St-Nazaire inland to Nantes, it flows sluggishly between widely separated banks, its course broken at low tide with sandy bars and spits which are the delight of fishermen and a constant headache to unwary navigators. Upstream again to a short way beyond Ancenis, it splits the département of Loire-Atlantique into two parts, which remained largely separate worlds until the St-Nazaire bridge was built in the 1970s.

South of the Loire is a gentle country of vineyards, where the grapes that make the white wines of the Loire grow in a more temperate climate than that of Burgundy further inland, or Bordeaux to the south. Immediately north of the river the landscape is far more industrialised, with the petrol installations of Donges and the shipyards of St-Nazaire. There is a difference too in the houses: to the north they are roofed in the dark slate of Brittany, while to the south they are roofed with red tiles and have an almost Mediterranean look.

In recent years the département has become embroiled in regional politics. Until the 1960s it was a part of Brittany, but under a reorganisation scheme it was transferred to a new region, the Pays de la Loire. So Brittany, instead of having five départements, was cut down to four, and lost its magnificent historical capital city of Nantes. This has left a legacy of nostalgia and bitterness among the inhabitants of Loire-Atlantique, who will tell you that Rennes may be the administrative centre of Brittany but Nantes is still its spiritual capital.

Conflict of one sort or another is nothing new in Loire-Atlantique. For centuries the Loire acted as a barrier separating the dukes of Brittany from their enemies to the south, while on the east the castle of Châteaubriant was one of a chain that guarded Brittany's eastern border. Earlier, in the Dark Ages, the Norsemen had sailed their fearsome longships up the Loire to Nantes and beyond, plundering, burning and cutting down the vineyards with their battleaxes. In later times the region saw some of the fiercest fighting of the Revolutionary period, while in March 1942 St-Nazaire was the target of a heroic commando raid on the German submarine pens that still loom over the harbour.

For the tourist and holidaymaker, Loire-Atlantique has a bewildering variety of choice. In its north-west corner are concentrated the sophisticated delights of La Baule, the Medieval walled town of Guérande above a moonscape of saltpans, and the forgotten watery expanse of the Grande Brière. Inland are woodlands, ancient abbeys and castles, and small villages where time seems to have stopped for half a century. As for Nantes itself, it is a superb city, full of life and vigour, looking half towards Brittany and half towards the wider world of France.

Note This book covers only the part of Loire-Atlantique north of the Loire. The main map shows the whole département, for clarity; the inset map shows the area covered in the text.

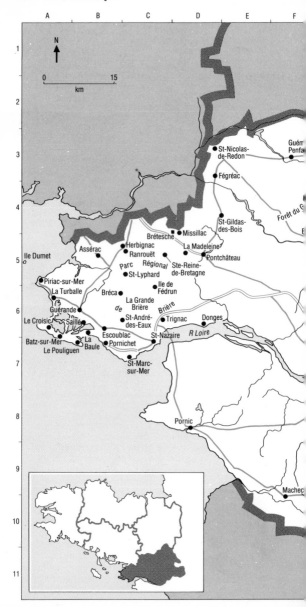

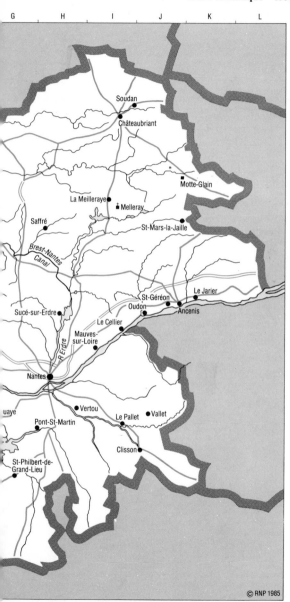

G H I J K L

Soudan

Châteaubriant

Motte-Glain

La Meilleraye ● Melleray

Saffré

St-Mars-la-Jaille

Brest-Nantes
Canal

St-Géréon ● Le Jarier

Sucé-sur-Erdre

Oudon ● Ancenis

Le Cellier

Mauves-
sur-Loire

R. Erdre

Nantes

uaye

Vertou

Pont-St-Martin

Le Pallet ● Vallet

Clisson

St-Philbert-de-
Grand-Lieu

© RNP 1985

Towns & villages

Ancenis   **J 6**
On Loire, 24mi/38.5km NE of
Nantes. Pop 7300. MD Thur.
Looking south across the tidal
shoals of the Loire, this attractive
little town has played its part in
history, since it was a frontier town
between Brittany and Anjou. In the
13th century it was captured by the
English; later it became a
smuggling centre, and it saw fierce
fighting and massacres during the
French Revolution. Near the huge
bridge across the Loire is a statue
to the poet Joachim du Bellay
(1522–1560), born in Liré on the
south side of the river.
There are a few steep streets of old
houses leading down to the Loire.
The massive 15thC château is now
a girls' school and is *not open to the
public.*
Ancenis is an excellent walking
centre, with paths along both
banks of the Loire and to the
villages and country on either side.
The Syndicat d'Initiative produces
a map giving a wide choice of
routes. Boating and fishing facilities
are available *in summer.*
As one of the chief towns of the
wine-growing region round the
Loire, Ancenis has a four-day wine
fair each *Dec.* It is also on the
tourist route called the 'Route
du Vin'.

Batz-sur-Mer   **A 6**
5mi/8km SW of Guérande. Pop
2300. The village of Batz
(pronounced 'Ba'), with its granite
houses, is dominated by the
mighty belfry of St-Guénolé Church
(197ft/60m high). Seaside Batz
consists of three small beaches
separated by rocks. During the
1830s the great French novelist
Honoré de Balzac spent some time
here.
Near the church is the 15thC
Chapel of Notre-Dame-du-Mûrier
(Our Lady of the Mulberry Tree).
The story goes that the builder of
the chapel was caught in a storm at
sea, and guided safely to harbour
by a tree that miraculously caught
fire—hence the dedication.

La Baule   **B 6**
On coast, 15.5mi/25km W of St-
Nazaire. Pop 15,200. MD daily in
summer. The only resort in

Brittany to rival the Côte d'Azur, La
Baule's superb sandy beach, south-
facing and 4mi/6.5km long, has
made it the leading holiday centre
of the region. It offers swimming,
water-skiing and windsurfing, golf,
tennis, shopping and nightlife –
every aspect of holidaymaking is
catered for. Although the seafront
is sophisticated, with new high-rise
hotels, apartments and shops, the
streets away from the front are still
very much those of a small
traditional resort, where 19thC
villas among the pine trees hark
back to the days when La Baule was
a quiet summer retreat for Nantes
businessmen. The town's full name
is La Baule–Escoublac, recalling a
village that was buried under the
sand-dunes in the 18th century.
La Baule's many attractions include
a sailing school, a yachting marina,
a golf-course, a rifle range, a centre
for *thalassothérapie* (seawater cure),
horseriding, tennis and squash
clubs, and courses in flying at the
local aerodrome. During the
summer there are cinemas,
theatres, concerts, and traditional
Breton music and dancing.

Châteaubriant   **I 2**
41mi/65.5km N of Nantes. Pop
13,800. MD Wed. A prosperous
town, on the borders of Anjou and
Brittany, climbing from its smart
main square to the imposing
château on top of the hill. It was
originally called Château-Brient,
after a local leader, Brient, who
built the first castle here in the 11th
century. The town is now an
important commercial and
agricultural centre, with a trade fair
(the Foire de Béré) held each *Sep.*
In a quarry just east of the town
(the Carrière des Fusillés) is an
impressive monument to 27
hostages shot by the Nazis on 22
Oct 1941.

Le Croisic   **A 6**
6mi/9.5km W of La Baule. Pop
4400. MD Thur. This attractive
harbour town stands at the end of
the Guérande Peninsula, looking
north east across the salt marshes
to the town of Guérande. It is very
much an active port rather than a
holiday resort, with fish markets
daily, beginning as early as *03.00,*
when the *langoustine* (large prawn)
catch is sold. On the other side of

the peninsula is a picturesque and rugged stretch of coast (La Grande Côte), facing the Atlantic.
Its strategic position guarding the valuable salt marshes meant that Le Croisic was often attacked in earlier times. It was bombarded by the British navy in 1759, but after three days the siege was called off. One of the viewpoints of the town, the Mont Esprit, is an artificial hill constructed in 1816 from ballast brought by ships sailing to Le Croisic to collect cargoes of salt; the French for ballast is *lest*, and the name Esprit derives from *lest pris*, meaning 'ballast removed'.
There is a small naval museum in the town hall (the Hôtel d'Aiguillon, built in the 17th century in Classical style). The town centre is dominated by the lofty lantern tower of the Church of Our Lady of Pity.
During the winter months, grey seals are sometimes washed up on the Atlantic coast of Le Croisic.

Donges   D 6
31mi/49.5km W of Nantes. Pop 6300. A centre of oil-refining and the petrochemical industry, with jetties that can take tankers of the largest size, Donges is an industrial sprawl on the north bank of the Loire. It was largely destroyed during World War II and has been almost entirely rebuilt. The church is ultra-modern, with a needle spire, and a main façade consisting of a huge parabolic arch, filled with a calvary carved in traditional Breton style.

Guérande   B 6
10mi/16km W of St-Nazaire. Pop 9400. MD Wed & Sat. The walled town of Guérande is like a smaller northern version of Carcassonne, with its Medieval battlemented walls, turrets and fortified gateways kept miraculously intact down the centuries. It owes its prosperity to salt, which was being collected from the nearby salt marshes (the *marais salants*) as far back as Roman times. The criss-cross pattern of low embankments, separating small, square reservoirs where the water evaporates leaving the salt behind, gives the look of a giant chessboard to the outskirts of the town.
Much of the town centre within the

walls is now pedestrianised, making Guérande an excellent shopping centre for antiques and local products. At its heart is the noble Romanesque Church of St-Aubin. There is a good museum in one of the Medieval gate-towers (the Porte St-Michel). During the 18th century the moat was mainly filled in, forming an attractive walk right round the circuit of the walls. Just north of the town is the 'Devil's Windmill' (Moulin du Diable). According to legend, it was built by Satan for a Guérande miller, who promised his soul in exchange. But just as the Devil was putting the last stone in place, the wily miller substituted a statue of the Virgin, thus foiling Satan and saving his soul at the same time.

Moulin du Diable, Guérande

Nantes   H 7
66mi/105km S of Rennes. Pop 420,000. MD daily. The most cosmopolitan city in Brittany, and indeed in the whole of north-west France, Nantes has an elegance and style all its own. Yet, though for centuries it was the spiritual, social and intellectual centre of Brittany and the headquarters of the dukes of Brittany, who lived in its mighty castle, it is now in an uneasy situation, since administratively it is no longer in Brittany but in a group of départements lumped together under the regional title of the Pays de la Loire. Due to its geographical position near the mouth of the Loire, Nantes has always looked in several directions at once: upstream to the heartlands of France, out to sea towards the Atlantic from which its prosperity derived, north to Brittany, and south to the Vendée and beyond.

It is a wine-growing centre in a cider-producing country, and even its older buildings (most notably the castle and the cathedral) are a compromise between north and south, since the lower courses of masonry are built of Breton granite, while the upper parts are limestone from the Loire valley.

Nantes was already an important town before 56BC, when the Romans conquered the region; its name derives from the Namnetes, a powerful Gaulish tribe. Under the Romans it became the commercial and administrative centre of the province of Armorica, but when the Roman empire collapsed in the 5th century it lay wide open to attacks by the pirate ships of the Saxons and Norsemen. Centuries of raids and pillage were finally brought to an end in AD939, when Alain Barbe-Torte routed the Norsemen and declared himself the first duke of Brittany. Under successive dukes Nantes grew prosperous, culminating in the rule of the great Duchess Anne at the end of the 15th century.

The city reached the height of its wealth and prestige in the 18th century, when its merchants and shipowners grew fat on the slave trade. Known as the *commerce triangulaire*, the 'three sides' of this trade consisted of a voyage to Africa with brandy, guns and other manufactured goods to exchange for slaves; the slave run to the West Indies; and then the return voyage to Nantes, laden with cotton, spices and sugar. During the French Revolution, Nantes became notorious as the scene of the *noyades* or drownings, in which people suspected of being against the Revolution were loaded into barges, which were then scuttled in the Loire.

After stagnating somewhat in the 19th century, Nantes recovered its position and prosperity during the 20th. During World War II it was a centre of resistance against the Germans, as is recalled by the name of one of the main streets, the cours des 50 Otages, so called in memory of 50 hostages shot by the Nazis. Nowadays it is a flourishing modern city, with industrial areas, 3mi/5km of harbour and wharves, an up-to-date university and high-rise flats and office buildings. From the tourist's point of view, it is an excellent city to shop in, and the restaurants offer cuisines ranging from Russian to Cambodian. There are theatres both regular and fringe and the city is host to international get-togethers of all sorts—like the Floralies, held every seven years in one of the city parks, at which flower-growers and buyers from all over the world meet at a kind of Chelsea-by-the-Loire. (The next Floralies is due in 1991.)

At first sight, Nantes can be a confusing city to find one's way around in, especially for the car-driver, as the centre is largely one-way. It owes much of its present layout to the Loire and its tributaries, though this may not be obvious at first. For example, the cours des 50 Otages follows the course of the Erdre, which runs in pipes under the city centre down to the Loire; and several branches of the Loire itself have been filled in down the years. Thus the most elegant section of the city, the Ile Feydeau, formerly stood on a proper island with wharves on either side; while a branch of the river once ran directly below the castle walls, in a bed now covered by the tarmac of the cours John Kennedy. The cours des 50 Otages is also the boundary between Medieval and 18thC Nantes. On its east side are the castle and cathedral; and on its west are the Classical 18thC streets which radiate from the pl Graslin, with its elegant theatre, built in 1788.

Statue of Jules Verne, Jardin des Plantes, Nantes

East of the castle it is well worth the short walk to the Jardin des Plantes, a quiet oasis of flowers and fine trees, with a magnificent conservatory. The gardens also contain a statue to Jules Verne, born in Nantes in 1828 and the city's most famous literary figure. Apart from its own attractions, Nantes is a centre for excursions to La Baule and the smaller coastal resorts, through the Loire vineyards with their small towns and villages, and by boat along the valley of the Erdre.

Piriac-sur-Mer A 5

9mi/14.5km NW of Guérande. Pop 1200. A small resort and fishing port, Piriac is at the northern extremity of the Guérande Peninsula, near the Pointe du Castelli. It was founded as long ago as the 6th century by Bretons from the interior of the country, and in earlier times was a prosperous fishing town, sending boats across the Atlantic for cod. It still has a small fishing fleet. On the coast round Piriac are strange rock formations, among them the 'Tomb of Almanzor' and 'Madame's Grotto'.

Offshore is the little Ile Dumet, now a sanctuary for seabirds. Dumet has another claim to fame: it is said by some geologists to be at the exact centre of the world's continents, though one wonders how they arrived at this conclusion. Two famous 19thC writers, Alphonse Daudet and Emile Zola, both spent some time at Piriac and describe it in their writings.

Pornichet B 7

6mi/9.5km W of St-Nazaire. Pop 7400. MD Wed & Sat. Though Pornichet adjoins La Baule and today appears almost to be part of the bigger resort, it is in fact very much a place in its own right, with its own individuality. Until the 1860s it was a small fishing village; but after its discovery by wealthy Parisians it became a popular summer resort, 20 years or so before La Baule. Modern Pornichet has an excellent marina, two fine beaches, a casino, and a centre for *thalassothérapie* (seawater cure). As it is so near La Baule, summer visitors can take advantage of La Baule's facilities, too.

Le Pouliguen B 7

10mi/16km W of St-Nazaire. Pop 4900. MD Tue & Fri. Le Pouliguen adjoins La Baule on its western side, corresponding to Pornichet on its east. But it is quite distinct geographically, as it is separated from La Baule by a harbour channel, and is in fact on the Guérande Peninsula. Far more than the other two towns, it is a sailing rather than a beach resort, with small boats moored along its 0.5mi/1km of quayside; it does, however, have its own small beach outside the harbour mouth. In summer, the small streets at its centre are largely pedestrianised.

At low tide it is possible to walk along the beach from the Pointe de Penchâteau, just south of Le Pouliguen, to Batz-sur-Mer, passing an amazing variety of caves and smaller holes in the rock. Most visited is the Grotte des Korrigans, named after Brittany's own breed of gnome, said to live in rocky clefts where they store their treasure.

Saillé B 6

2mi/3km S of Guérande. Pop 800. This little town of salt-workers stands on a rocky islet, with a chessboard of saltpans on either side. It has kept its old traditions more than any other village of the Guérande Peninsula, and recalls them in a small museum, the 'House of the Marsh-dwellers' (Maison des Paludiers). In former times the men of Saillé wore different costumes depending on whether they were single, married or widowers.

St-Marc-sur-Mer C 7

4mi/6.5km SW of St-Nazaire. Pop: *see St-Nazaire*. A tiny seaside resort, with a small beach hemmed in by rocks. In the 1950s it became familiar to film-goers as the setting for Jacques Tati's comedy 'Monsieur Hulot's Holiday' ('Les Vacances de Monsieur Hulot').

St-Nazaire C 7

37.5mi/60km W of Nantes. Pop 70,000. MD Tue, Fri & Sun. Today one of the main shipbuilding centres of western France, and a major port, St-Nazaire was virtually obliterated at the end of World War II, during the last-ditch struggles of the Germans against the Allied forces. Over 80% of the buildings were destroyed, which means that St-Nazaire is today an entirely modern town, of little tourist interest.

It owes its prosperity to its position at the mouth of the Loire, well downstream from Nantes, which it ousted as a major harbour towards the end of the 19th century as ships grew too large to negotiate the shoals and shallows further upstream. Excavations have shown that St-Nazaire is probably on the site of the Gallo-Roman port of Corbilo, making it 2000 years old as a harbour town. The only visible relic of the past is in the pl du Dolmen, where a dolmen (pair of standing stones with a third stone laid across the top) stands beside a menhir (single standing stone), forming an incongruous group among the modern housing. In 1975 the position of St-Nazaire was further enhanced, when a giant suspension bridge, the Pont de St-Nazaire, was built across the Loire estuary, obviating the need for southbound traffic to go 37.5mi/ 60km upstream to Nantes, before it could cross the river.

Visitors to St-Nazaire go there mainly for its wartime reminders, notably the huge submarine pens where Hitler kept the U-boats that harried the Atlantic convoys. Rust-streaked and hideous, they are far too solidly built to be removed by anything short of an atom bomb; so St-Nazaire has made the best of them, by using their cavernous interiors for cold storage, and even creating a 'panoramic terrace' and roof garden on top of one of them. Just to the north of the harbour entrance are two good beaches. Above them, at the harbour end, is a granite column commemorating one of the most daring exploits of World War II—the commando raid in Mar 1942 on the harbour installations of St-Nazaire. Known as 'Operation Chariot', it was carried out by Anglo-Canadian troops, who penetrated the harbour defences, proving that the German invaders were not invulnerable. St-Nazaire is one of the *communes* of the Brière (*see Countryside*), which lies just inland across the ring road and is easily reached from the town.

La Turballe　　　　　　　**A　6**
4mi/6.5km W of Guérande. Pop 3200. A small resort and fishing port, half-way between Le Croisic and Piriac. It has a brightly painted harbour building and a modern church, in which contemporary ideas are combined with Breton architectural traditions.

Interesting buildings

Churches and other ecclesiastical buildings are normally *open 10.00–12.00, 14.00–17.00 (18.00 in summer)*.

Abbaye de la Melleray　　　**I　2**
Meilleraye, 12mi/19km S of Châteaubriant. This remote and peaceful abbey stands by a lake among trees, a few kilometres from the hamlet of La Meilleraye. It was founded by Cistercians in the 12th century, but most of the existing buildings are 18th and 19thC. The abbey is now occupied by the silent Trappist order, and is *not open* except for the church, which can be seen at the hours of morning and evening Mass (*Sun 10.30 & 16.30; Mon–Sat 07.30 & 18.15*)

Base Sous-Marine　　　　　**C　7**
St-Nazaire. Submarine pens beside St-Nazaire harbour. The roof of one of the massive concrete submarine pens, which during World War II sheltered the German U-boats, has been turned into a roof garden. This *'terrasse panoramique'* gives wide views over the harbour and shipping of St-Nazaire, the Loire estuary, and the magnificent suspension bridge across the river. Associated with the terrace are rooms with temporary local exhibitions of costume, ship models etc, and a rooftop café. *Open Jul & Aug, daily 09.30–19.30; Jun & Sep 09.30–12.00, 14.00–18.00, closed Mon.* **Charge**

Cathédrale St-Pierre　　　**H　7**
Nantes. In centre of town. Founded as far back as the 4th century, this Gothic cathedral dates mainly from the 15th. In 1972 it was devastated by fire, and much of it has been closed off ever since. At present, only the lofty nave is open to view. The south transept contains the

tomb of Duke François II (died 1488) and his second wife, Marguérite de Foix; the tomb is a Renaissance masterpiece by the sculptor Michel Colombe. In the north aisle is a well, said to have been used by pilgrims on their way to Santiago de Compostela, in northern Spain.

Château de Châteaubriant   I 2
Rue du Château, Châteaubriant. A fascinating complex of buildings of different periods, today used mainly as local government offices. The base of the massive 11thC keep survives, but most of the château is 16thC Renaissance, with a splendid open arcade. It was built by Jean de Laval for his young wife Françoise de Foix, who died in the château in 1537 under mysterious circumstances, perhaps murdered by her jealous husband—though this story now tends to be discounted. *Free guided tours 10.00–12.00 & 14.00–19.00. Closed Tue & Sun morn.*

Château, Châteaubriant

Château des Ducs de Bretagne   H 7
Nantes. In centre of town. Tel (40) 47 18 15. Fortified by two of the dukes of Brittany in the 15th century, this magnificent castle reflects the final years of Breton independence from French control. Traces of an older castle are marked out in the middle of the courtyard, and a single tower, the Vieux Donjon, remains from the 13th and 14th centuries. The fanciful Renaissance interior, contrasting with the massive strength of the outer walls, is largely the work of Duchess Anne (1477–1514), the last of the ducal line. She commissioned the Renaissance façade of the Grand Logis, the well with its ornate canopy (the 'Golden Crown', or Couronne d'Or), and the Tour de

la Couronne d'Or, from which Anne and her ladies could watch the tournaments in the courtyard below.
The castle was the setting for many great state occasions, most notably in 1598, when Henri IV came here to sign the Edict of Nantes, which guaranteed freedom of worship to Catholic and Protestant alike. When Henri saw the fortifications, he is said to have exclaimed: *"Ventre Saint-Gris, les ducs de Bretagne n'étaient pas des petits compagnons!"* (Roughly translated, "the dukes of Brittany were certainly something!") A large plaque on the wall inside the castle commemorates the linking of Brittany to France in 1532, by an act of union which put an end to Breton independence. There are three museums in the castle (*see Museums section*). *Open 10.00–12.00, 14.00–16.00. Closed 1 Jan & Tue Sep–Jun.* **Charge**

Château de la Motte-Glain   I 2
11.5mi/18.5km SE of Châteaubriant. A superb Renaissance château on the borders of Brittany and Anjou, reflected in the lake at its foot. The present castle was built in 1496 by Pierre de Rohan. It contains fine Renaissance fireplaces, and a collection of African big-game trophies. *Open 15 Jun–15 Sep 14.30–18.30, closed Tue; Easter–end Sep, Sat, Sun & hols only.* **Charge**

Château de Ranrouët   C 5
Near Herbignac. 10.5mi/17km NE of Guérande. Tel (40) 70 28 10. Standing on the north side of the Grande Brière, the château was built in the 12th and 13th centuries and abandoned in the 18th. The main fortification consists of six towers linked by a curtain wall. *Open Sun aft & hols, & Sat on request.*

Collégiale de St-Aubin   B 6
Guérande. From its foundation in the 9th century until the French Revolution in 1789, this imposing church at the centre of the walled town of Guérande was run by a College or group of canons—hence the name. The present building, dedicated to St-Aubin, is a medley of architectural styles from the 12th to the 17th century. The main

façade, with its gables and gargoyles, is in 15thC Flamboyant Gothic style, and the external pulpit is from the same period. Inside the church, the nave is in Romanesque style, with small devils carved on the capitals. Some of the stained glass dates from the 13th century.

Cours Cambronne　　　　**H　7**
Nantes. In centre of town. Perhaps the most Parisian-looking architectural group in Nantes, the 18thC cours Cambronne consists of two rows of elegant houses facing each other across a wide rectangle of gravel. It gets its name from General Cambronne, a hero of Napoleon's army, born near Nantes in 1770. As commander of the Imperial Guard at Waterloo, he was called upon to surrender, and replied with the single swear-word "*Merde!*", which has been known as the '*mot de Cambronne*' ever since.

Donjon d'Oudon　　　　**J　6**
14.5mi/23km NE of Nantes. The little town of Oudon, on the north bank of the Loire, is dominated by a strange octagonal tower, rising above the ruins of a 13thC castle. Dating from the 14th century, the tower is over 98ft/30m high, and from its top there are wide views over the Loire valley.

Eglise de St-Gildas　　　　**D　4**
St-Gildas-des-Bois. 11mi/17.5km S of Redon. A Romanesque church of the 12th–13th century, originally belonging to a Benedictine abbey. It was much damaged at the end of World War II, but has been completely restored, with stained glass dating from 1956.

Eglise de St-Jean-de-Béré　　**I　2**
Châteaubriant. This 11thC Romanesque church is on the north-west side of the town, off the Rennes road. The south façade is decorated with Medieval relief carvings of the Virgin. The open-air pulpit was used by preachers during periods of bubonic plague. Inside there are a number of wooden statues of the 15th and 17th centuries, and a Baroque high altar and reredos.

Ile Feydeau　　　　**H　7**
Nantes. In centre of town. Though this 'island' of splendid 18thC

houses is now landlocked, when first built it was surrounded by water, with quays on either side. The houses were built for the *armateurs* (shipowners) and merchants who prospered from the slave trade; many of them have now been turned into shops and restaurants.

Passage Pommeraye　　　**H　7**
Off rue Crébillon, Nantes. A pretty 19thC shopping arcade, on two levels. Its cast-iron columns, glass roof-span and drooping statues were restored, cleaned and repainted in the 1970s.

Pontchâteau, calvary　　　**D　5**
31mi/49.5km NW of Nantes. Pontchâteau's calvary, unusual in its size and complexity, is near the hamlet of La Madeleine, 2.5mi/4km W of the town. The first calvary was constructed here in 1709 by the preacher Louis-Marie Grignion de Montfort, who founded his own religious order, the Montfortains. This calvary was demolished by order of Louis XIV; the present complex was begun in 1821, by the local priest. It consists of an artificial hill, some 98ft/30m high, with the crosses of Christ and the two thieves at its summit. All round are small shrines and grottoes devoted to Bible themes (the caves of Adam and of Bethlehem, the cave of the Agony, the Stations of the Cross etc). The calvary is much visited by pilgrims, especially at Whitsun. Nearby is a tall standing stone called the 'Fuseau de la Madeleine' (Mary Magdalene's Spindle).

Saffré, Resistance monument　　　　**H　4**
25mi/40km N of Nantes. This impressive monument to the French Resistance stands at the end of a lane east of the village of Saffré. In June 1944, after the Allied invasion of France, the local *maquis* rose against the Germans, who captured a number of them and shot 27 after a farcical trial. The monument's inscription reads: "To the men of the *maquis* who fell gloriously so that France could be reborn free".

Théâtre Graslin　　　　**H　7**
Pl Graslin, Nantes. Built in the 1780s, this building, with its

Corinthian portico has been the city's leading theatre for 200 years. As well as plays, the company puts on operas and ballets.

Museums & galleries

Aquarium Marin de la Côte d'Amour   A 6
6 quai du Port Ciguet, 44490 Le Croisic. Tel (40) 23 02 44. On the quayside of Le Croisic's pretty little harbour, this privately owned aquarium has three rooms with more than 250 types of marine life, including fish from the Indian Ocean and the Pacific. *Open Jul & Aug 10.00–20.00; 1 Sep–30 Jun 10.00–12.00, 14.00–19.00.* **Charge**

Archéologique, Musée   H 7
Pl Jean V, 44000 Nantes. Tel (40) 89 34 32. A collection of antiquities from the lower Loire region, dating from prehistoric, Gaulish and Gallo-Roman times. Also exhibits from other parts of the world (ancient Egypt, Oceania). *Open 10.00–12.00, 14.00–18.00. Closed Tue.* **Charge**

Art Populaire Régional, Musée d'   H 7
Château des Ducs de Bretagne, 44000 Nantes. Tel (40) 47 18 15. Housed in the Grand Logis (main building) of the château, this is a comprehensive collection of Breton clothes, *coiffes* (traditional lace head-dresses) and furniture from the 16th to the early 20th century. Rooms opened in 1982 contain pottery and ironwork. *Open Jul & Aug, daily 10.00–12.00, 14.00–18.00. Closed Tue 1 Sep–30 Jun.* **Charge**

Arts Decoratifs, Musée des   H 7
Château des Ducs de Bretagne, 44000 Nantes. Tel (40) 47 18 15. One of the three museums in the château, this collection is housed in the 15thC Tour du Fer à Cheval ('Horseshoe Tower'). It contains decorative art of all kinds, including a section of contemporary textile art. *Open Jul & Aug, daily 10.00–12.00, 14.00–18.00. Closed Tue 1 Sep–30 Jun.* **Charge**

Arts et Traditions Populaires du Pays Blinois, Musée des   F 5
13 rue de Nantes, 44130 Blain. Tel (40) 79 00 04. Blain is a small

country town 22.5mi/36km N of Nantes. This varied museum displays local archaeology, traditional crafts with re-creations of sabot-maker's workshop, bakery etc, historical postcards, clothes and furniture. *Open Sat 14.00–18.00; Sun 09.00–12.00, 14.00–18.00.* **Charge**

Beaux Arts, Musée des   H 7
10 rue Georges Clemenceau, 44000 Nantes. Tel (40) 74 53 24. One of the finest French art galleries outside Paris, with paintings from the 13th century to the present. Five rooms on the first floor give a historical survey of French art from the 17th to the early 19th century, including a famous portrait by Ingres and three works by Georges de la Tour. *Open Mon & Wed–Sat 10.00–12.00, 13.00–17.45; Sun 11.00–17.00. Closed Tue.* **Charge** (free Sat & Sun)

La Chaumière Brièronne   C 5
180 Ile de Fédrun, 44720 St-Joachim. Tel (40) 88 42 72. One of the small museums of the Grande Brière (its name means 'Cottage of the Brière'). A typical cottage interior, with old tools and traditional costumes, recalling the life of the marsh-dwellers of the Ile de Fédrun at the beginning of the 20th century. *Open 1 Jul–30 Sep 10.00–12.30, 15.00–19.00.* **Charge**

Porte St-Michel, Guérande

Guérande, Musée Régional de   B 6
1 pl du Marhallé, 44350 Guérande. No tel. A museum of regional and local history housed in the Porte St-Michel, one of the 15thC gateways of this splendid Medieval town. It includes costumes of the salt-workers and marsh-dwellers of the region, typical red-varnished furniture, pottery, and weaving. *Open Easter–30 Sep 09.30–12.00, 14.00–19.00.* **Charge**

Histoire Naturelle, Muséum d'   **H 7**

12 rue Voltaire, 44000 Nantes. Tel (40) 73 30 03. Founded as long ago as 1799, this is now an up-to-date natural history museum with the latest audio-visual facilities and an extensive library. There are exhibits of comparative anatomy, pre-history, a 'vivarium' with live insects and reptiles etc. *Open Tue–Sat 10.00–12.00, 14.00–18.00; Sun 14.00–18.00.* **Charge**

Jules Verne, Musée   **H 7**

3 rue de l'Hermitage, 44000 Nantes. Tel (40) 89 11 88. Jules Verne, the pioneer of science fiction, was born in Nantes in 1828 and this museum was opened in 1978 to mark the 150th anniversary of his birth. It includes models, 19thC books and posters, old photographs, letters, and some of Verne's furniture. *Open 10.00–12.30, 14.00–17.00. Closed Tue & hols.* **Charge**

Kerhinet, Musée de   **C 5**

180 Ile de Fédrun, 44720 St-Joachim. Tel (40) 88 42 72. At St-Lyphard (though managed from Fédrun), a village on the west side of the Grande Brière. Kerhinet consists of a group of 18 cottages on either side of a central path. In summer they are used for exhibitions and traditional handicrafts. *Open 1 Jun–30 Sep 10.00–12.30, 15.00–19.00.* **Charge**

La Maison de l'Eclusier

La Maison de l'Eclusier   **C 5**

180 Ile de Fédrun, 44720 St-Joachim. Tel (40) 88 42 72. The 'Sluice-keeper's House' is in the Brière hamlet of Rozé. In former times the regulation of water level in the Brière was of great importance, and control of the sluice gates was a highly responsible job. This keeper's house is now a museum tracing the history of water control. *Open*

1 Jun–30 Sep 10.00–12.30, 15.00–19.00. **Charge**

La Maison de la Mariée   **C 5**

130 Ile de Fédrun, 44720 St-Joachim. Tel (40) 88 42 04. The 'House of the Bride' is a small private museum, celebrating the 19th and early 20thC marriage customs of the Brière. Wax flowers were a speciality, and after the wedding the bouquets and other souvenirs were kept under glass cases in the home. *Open 1 Mar–31 May 09.00–12.30, 13.30–19.30; 1 Jun–30 Sep 09.00–19.30.*

La Maison des Paludiers   **B 6**

35 rue du Ber, Saillé, 44350 Guérande. Tel (40) 42 22 28. The little town of Saillé, near Guérande, has lived for centuries on the salt industry. This museum is a guide to the skills of the salt-marshes, with tools, models and furniture. *Open Jul & Aug, daily 10.00–12.00, 14.00–19.00; Jun & Sep, daily 14.00–18.00.* **Charge**

Naval, Musée   **A 6**

Mairie, 44490 Le Croisic. Tel (40) 42 91 17. On the ground floor of the town hall, the Naval Museum consists mainly of models of old warships and merchantmen. There are also exhibits of sextants and other aids to navigation, sabres and pistols, documents and engravings of naval actions. *Open 1 May–30 Sep 10.00–12.00, 15.00–19.00, Mon & Thur aft only.* **Charge**

Planétarium   **H 7**

Square Moysan, rue le Huedé, 44000 Nantes. Tel (40) 73 99 23. Opened in 1981, the planetarium is conveniently near the Jules Verne Museum. There are three sessions a day, on different astronomical themes. *Open Wed–Sat & Sun aft. Sessions at 10.30, 14.15 & 15.45.* **Charge**

Salorges, Musée de   **H 7**

Château des Ducs de Bretagne, 44000 Nantes. Tel (40) 47 18 15. A fascinating museum in the château, created in the 1920s and devoted to seafaring and trade, in particular the *'commerce triangulaire'* (a run to Africa to buy slaves, across the Atlantic to sell them, then back from the West Indies with cotton and sugar). In the same building is an auditorium where audio-visual displays are regularly shown. *Open Jul & Aug, daily 10.00–12.00, 14.00–18.00. Closed Tue 1 Sep–30 Jun.* **Charge**

Thomas Dobrée, Musée   **H 7**
Pl Jean V, 44000 Nantes. Tel (40) 89 34 32. The Dobrée family were *armateurs* (shipowners) of Nantes in the 18th and 19th centuries, and this museum represents the collection of the last of them. Rare books and manuscripts, enamels, alabasters, paintings. *Open 10.00–12.00, 14.00–18.00. Closed Tue.* **Charge**

Accommodation

Campsites

Prices at campsites vary according to the facilities available but seldom exceed ten francs per person at present. There will usually also be a charge for the car and for the site.

Ancenis   **J 6**
Municipal de l'Ile Mouchet
44150 Ancenis. Tel (40) 83 00 06. This site, on the west side of the town, is grassy and tree-shaded, and has direct access to the banks of the Loire. *Open mid-May–mid-Sep.*

Assérac   **B 5**
Le Traverno
Assérac, 44410 Herbignac. 4mi/6.5km W of Herbignac. Tel (40) 88 98 82. A site near the Grande Brière, and within easy reach of the sea. *Open 1 Jun–30 Sep.*

La Baule   **B 6**
Les Ajoncs d'Or
Chemin du Rocher, 44500 La Baule. Tel (40) 60 33 29. On the north side of the town, this is a medium-sized site with bar, food shop and many other amenities. *Open 1 Apr–30 Sep.*
Municipal
Av Paul Minot, 44500 La Baule. Tel (40) 60 17 40. A site in two separate parts, one for caravans and the other for tents. *Open 1 Apr–30 Sep.*

Le Croisic   **A 6**
L'Océan
44490 Le Croisic. Tel (40) 23 07 69. Only 220yds/200m from the sea, in the direction of the Pointe du Croisic, this is a flat, grassy site, with many amenities. *Open 1 Apr–mid-Nov.*

La Pierre Longue
44490 Le Croisic. Tel (40) 23 13 44. A fairly large site, west of the town in the direction of the Pointe, and 550yds/500m from the sea. *Open Easter–mid-Sep.*

Fégréac   **D 3**
Municipal le Bellion
Fégréac, 44460 St-Nicolas-de-Redon. Tel (40) 88 71 09. About 4mi/6.5km S of Redon, this quiet inland site is near both the Vilaine River and the Nantes–Brest Canal. *Open mid-Jun–mid-Sep.*

Guémené-Penfao   **F 3**
L'Hermitage
44290 Guémené-Penfao. Tel (40) 79 23 48. A peaceful, attractive site outside Guémené, which is 12.5mi/20km E of Redon on the D775. *Open all year.*

Guérande   **B 6**
Le Crémeur
44350 Guérande. Tel (40) 24 93 12. A gently sloping site, 1.5mi/2.5km NE of the town. *Open 1 Apr–30 Sep.*

Nantes   **H 7**
Municipal du Val du Cens
Bvd du Petit-Port, 44000 Nantes. Tel (40) 74 47 94. This site is on the north side of the city, by the Cens (a small tributary of the Erdre). It is planted with flowers, and has separate plots for tents. *Open all year.*

Piriac-sur-Mer   **A 5**
Pouldroit
Piriac, 44420 La Turballe. Tel (40) 23 50 91. A flat, grassy site, 325yds/300m from the sea. It has many facilities, including a common-room. *Open mid-May–mid-Sep.*

Le V</sub>éridet
Piriac, 44420 La Turballe. No tel. A small site 0.5mi/1km S of the village, with direct access to the sea. *Open all year.*

Pornichet **B 7**

Le Clos Oral
44380 Pornichet. No tel. A
centrally placed site, 435yds/400m
from the sea and near shops and
supermarkets. *Open mid-Jun–
mid-Sep.*

St-Lyphard **C 5**

Les Brières du Bourg
St-Lyphard, 44410 Herbignac. Tel
(40) 45 83 13. An inland site, on the
edge of the Grande Brière, beside a
lake, with swimming nearby. *Open
mid-Jun–mid-Sep.*

St-Marc-sur-Mer **C 7**

L'Eve
St-Marc-sur-Mer, 44600 St-
Nazaire. Tel (40) 45 92 65. A large
site, with its own tunnel under the
road giving convenient access to
the beach. *Open mid-May–
mid-Sep.*

St-Mars-la-Jaille **J 4**

L'Erdre
44540 St-Mars-la-Jaille. No tel. On
the eastern fringe of Brittany, this
small site is about 15.5mi/25km
SE of Châteaubriant, beside
the Erdre River. *Open Easter–
31 Oct.*

Ste-Reine-de-Bretagne **C 5**

Château du Deffay
Ste-Reine-de-Bretagne, 44160
Missillac. Tel (40) 45 63 84. On the
north-east side of the Brière
Regional Park, this site is a
member of the prestigious 'Castels
et Camping' association. The site
is in the grounds of a small stone-
built château, now used in part as
a restaurant, recreation rooms etc,
and has swimming and riding
facilities. To one side is a large lake.
Open 1 Jun–31 Aug.

La Turballe **A 6**

La Falaise
44420 La Turballe. Tel (40) 23 32
53. This site opens directly on to
the beach, and is only 220yds/200m
from the village centre. *Open
1 Apr–31 Oct.*

Parc Ste-Brigitte
44420 La Turballe. Tel (40) 23 30
42. A fairly small, quiet site, 2mi/
3km from the beaches, with its own
swimming pool for those who
prefer unsalted water. *Open 1 Apr–
30 Sep.*

Hotels

Ancenis **J 6**

Hôtel du Soleil Levant
Barrière St-Pierre, 44150 Ancenis.
Tel (40) 83 11 36. A small (six-
bedroom) hotel near the town
centre. Its restaurant specialises in
fish from the Loire. **F**

Hôtel du Val de Loire
Le Jarier d'Ancenis, 44150
Ancenis. Tel (40) 96 00 03. 1.5mi/
2.5km E of Ancenis along the
Angers road, this modest-sized (30-
bedroom) hotel has its own
restaurant. *Restaurant closed Sat
1 Oct–31 May* A.V. **FF**

La Baule **B 6**

Castel Marie-Louise
Esplanade du Casino, 44504 La
Baule. Tel (40) 60 20 60. A
member of the 'Relais et Châteaux'
association, this mock-baronial
hotel is in its own grounds near the
casino and the sea. *Closed Jan.*
Ax.Dc.V. **FFF**

L'Hermitage
Esplanade François-André, 44504
La Baule. Tel (40) 60 37 00. The
grandest hotel in La Baule, it stands
at the west end of the front with
private gardens leading to the
beach. Private swimming pool.
Closed mid-Oct–mid-Apr.
Ax.Dc.V. **FFF**

Hôtel Alcyon
19 av des Pétrels, 44500 La Baule.
Tel (40) 60 19 37. A short way
from the seafront, this hotel is a
member of the 'Petits Nids de
France' group. No restaurant. *Open
all year.* V. **FF**

Ty Gwenn
25 av de la Grande Dune, 44500 La
Baule. Tel (40) 60 37 07. A small
hotel among pine trees near the sea.
Closed Oct. **F**

Châteaubriant **I 2**

Hostellerie de la Ferrière
Rte de Nantes, 44110
Châteaubriant. Tel (40) 28 00 28.
Set in its own park-like grounds on
the south side of the town, this
hotel is a member of the 'Petits
Nids de France' association. *Open
all year.* Ax.Dc. **FF**

Hôtel Armor
19 pl de la Motte, 44110
Châteaubriant. Tel (40) 81 11 19. A

modern hotel (without restaurant) in the town centre. *Open all year.* A. **FF**

Hôtel L'Estacade
4 quai Lénigo, 44490 Le Croisic. Tel (40) 23 07 77. Small hotel at the western end of the harbour area. *Closed mid-Nov–mid-Dec.* V. **F**

Hôtel Les Nids
Bvd Général Leclerc, 44490 Le Croisic. Tel (40) 23 00 63. A quiet hotel, a little way inland from the harbour area. Its restaurant specialises in seafood. *Closed 1 Oct–Easter.* V. **FF**

Hôtel Le Roc Maria
Rue des Halles, 44350 Guérande. Tel (40) 24 90 51. A small hotel, with a crêperie for Breton pancake meals and snacks. *Closed 1 Oct–end Feb.* A. **FF**

Hôtel du Golf de la Breteshe
44160 Missillac. Tel (40) 88 30 05. The Château de la Bretesche, 0.5mi/1km W of the little town of Missillac, is a Medieval fantasy of pointed turrets and gables reflected in a calm lake. Dating from the 15th century, it was burnt during the French Revolution, but was restored in the 19th and 20th centuries. The 19th century stable block is now a luxury hotel, and an 18-hole golfcourse has been laid out in the grounds. *Closed Feb.* V. **FFF**

Hôtel Frantel
Ile Beaulieu, 44000 Nantes. Tel (40) 47 10 58. A large, modern, luxury hotel, in the business quarter of the Ile Beaulieu, about 0.5mi/1km from the château and city centre. The restaurant specialises in regional dishes. *Open all year. Restaurant closed Sun.* A.Ax.Dc.V. **FFF**

Hôtel des Trois Marchands
26 rue Armand Brossard, 44000 Nantes. Tel (40) 47 62 00. Hotel of moderate size, in a quiet street in the old town, near the cathedral and castle. *Open all year.* Ax.Dc.V. **FF**

Hôtel de la Vendée
8 allée du Cdt Charcot, 44000 Nantes. Tel (40) 74 14 54. A hotel without a restaurant, between the castle and botanic gardens, and so convenient for sightseeing. *Open all year.* Ax.Dc.V. **FF**

Hôtel-Restaurant de la Poste
26 rue de la Plage, Piriac, 44420 La Turballe. Tel (40) 23 50 90. A small hotel in the road leading down to the beach. *Closed mid-Oct–end Feb.* **F**

Hôtel des Charmettes
7 av Flornoy, 44380 Pornichet. Tel (40) 61 04 30. A quiet hotel with a shady garden, 220yds/200m from the sea. *Closed mid-Sep–31 May.* V. **FF**

Hôtel de France
2 av de Gaulle, 44380 Pornichet. Tel (40) 61 08 68. A small hotel near the station and a short walk from the beach. *Closed mid-Sep–mid-May.* **F**

Hôtel Jules Verne
2 rue d'Alger, 44510 Le Pouliguen. Tel (40) 42 32 79. A small hotel with restaurant near the harbour. English spoken. *Open all year.* V. **F**

Hôtel de la Plage
St-Marc-sur-Mer, 44600 St-Nazaire. Tel (40) 45 92 82. The hotel of Jacques Tati's film comedy, 'Monsieur Hulot's Holiday' ('Les Vacances de Monsieur Hulot'), it opens directly on to the main sandy beach. *Open all year.* **FF**

Hôtel Armoric
92 av de la République, 44600 St-Nazaire. Tel (40) 22 51 31. In the busy centre of the town on the main street, this medium-sized hotel and restaurant is convenient for the beaches and for sightseeing. *Open all year.* **FF**

Hôtel du Berry
1 pl de la Gare, 44600 St-Nazaire. Tel (40) 22 42 61. One of the 'Inter-Hotel' association. *Closed Xmas–New Year.* Ax.Dc.V. **FF**

Restaurants

Ancenis J 6

Auberge de Bel Air
Rte d'Angers, 44150 Ancenis. Tel
(40) 83 02 87. A moderately priced
restaurant, 0.5mi/1km E of the
town along the Angers road. *Closed
Aug, Mon & Sun eve.* V. **FF**

La Charbonnière
Bvd Joubert, 44150 Ancenis. Tel
(40) 83 25 17. This restaurant has
panoramic views of the Loire. **FF**

La Baule B 6

Chez Henri
161 av de Lattre-de-Tassigny,
44500 La Baule. Tel (40) 60 23 65.
Restaurant popular with locals.
Closed Tue. A.Ax.Dc.V. **FF**

L'Ankou
38 av de l'Etoile, 44500 La Baule.
Tel (40) 60 22 47. Named for some
obscure reason after the Breton
figure of death, this is a cheerful
restaurant in the middle of town.
*Closed Jan, & Mon & Tue 11
Sep–31 Dec & 1 Feb–30 Jun.* **FF**

L'Espadon
Résidence du Golfe, 2 av de la
Plage, 44500 La Baule. Tel (40) 60
05 63. On the fifth floor with a wide
view over the bay, this is a
luxurious restaurant specialising in
seafood. *Closed 1 Nov–31 Jan, Sun
eve & Mon 1 Sep–31 Oct & 1 Feb–
30 Jun.* Dc.V. **FFF**

Châteaubriant I 2

Auberge Bretonne
23 pl de la Motte, 44110
Châteaubriant. Tel (40) 81 03 05. A
restaurant and bar in the town
centre, specialising in charcoal
grills. *Closed Sat.* A. **F**

La Petite Chaumière
Pl de l'Eglise St-Nicolas, 44110
Châteaubriant. Tel (40) 81 05 17.
Small restaurant in the town centre,
with regional specialities. *Closed
Sun.* **F**

Le Croisic A 6

Le Bretagne
Quai de la Petite Chambre, 44490
Le Croisic. Tel (40) 23 00 51.
Quayside restaurant specialising in
locally caught fish, lobsters and
other seafood. *Closed 1 Nov–end
Feb.* **FF**

Les Filets Bleus
12 rue de la Marine, 44490 Le
Croisic. Tel (40) 23 07 42.
Centrally placed seafood restaurant
near the inner harbour. *Closed Dec,
Jan & Sun out of season.* V. **FF**

Guérande B 6

Ti Marok
Pl du Marhallé, 44350 Guérande.
Tel (40) 24 92 08. A restaurant
specialising in *couscous*, just outside
the old walls of the town. *Closed
Oct, & Tue & Wed 1 Nov–31
May.* **FF**

Nantes H 7

Le Carabi
9 rue Ste-Croix, 44000 Nantes. Tel
(40) 47 74 14. A small, candle-lit
restaurant in the Medieval part of
the city, formed from a roofed-over
section of an old street. *Open all
year.* **FF**

Le Poivre et Sel
13 rue Kervégan, 44000 Nantes.
Tel (40) 47 02 35. In a fine 18thC
house on the Ile Feydeau, with
stone heads carved over the lower
windows. Fish a speciality. *Open all
year.* A.Dc.V. **FF**

La Reine Margot
8 rue de la Juiverie, 44000 Nantes.
Tel (40) 47 43 85. As the name of
the street (now pedestrianised)
suggests, in the Middle Ages this
was the Jewish ghetto of Nantes.
Restaurant specialising in meat
dishes. *Closed Aug.* A. **F**

La Sirène
4 rue Kervégan, 44000 Nantes. Tel
(40) 47 00 17. A restaurant in an
18thC street on the Ile Feydeau,
specialising in lobster and
other kinds of seafood. It has
been a restaurant since the
beginning of the century. *Closed
Sun.* V. **FF**

Oudon J 6

Chez Lulu
44980 Oudon. Tel (40) 83 60 26. A
small restaurant beside the Loire,
near the station. Specialities include
eels and frogs' legs. **F**

Piriac-sur-Mer A 5

Café-Restaurant de l'Océan
Lerat, 44420 La Turballe. 2mi/3km
SE of Piriac. Tel (40) 23 31 30.
Seafront restaurant specialising in
mixed seafood (*fruits de mer*). *Open
all year.* **F**

Pornichet   **B 7**

Le Danicheff
45 ave Gén-de-Gaulle, 44380
Pornichet. Tel (40) 61 07 32. An
attractive restaurant in the town
centre, specialising in seafood.
(Some rooms above restaurant.)
Open all year. **FF**

La Goulette
126 av de Mazy, 44380 Pornichet.
Tel (40) 61 27 08. A restaurant
serving international dishes such as
couscous and paella. *Closed Sat &
Sun out of season.* V. **FF**

Le Pouliguen   **B 7**

Le Boucanier
5 pl des Halles, 44510 Le
Pouliguen. Tel (40) 42 31 98. Only
55yds/50m from the port, this
restaurant serves fish fresh from its
own tank. *Open all year.* **FF**

Le Rallye
Pl de la Duchesse Anne, 44510 Le
Pouliguen. Tel (40) 42 30 71. A
short way from the port, on the
main road, this restaurant
specialises in grills served on vine
leaves. *Open all year.* V. **FF**

St-Nazaire   **C 7**

Bon Accueil
39 rue Marceau, 44600 St-Nazaire.
Tel (40) 22 07 05. Traditional
restaurant with a few rooms near
the submarine pens and the beach.
The proprietor also supervises the
kitchens, so the food is good.
Closed Jul & Sat. Ax.Dc.V. **FF**

Le Trou Normand
60 rue de la Paix, 44600 St-Nazaire.
Tel (40) 22 46 24. Named after the
mid-meal drink of Calvados popular
in Normandy, this is a cheerful
restaurant in the town centre.
Closed Mon. V. **F**

Countryside

La Brière (Grande Brière)   **C 6**
31mi/49.5km NW of Nantes.
Inland from La Baule and St-
Nazaire, most of the peninsula
between the Loire on the south and
the Vilaine on the north is a
marshy, low-lying area recalling
the Fens of East Anglia. Here
100,000 acres/40,500 hectares have
been designated a Nature Park
(Parc Naturel Régional), which
contains at its heart the unique

survival known as La Grande
Brière, some 17,500 acres/7000
hectares of water, reedbed, disused
peat workings, and isolated villages.

Ruined cottages, Grande Brière

Until the early years of this century
the Briérons lived from the
marshes, fishing, shooting, and
raising a few cattle, and cutting
peat which they either burnt
themselves or sold in Nantes. But
from 1900 the Brière declined, as
the population died or drifted
away. The carefully maintained
system of watercourses silted up,
the thatched roofs of the cottages
fell in and were not repaired, and
all the old fishing and boating skills
were lost. This was the situation
when the Parc Régional was set up
in 1970, and since then the Brière
has begun to recover. Cottages have
been renovated as second homes,
or as first homes by people who
have chosen to live here. Small
museums have been opened, which
tell the story of the Brière and its
skills, with active craftsmen
participating. Today a wider
public than ever before can
experience the Brière at first hand
by going out with a boatman on one
of the traditional flat-bottomed
chalands or punts, to enjoy the
wildlife and peaceful atmosphere.

Forêt de Gâvre   **F 4**
22mi/35km NW of Nantes. This is
the largest stretch of woodland in
the département, covering about
11,050 acres/4500 hectares. It still
contains a few wild boar, as well as
quantities of deer; the name Gâvre
is said to come from the Breton *karv*
(French *cerf*), meaning deer.

Vallée d'Erdre
Due north of Nantes. The Erdre
Valley is an open-air playground for
the Nantais, and one of the prettiest
areas around their city. The river
runs north from the centre of
Nantes for about 15.5mi/25km,
widening here and there into

lagoons, and passing villages like Sucé-sur-Erdre, a great centre for sailing and other water sports. During the 17th century, the famous philosopher René Descartes lived for a while at Sucé.

Entertainment

Casinos

Casino de la Baule　　　　**B 6**
Esplanade François-André, 44504 La Baule. Tel (40) 60 22 80. This casino has a cinema, restaurant, theatre and two nightclubs (*see below*), in addition to gambling. *Open Easter & 1 May–30 Sep, nightly from 16.30.*

Casino de Pornichet　　　**B 7**
Bvd des Océanides, 44380 Pornichet. Tel (40) 61 05 48. Casino with cinema and nightclub. *Open 1 May–30 Sep, nightly.*

Discothèques

L'Ange Bleu　　　　　　　**H 7**
15 rue Kervégan, 44000 Nantes. Tel (40) 89 58 30. On Ile Feydeau. *Open 21.30–04.00. Closed Sun.* **Charge**

Les Bermudes　　　　　　　**J 6**
St-Géréon, 44150 Ancenis. Tel (40) 96 09 06. Beside the N23, 1.5mi/2.5km W of Ancenis. *Open Thur–Sun.* **Charge**

La Clé des Champs　　　　**I 2**
Soudan, 44110 Châteaubriant. Tel (40) 81 22 37. In the village of Soudan, 4mi/6.5km E of Châteaubriant. *Open nightly.* **Charge**

Le Marais　　　　　　　　　**B 6**
Rte de Congor, 44350 Guérande. Tel (40) 24 93 08. Disco and restaurant. *Disco open 1 Jun–30 Sep, 22.30–dawn; 1 Oct–31 May, Sat & Sun only.* **Charge**

The Navy Club　　　　　　　**C 7**
10 rue de Maudes, 44600 St-Nazaire. Tel (40) 22 40 32. Disco with grill and pizzeria. *Open nightly to 04.00.* **Charge**

Le Petit Club　　　　　　　**H 7**
1 rue de l'Héronnière, 44000 Nantes. Tel (40) 89 45 43. Disco and cabaret. *Open 22.00–04.00. Closed Sun.* **Charge**

Sako　　　　　　　　　　　　**B 6**
Casino de la Baule, Esplanade François-André, 44504 La Baule. Tel (40) 60 22 80. *Open Easter & 1 May–30 Sep, nightly from 22.00.* **Charge**

Le Samba　　　　　　　　　　**H 7**
8 rue Fouré, 44000 Nantes. Tel (40) 20 09 32. African and Afro-Cuban music. *Open nightly.* **Charge**

Le Tropicana　　　　　　　**B 6**
Casino de la Baule, Esplanade François-André, 44504 La Baule. Tel (40) 60 20 14. A smart nightclub and disco. *Open Easter & 1 May–30 Sep, nightly.* **Charge**

Leisure activities

Flying

Aéro-club de la Côte d'Amour　　　　　　　**B 6**
Aérodrome de la Baule–Escoublac, 44500 La Baule. Tel (40) 60 23 84. A club for experienced flyers and learners, also an aero-model club.

Golf

Golf de la Baule　　　　　**C 6**
Domaine de St-Denac, St-André-des-Eaux, 44600 St-Nazaire. Tel (40) 60 46 18. An 18-hole course well planted with trees. **Charge**

Golf de la Bretesche　　　**D 4**
44160 Missillac. Tel (40) 88 30 05. An 18-hole course in the magnificent park of the Château de la Bretesche. **Charge**

Horseriding

Centre Equestre de la Baule B 6
44500 La Baule. Tel (40) 60 39 29. In the heart of La Baule, catering for riders of all grades.

Rifle-shooting

Stand de Tir d'Escoublac　**B 6**
Complexe Sportif d'Escoublac, rue Jean Sohier, 44500 La Baule–Escoublac. Tel (40) 24 43 22. An up-to-date rifle and pistol range, with Olympic capabilities, for marksmen of any standard. *Open summer 09.00–12.00, 15.00–17.00, closed Fri; out of season Sat–Mon only 09.00–12.00, 15.00–18.30.*

Sailing

Centre Nautique Valentin   A 6
Plage Valentin, 44490 Le Croisic.
Tel (40) 23 92 17. The centre runs
courses of one or two weeks, at all
levels, in *Jul & Aug.*

Chil's Club   B 7
Av des Grèves, 44380 Pornichet.
No tel. The sailing school takes
learners from the age of six up, and
also hires out boats of all kinds
(catamarans, windsurfers etc).
Open daily.

There are sailing schools at La
Baule, Batz-sur-Mer and Le
Pouliguen.

Seawater cure (thalassothérapie)

Les Thermes des Océanides B 7
44380 Pornichet. Tel (40) 61 07 55.
A large establishment on the
seafront, with a variety of
treatments for rheumatic and other
complaints. *Open all year.*

Excursions

Bicycle excursions

Loire-Atlantique is an excellent
département for the cyclist as much
of it, especially on either side of the
Loire, is flat. Ancenis is a good
cycling centre for the Loire wine
country. La Baule is another good
centre, convenient for the Grande
Brière and the Guérande
Peninsula.

Boat trips

Erdre Valley
Armement Lebert-Buisson, 24 quai
de Versailles, 44000 Nantes. Tel
(40) 20 24 50. Cruises along the
River Erdre, the water playground
of Nantes, take place *1 Feb–31 Dec.*
Timing and frequency depend on
season. A number of evening
cruises include dinner.

Grande Brière
By far the best way of seeing this
unique area of waterways, reeds,
ancient thatched cottages and
wildlife is from water-level, in a
chaland or punt. A good many of
these are now motorised, though
the old-fashioned craft, propelled
quietly by punt-pole, are far more
enjoyable. Centres are the villages

of Fédrun and St-Lyphard, where
it is best to enquire locally, as the
boatmen work for themselves and
their times are unpredictable.

Ile Dumet
A three-hour cruise (*summer only*)
from Le Croisic to this island
seabird sanctuary. Also one-hour
offshore cruises from Le Croisic.
Tel (40) 23 12 27.

Tours by car (one-day trips)

Around La Baule & St-Nazaire
Coast & beaches
Starting from La Baule, cross the
harbour inlet to Le Pouliguen,
then along the Côte d'Amour with
its rocks and grottoes (Grotte des
Korrigans etc). To Le Croisic,

Pont du Diable, Côte d'Amour

pretty old harbour town with
aquarium. Skirt the Guérande
saltmarshes to Guérande (walled
Medieval town), then along the
coast to La Turballe and Piriac.
From Piriac, take coast road up to
Pénestin (in Morbihan), then by
Vilaine estuary to La Roche-
Bernard (Morbihan). Head south
to St-Nazaire through Herbignac
(ruins of Château de Ranrouët),
along west edge of Brière Natural
Park through St-Lyphard and St-
André-des-Eaux. In St-Nazaire,
German submarine pens and
Commando memorial. Back to La
Baule along coast via St-Marc-sur-
Mer and Pornichet.
Grande Brière
From La Baule, through Escoublac
to St-André-des-Eaux. Then skirt

Chalands, Grande Brière

the Brière in a clockwise circuit, as follows, if possible allowing time for an hour's water trip on a punt (*chaland*): Bréca, St-Lyphard, Mayun, Camerun, St-Joachim, Ile de Fédrun, Rosé, Trignac, La Baule. There are small museums on different aspects of the Brière in St-Lyphard, St-Joachim and Fédrun.

Loire Valley Wine Routes

Though this book only covers the north bank of the Loire, obviously no-one with a car would ignore the south bank. So these routes, starting from Nantes, take in the south bank as well.
Since this is mainly wine-growing country, the routes take in three of the Loire wines: Muscadet, Gamay and Gros-Plant.

Gamay route

Gamay is the main non-white wine of the region. It is a rosé, produced from a small area (only 500 acres/

200 hectares) round Ancenis, and thus largely within Loire-Atlantique.
From Nantes, take the main road (N23) along the north bank of the Loire. Then by lanes along the river through wine villages like Mauves and the suitably named Le Cellier ('cellar'). Through Oudon, with its mighty octagonal tower, to Ancenis. Then cross the river to Liré, and back along the south bank through Champtoceaux (fine views of the Loire) to Nantes.

Gros-Plant route

Like Muscadet, Gros-Plant is a dry white wine, produced mainly south of the Loire from 6500 acres/2630 hectares of vineyard.
From Nantes, take the Pornic road (D751) to Bouaye, then head south to Machecoul. West on D117 to St-Philibert-de-Grand-Lieu (superb abbey and lake). Back to Nantes along D65 through Pont–St-Martin.

Muscadet route

Muscadet is the most popular of the Loire wines, and the most widely grown. It is a white, fairly dry wine, and its vines cover by far the largest area—24,000 acres/9720 hectares.
Starting from Nantes on the Clisson road (N148), turn off to Vertou, then on to Clisson, a market town with a magnificent ruined castle. Then north to Vallet, and back to the main road at Le Pallet, the birthplace of Peter Abelard, the 12thC teacher and philosopher whose tragic love for Heloïse has inspired writers since the Middle Ages. From Le Pallet, back to Nantes.

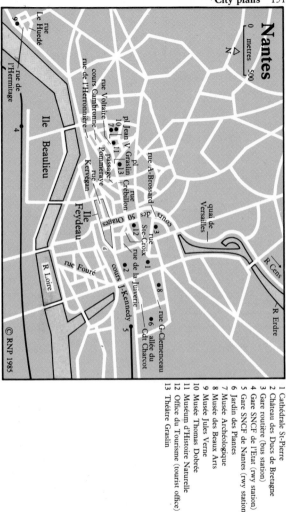

Nantes

0 metres 500

N

rue Le Huede

rue de l'Hermitage

Ile Beaulieu

Ile Feydeau

rue de l'Hermitière

cours Cambronne

rue Voltaire

pl Jean V Graslin

rue Crébillon

pl Ste-Croix

rue Kervégan

passage Pommeraye

rue A-Brossard

cours des Otages

rue des 50 Otages

rue Ste-Croix

rue de la Juiverie

cours J-Kennedy

rue Fouré

R Loire

quai de Versailles

R Cens

R Erdre

allée du Cdt Charcot

rue G-Clemenceau

© RNP 1985

10 • 7 • 11 • 13

3 •

12 •

1 •

2 •

8 •

6 •

5

4

9 •

1 Cathédrale St-Pierre
2 Château des Ducs de Bretagne
3 Gare routière (bus station)
4 Gare SNCF de l'État (rwy station)
5 Gare SNCF de Nantes (rwy station)
6 Jardin des Plantes
7 Musée Archéologique
8 Musée des Beaux Arts
9 Musée Jules Verne
10 Musée Thomas Dobrée
11 Muséum d'Histoire Naturelle
12 Office du Tourisme (tourist office)
13 Théâtre Graslin

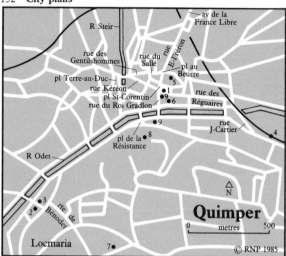

1 Cathédrale de St-Corentin
2 Eglise de Notre-Dame
3 Faïencerie
4 Gares SNCF & routière
  (bus & rwy stations)

5 Musée des Beaux Arts
6 Musée Breton
7 Musée de la Faïence
8 Mont Frugy
9 Syndicats d'Initiative (tourist offices)

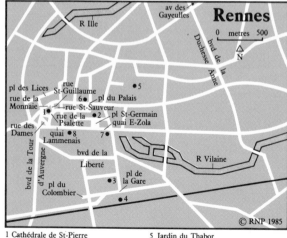

1 Cathédrale de St-Pierre
2 Eglise St-Germain
3 Gare routière (bus station)
4 Gare SNCF (rwy station)

5 Jardin du Thabor
6 Palais de Justice
7 Palais des Musées
8 Syndicat d'Initiative (tourist office)

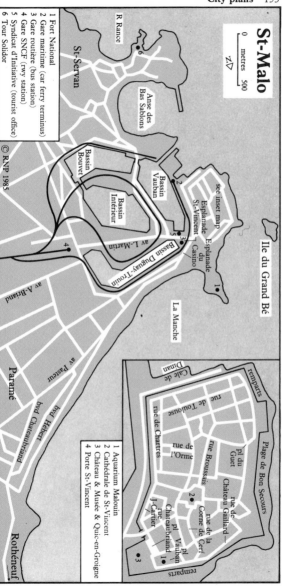

St-Malo

0 — metres — 500

N▽

© RNP 1985

1 Fort National
2 Gare maritime (car ferry terminus)
3 Gare routière (bus station)
4 Gare SNCF (rwy station)
5 Syndicat d'Initiative (tourist office)
6 Tour Solidor

R Rance

St-Servan

Anse des
Bas Sablons

Bassin
Bouvet

Bassin
Vauban

Bassin
Intérieur

Bassin Duguay-Trouin

av L-Martin

av A-Briand

av Pasteur

bvd Hébert

bvd Chateaubriand

Paramé

Rothéneuf

Esplanade
du
St-Vincent

Esplanade
St-Vincent
Casino

see inset map

Ile du Grand Bé

La Manche

1 Aquarium Malouin
2 Cathédrale de St-Vincent
3 Château & Musée & Quic-en-Groigne
4 Porte St-Vincent

Cale de
Dinan

remparts

rue de Toulouse

rue de Chartres

rue de
l'Orme

rue Broussais

pl du
Guet

Plage de Bon Secours

rue de
Château Gaillard

rue de la
Corne de Cerf

pl
Vauban

rue
J-Cartier

rue
Chateaubriand

remparts

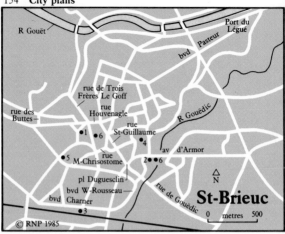

© RNP 1985

1 Cathédrale St-Etienne
2 Gare routière (bus station)
3 Gare SNCF (rwy station)

4 Grandes Promenades
5 Notre-Dame-de-l'Esperance
6 Offices du Tourisme (tourist offices)

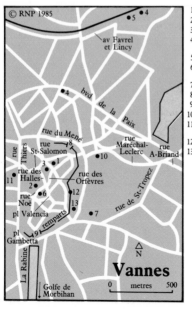

© RNP 1985

1 Cathédrale de St-Pierre
2 Château Gaillard & Musée
3 La Cohue
4 Gares routières (bus stations)
5 Gare SNCF (rwy station)
6 Hôtel de Roscanvec & Musée
7 Jardins de la Garenne
8 Porte Prison
9 Porte St-Vincent
10 Préfecture
11 Syndicat d'Initiative (tourist office)
12 Tour du Connétable
13 Vieux lavoirs

Index